VOYAGES
IN ENGLISH

Writing and Grammar

Elaine de Chantal Brookes

Patricia Healey

Irene Kervick

Catherine Irene Masino

Anne B. McGuire

Adrienne Saybolt

LOYOLAPRESS.

CHICAGO

Cover Design/Production: Loyola Press
Cover Illustration: Jeff Parks, Anni Betts
Interior Design/Production: Loyola Press, Think Design Group

Acknowledgements to copyright holders appear on page 326, which is to be considered a continuation of the copyright page.

Loyola Press has made every effort to locate the copyright holders for the cited works used in this publication and to make full acknowledgment for their use. In the case of any omissions, the Publisher will be pleased to make suitable acknowledgments in future editions.

ISBN-10: 0-8294-2360-5
ISBN-13: 978-0-8294-2360-0

Manufactured in the United States of America.

LOYOLAPRESS.

3441 N. Ashland Avenue
Chicago, Illinois 60657
(800) 621-1008
www.loyolapress.com

11 12 13 14 15 Web 10 9 8 7 6 5 4 3

VOYAGES IN ENGLISH
WRITING AND GRAMMAR

Welcome to

Inside the Student Book

The Teacher Planning Pages

Inside the Teacher Guide

Parent Letter

Scope and Sequence of Skills

Grade 1 Contents

CHAPTER 3   Verbs and How-to Articles   74

CHAPTER 4   Pronouns, Adjectives, and Descriptions   108

CHAPTER 5   Contractions and Book Reports   142

CHAPTER 6   Word Study and Research Reports   176

Welcome to VOYAGES IN ENGLISH
WRITING AND GRAMMAR

A SIXTY-YEAR LEGACY

Sixty years ago a handful of highly experienced grammar and writing teachers set out on a quest—to develop a curriculum for teaching English to immigrant children. They knew that language is critical to finding a place in the world. They knew that communication cannot be separated from critical thinking. They knew that fluency, creativity, communication, and elaboration cannot be successfully separated from grammar, mechanics, syntax, and semantics.

Today our eyes are filled with color television and computer graphics. Our minds are filled with ever-changing information. Our e-mails carry important news of business and too often serve as the only connection to our extended families. Still, as it was six decades ago, our first impression of a person's skills and intelligence is firmly set in how well the person communicates— in conversation and in writing.

VOYAGES IN ENGLISH IN THE 21ST CENTURY

We at Loyola Press worked with the Sisters, Servants of the Immaculate Heart of Mary, Immaculata, Pennsylvania, the program authors, for two years to conceptualize this edition of *Voyages in English*. We realized that more than ever students and teachers need the values of the past to carry us all into the future. Through that collaboration, we forged this shared vision to

- uphold the strength and rigor of the original *Voyages* program,

- provide all students (and teachers) with proficiency in the foundations of grammar; and to provide the tools needed to master each writing genre, enabling them to communicate successfully with any audience, and

- reintegrate the writing process with its structural underpinnings at the word level, the sentence level, and the idea level (beyond the paragraph level).

We bring the best values of the past to the 21st century, empowering students as critical thinkers who can achieve their full potential.

FOCUS ON GRAMMAR

In every grade, growth in oral and written language skills is of paramount importance. Language is a vehicle for expressing wonder and delight, a tool for exchanging ideas, a medium for transmitting information, and a resource for bridging the differences among people. It is the underlying philosophy of *Voyages in English* to help students recognize these goals of language and to provide them with the skills to attain these goals.

Voyages in English includes the major areas of grammar: correct usage, mechanics, and dictionary skills. Each chapter incorporates a grammar concept with one of the following writing genres: personal narratives, friendly letters, how-to writing, descriptions, book reports, and research reports. For purposes of instruction, the grammar skills are often taught in isolation, but they should not be considered separate and distinct from one another.

Students at the primary level are just becoming acquainted with the tools of language. They are eager to express themselves orally and in written form. In these activities, spontaneity and creativity are encouraged. Grammar, correct usage, mechanics, and spelling are taught primarily to enhance the students' oral and written expression. Becoming proficient in language is a process. As students mature, their knowledge and use of the language should mature as well.

Voyages in English will provide a foundation for the further development of language skills. A textbook, coupled with a teacher's own love of language, is a vehicle for transmitting to the students an appreciation for the written word.

INSIDE THE STUDENT BOOK

Grammar Study

Each chapter of the student book provides comprehensive practice of each grammar concept. These practice pages can be used to introduce and reinforce concepts in class, or can be sent home with students as homework.

Grammar Practice: Students practice each grammar skill using a variety of activities.

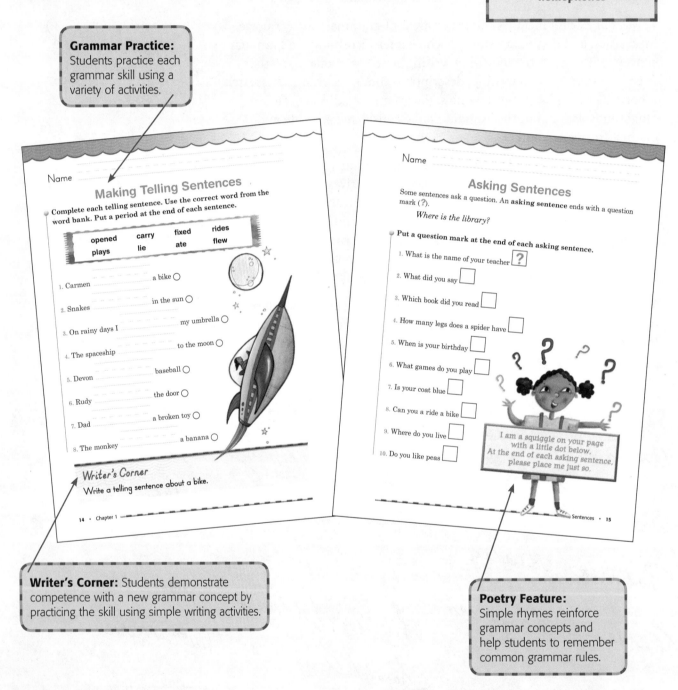

Writer's Corner: Students demonstrate competence with a new grammar concept by practicing the skill using simple writing activities.

Poetry Feature: Simple rhymes reinforce grammar concepts and help students to remember common grammar rules.

Grammar Assessment

Two Show What You Know pages are provided at the end of each grammar chapter and can be used as reinforcement or as review. A Cumulative Review is offered at the end of the book to test students' mastery of the primary grammar concepts they must know at the end of the year.

Show What You Know:
Use as a review of the chapter's major concepts or to test students' mastery of the chapter's grammar skills.

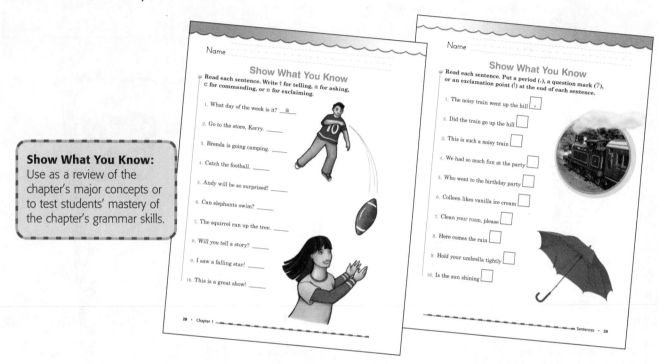

Grammar Review:
Use as a cumulative test to determine students' mastery of the program's grammar skills.

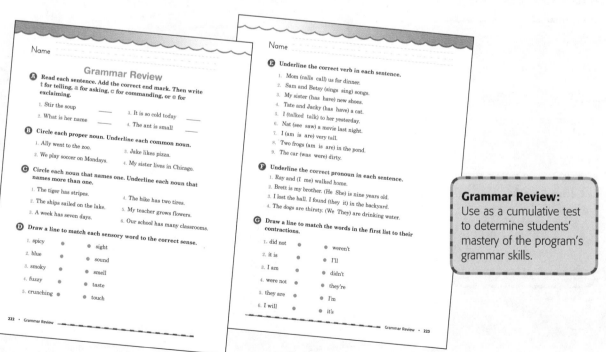

Get Ready to Write

Get Ready to Write introduces students to each chapter's writing genre. Students learn about the elements and characteristics of each genre, and workbook practice helps to illustrate how those elements and characteristics are applied to writing.

6 Genres

personal narratives
friendly letters
how-to articles
descriptions
book reports
research reports

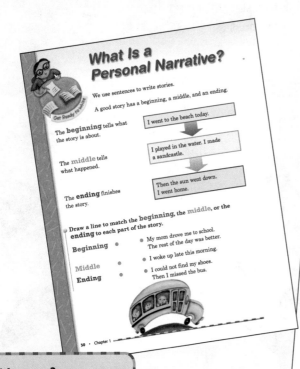

What Is a . . . ?:
Students learn clear definitions of the elements and the characteristics of the genre.

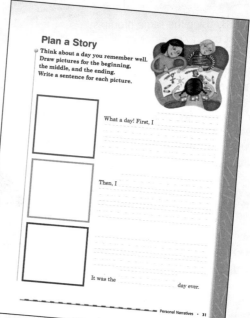

Genre Practice:
On subsequent pages, students practice the skills they will need to write a complete portfolio piece for each genre.

Writer's Workshop

The Writer's Workshops are the writing process in action. The stages of the workshop illustrate how the writing process moves the work forward. Prewriting, Drafting, Revising, and Publishing help young writers develop and express their ideas. Editing and Proofreading help students check their work for clarity, logic, and accuracy.

Learn by Example: A virtual student guides students through the writing process. Achievable examples are modeled to illustrate the process in action.

Prewriting: By using the same prompts the virtual student uses to generate brainstorming ideas, students are able to brainstorm focused, age-appropriate topics. They are then challenged to use a graphic organizer to put thoughts and ideas into a coherent order.

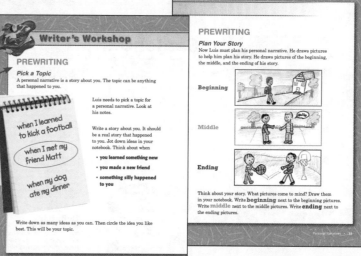

Drafting: An age-appropriate first draft allows students to see the relationship between prewriting and drafting. This "sloppy copy" helps emphasize the importance of capturing ideas at this stage of the writing process.

Editing and Revising: Students use a professional, yet achievable checklist to edit the ideas and the flow of their draft. They are then guided to develop a new draft to better catch errors and to improve the draft as a whole.

Proofreading: Students use a second checklist to edit the grammar and conventions in their draft.

Publishing: Students create a final portfolio piece that is both audience- and age-appropriate. A variety of publishing suggestions are offered in each chapter.

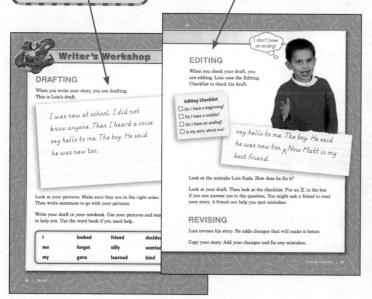

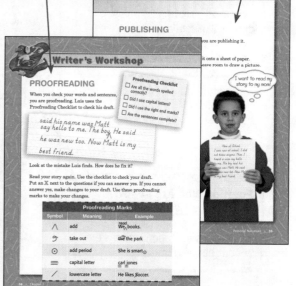

THE TEACHER PLANNING PAGES

Preceding each chapter is a brief seminar for teachers. These planning pages provide background, activities, and guidance for each grammar skill and writing genre. The guidance of curriculum planners and grammar experts helps teachers approach each chapter with confidence.

Grammar Focus: The specifics of the grammar study allow teachers to plan around students' needs.

A Visual, Please: Teachers can use this feature to demonstrate learning strategies that appeal to visual learners.

Grammar for Grown-ups: Teachers are given a concise review of each grammar topic so they can teach with confidence.

Common Errors: Grammar experts illustrate and explain common grammar mistakes heard or seen inside the classroom.

For Kids Who Are Ready: Teachers are given the tools to provide additional challenges and background to students who are curious about grammar.

Ask a Mentor: The Grammar Geek and Grammar Geezer offer workable solutions to grammar problems that students in this grade often encounter.

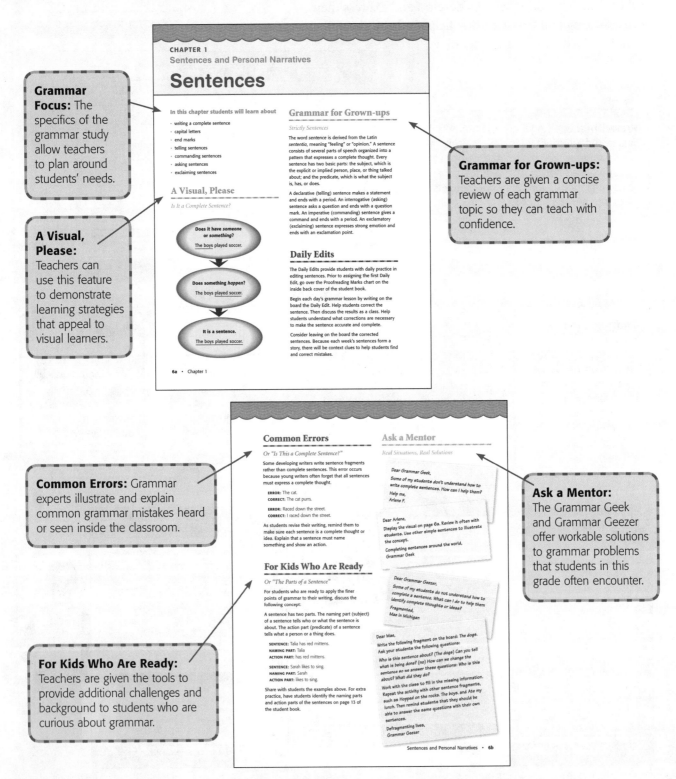

Genre Description:
A comprehensive explanation of the elements and characteristics of the writing genre helps teachers understand the relationship between grammar, mechanics, and writing.

Genre Characteristics:
Explicitly stated genre characteristics help to define the genre and allow teachers to teach with confidence and consistency.

CHAPTER 1
Sentences and Personal Narratives

Personal Narratives

Genre Characteristics

At the end of this chapter, students will write a personal narrative. They will be guided through the writing process in the Writer's Workshop. The completed personal narrative will include the following:

- a topic about something that really happened to the writer
- a first-person point of view
- a beginning that tells what the story is about
- a middle that tells what happened
- an ending that finishes the story
- time order
- correct grammar, spelling, capitalization, and punctuation

Daily Story Starters

The Daily Story Starters for this chapter provide students with practice writing about themselves. This daily practice helps to prepare students for writing their personal narratives.

Begin each day by writing on the board the Daily Story Starter. Allow time for students to complete the sentence. Then discuss the results as a class. Because the purpose of this activity is to practice brainstorming, talk to students about their ideas and whether the ideas are appropriate for the genre.

Taking It Personally

Personal narratives are written to share significant events in writers' lives. They are personal to the core, and at their best they are revealing and relevant to others.

A personal narrative has a clear focus on a particular topic. The topic is always a true story or event that the writer experienced. First-person point of view indicates to the reader that the writer is telling the story about himself or herself. The ideas in the narrative help express the importance of the topic to the writer.

Effective personal narratives are well organized. Ideas are usually presented in order. The main idea is often clearly explained in the beginning, while the ending of a personal narrative gives a sense of resolution.

The writer of an effective personal narrative knows how to let his or her personality shine through with the use of humor, phrasing, dialog, or a combination of these characteristics. Personal narratives have an honest voice—one that is authentic and true. Throughout a personal narrative, the writing is correct in grammar, punctuation, capitalization, and spelling.

Teacher's Toolbox:
Suggestions from professional educators offer ways to help students get the most out of their writing experience.

Reasons to Write:
Drawing on the practical applications of each genre, Reasons to Write offers examples of people who use writing in their jobs and everyday lives.

Literature Links:
Teachers can offer their students relevant and age-appropriate examples of the genre.

Teacher's Toolbox

Try the following ideas to help your students get the most out of the Writer's Workshop:

- Encourage students to keep a picture journal to record important or interesting personal experiences.
- Invite students to bring in pictures or drawings of favorite family events. Discuss how these events might make good personal narrative topics.
- Invite local officials or celebrities (such as the mayor, an entertainer, or the principal) to tell the class about an event they remember from their own childhood.

Reasons to Write

Share with your students the following times in which people write personal narratives. Talk about why it is important to become a good writer of personal narratives.

- a teacher writing about a classroom experience for a teaching journal
- a truck driver writing a description of her delivery
- a firefighter writing a report about a rescue operation

Literature Links

You can add the following titles to your classroom library to offer your students examples of well-written personal narratives:

My Name Is Yoon by Helen Recorvits

There's an Alligator Under My Bed by Mercer Mayer

Diary of a Spider by Doreen Cronin

Assessment

The student's scoring rubrics guide students to practice self-evaluation, as well as to see how well they understand the elements and characteristics of each writing genre. The teacher's scoring rubric provides teachers with a targeted and balanced tool for assessing student writing at the idea level, the sentence level, and the word level.

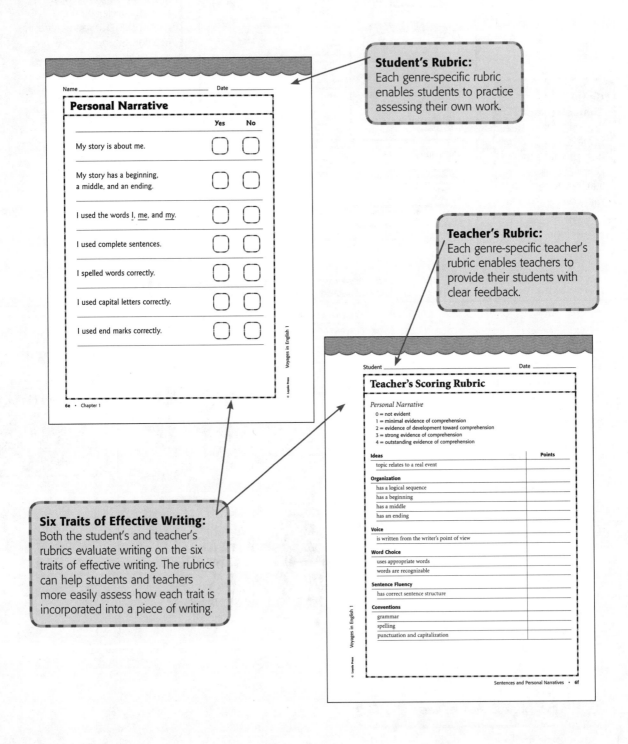

Student's Rubric:
Each genre-specific rubric enables students to practice assessing their own work.

Name _____ Date _____

Personal Narrative

	Yes	No
My story is about me.	☐	☐
My story has a beginning, a middle, and an ending.	☐	☐
I used the words I, me, and my.	☐	☐
I used complete sentences.	☐	☐
I spelled words correctly.	☐	☐
I used capital letters correctly.	☐	☐
I used end marks correctly.	☐	☐

6e • Chapter 1

Teacher's Rubric:
Each genre-specific teacher's rubric enables teachers to provide their students with clear feedback.

Student _____ Date _____

Teacher's Scoring Rubric

Personal Narrative

0 = not evident
1 = minimal evidence of comprehension
2 = evidence of development toward comprehension
3 = strong evidence of comprehension
4 = outstanding evidence of comprehension

	Points
Ideas	
topic relates to a real event	
Organization	
has a logical sequence	
has a beginning	
has a middle	
has an ending	
Voice	
is written from the writer's point of view	
Word Choice	
uses appropriate words	
words are recognizable	
Sentence Fluency	
has correct sentence structure	
Conventions	
grammar	
spelling	
punctuation and capitalization	

Sentences and Personal Narratives • 6f

Six Traits of Effective Writing:
Both the student's and teacher's rubrics evaluate writing on the six traits of effective writing. The rubrics can help students and teachers more easily assess how each trait is incorporated into a piece of writing.

Extensions

The Daily Edits, Daily Story Starters, and Chapter Adaptors provide teachers with a variety of ways to extend and reinforce each chapter's concepts. Teachers can use these features as class activities or as additional practice for students who are having trouble. Each chapter's extensions are tailored to the grammar skills and the writing genre that students are learning about, giving teachers a way to reinforce the connection between writing and grammar.

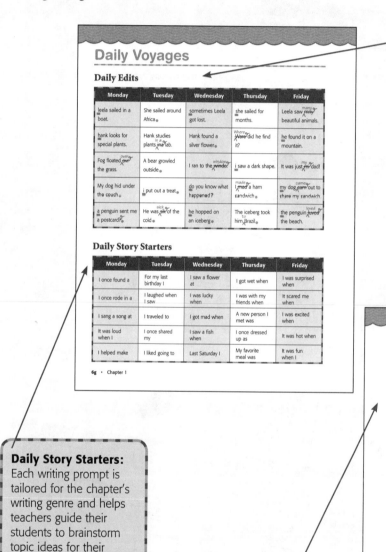

Daily Edits: Simple sentences provide practice for students to hone their editing skills. Teachers can guide students to correct the editing problems that the class may encounter when writing their portfolio pieces. Because each week's sentences form a story, students can use context clues to correct their mistakes.

Daily Story Starters: Each writing prompt is tailored for the chapter's writing genre and helps teachers guide their students to brainstorm topic ideas for their portfolio pieces. Students are encouraged to use the prompts to help consider possible topics, as well as the audience that is appropriate for the piece.

Chapter Adaptors: A variety of writing and grammar options help teachers extend, enrich, or reteach important concepts in each chapter. The options appeal to a variety of learning styles and help teachers provide new ways for students to practice major concepts.

INSIDE THE TEACHER GUIDE

Annotated Student Pages

The Teacher Edition of *Voyages in English* provides annotated student pages for quick reference and easy correction. Each clearly marked page can be easily referenced to its corresponding teaching at the back of the book.

Step-by-Step Teaching

The step-by-step teaching at the end of the Teacher Guide runs parallel to each student book chapter. The step-by-step teaching provides guidance, suggestions, and activities for the implementation of each chapter. Teachers are also equipped with flexible modeling ideas to ease the integration of grammar and writing. The teaching is clearly marked for easy reference to the annotated student book pages.

Teaching Grammar: Teachers can guide students through the elements of each grammar lesson, using the suggested activities and modeling techniques.

Introducing the Chapter: Each chapter opens with an age-appropriate model of the genre. Teachers can use the step-by-step plan to introduce the elements and characteristics of the genre and to show how grammar relates to writing.

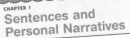

Get Ready to Write: Teachers can use these activities and modeling techniques to deepen students' understanding of the writing genre.

Writer's Workshop: This guide offers specific definitions of each stage of the writing process, as well as concrete examples and modeling activities. Teachers can use these suggestions to guide students as they work on their portfolio pieces.

Parent Letter

The reproducible parent letter on page xxii, which is intended to be sent home with students at the beginning of the school year, provides teachers with a way of informing parents about the writing process. It guides parents to understand that the development and exploration of ideas is as important as a polished final piece and a definitive grade. The parent letter also offers advice for how parents can become involved in guiding their children by assuming the roles of editor and advisor.

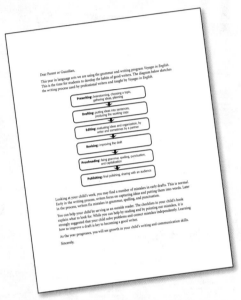

Blackline Masters

In addition to the comprehensive grammar practice provided in each student book, Loyola Press is proud to offer online additional practice pages for the grammar skills. The Blackline Masters can be used to reinforce or to assess the grammar concepts taught in the program.

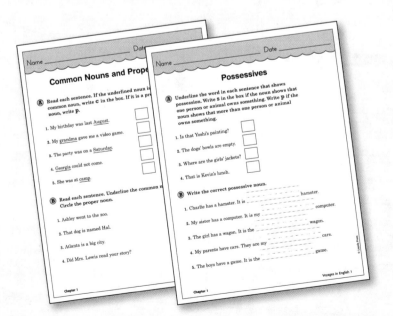

One Chapter, One Month

Each chapter in *Voyages in English* is a study of a grammar concept and a writing genre. The chapters are designed to cover about 25 class days—a chapter opener, grammar lessons presented across 22 days, and the genre Writer's Workshop across 18 days. By the final week, students should have a clear understanding of how the structure of grammar supports the expression of writing.

	MONDAY	TUESDAY	WEDNESDAY	THURSDAY	FRIDAY
WEEK 1	Grammar	Grammar	Grammar	Grammar	Grammar
WEEK 2	Grammar	Grammar	Grammar **Get Ready to Write**	Grammar **Get Ready to Write**	Grammar **Get Ready to Write**
WEEK 3	Grammar **Get Ready to Write**	Grammar **Prewriting**	Grammar **Prewriting**	Grammar **Drafting**	Grammar **Drafting**
WEEK 4	Grammar **Editing**	Grammar **Editing**	Grammar **Revising**	Grammar **Revising**	Grammar **Proofreading**
WEEK 5	Grammar **Proofreading**	Grammar **Publishing**	**Publishing**	**Presentations**	**Presentations**

Dear Parent or Guardian,

This year in language arts we are using the grammar and writing program *Voyages in English*. This is the time for students to develop the habits of good writers. The diagram below sketches the writing process used by professional writers and taught by *Voyages in English*.

Prewriting: brainstorming, choosing a topic, gathering ideas, planning

Drafting: putting ideas into sentences, producing the working copy

Editing: evaluating ideas and organization, by writer and sometimes by a partner

Revising: improving the draft

Proofreading: fixing grammar, spelling, punctuation, and capitalization

Publishing: final polishing, sharing with an audience

Looking at your child's work, you may find a number of mistakes in early drafts. This is normal. Early in the writing process, writers focus on capturing ideas and putting them into words. Later in the process, writers fix mistakes in grammar, spelling, and punctuation.

You can help your child by serving as an outside reader. The checklists in your child's book explain what to look for. While you can help by reading and by pointing out mistakes, it is strongly suggested that your child solve problems and correct mistakes independently. Learning how to improve a draft is key to becoming a good writer.

As the year progresses, you will see growth in your child's writing and communication skills.

Sincerely,

Scope and Sequence of Skills

Grammar	Grade Level		
	1	2	3
NOUNS			
common/proper	I	T	T
singular/plural	I	I	T
irregular			T
possessive		I	T
collective			T
as subjects			T
used in direct address			I
words used as nouns and verbs			I
words used as nouns and adjectives			I
PRONOUNS			
singular/plural	I	I	T
subject	I	I	I
object	I	I	I
possessive			I
as compound subjects			I
agreement with antecedent			I
ADJECTIVES			
descriptive	I	I	T
positive/comparative/superlative	I	I	T
articles			T
demonstrative			I
that tell how many	I		I
common/proper			I
as subject complements			I
position of			I
words used as nouns or adjectives			I
little, less, least			I
ADVERBS			
manner		I	I
time			I
place			I
negation			I

I = Introduced, **T** = Taught

Grammar *(continued)*	Grade Level		
	1	2	3
VERBS			
subject/verb agreement	I	I	T
action	I	I	T
being/linking	I	I	T
words used as nouns/verbs			I
regular/irregular	I	I	I
simple present	I	I	I
simple past	I	I	I
future with *will*			I
future with *going to*			I
helping (auxiliary)		I	I
principal parts			I
present progressive		I	I
past progressive		I	I
CONJUNCTIONS			
coordinating			I
SENTENCES			
declarative	I	I	I
interrogative	I	I	I
exclamatory	I	I	I
imperative	I	I	I
simple	I	I	I
compound (conjunctions)			I
PARTS OF SENTENCES			
subject and predicate		I	I
simple subject		I	I
simple predicate		I	I
compound sentence elements			I
subject complement			I
PUNCTUATION/CAPITALS			
end punctuation	I	I	T
capital letters	I	I	T
periods/capital letters in abbreviations		I	T
periods/capital letters in titles and initials		I	T
titles of books, stories, etc.	I	I	I
commas in series			I
commas in compound sentences			I
apostrophes	I	I	T
writing addresses			T
writing direct quotes			I
commas in direct address			I
commas after initial phrase			I

I = Introduced, **T** = Taught

Writing	Grade Level		
	1	2	3
GENRES			
Personal Narratives	X	X	X
Descriptions	X	X	X
Book Reports/Expository Writing	X	X	X
How-to Articles	X	X	X
Friendly Letters	X	X	X
Creative Writing			X
Persuasive Writing			X
Research Reports	X	X	X
GENRE SKILLS			
Plot Development			X
Organization	X	X	X
Ideas and Outlines	•	•	•
Spatial Order			•
Chronological Order	•	•	•
Comparing and Contrasting			•
Title	X	X	X
Topic	X	X	X
Introduction	X	X	X
Body	X	X	X
Conclusion	X	X	X
Audience	X	X	X
Purpose	X	X	X
Voice/Tone/Word Choice	X	X	X
Sentence Fluency	X	X	X
WRITING PROCESS			
Prewriting	X	X	X
Brainstorming	•	•	•
Free Writing	•	•	•
Organizing Ideas	•	•	•
Choosing a Topic	•	•	•
Drafting	X	X	X
Content Editing	X	X	X
Proofreading	X	X	X
Revising	X	X	X
Publishing	X	X	X

X = skill taught at grade level, **•** = topic taught at grade level

Writing (continued)	Grade Level		
	1	2	3
WRITING SKILLS			
Revising Sentences			X
Adjectives	X	X	X
Graphic Organizers	X	X	X
Five-Senses Chart	•	•	•
Idea Charts	•	•	
Storyboards	•	•	
Sentence Strips/Note Cards	•	•	•
Word Maps/Word Webs/Idea Webs			•
Expanding Sentences			X
Combining Sentences			X
Verbs			X
Dialog			X
Sentence Types			
Simple Sentences	•	•	•
Compound Sentences			•
Transition Words		X	X
WORD STUDY			
Prefixes			X
Number Prefixes			X
Antonyms	X	X	X
Synonyms	X	X	X
Exact Words	X	X	X
Nouns	•	•	•
Verbs	•	•	•
Adjectives	•	•	•
Adverbs			•
Homophones	•	•	•
Contractions	X	X	X
Transition Words		X	X
Suffixes			X
Noun and Adjective Suffixes	•	•	•
Adverb and Verb Suffixes	•	•	•

X = skill taught at grade level, • = topic taught at grade level

Writing	Grade Level		
	1	2	3
STUDY SKILLS LESSONS			
Dictionary	X	X	X
Pronunciation			•
Word Definition	•	•	•
Entry Words		•	•
Guide Words		•	•
Taking Notes	X	X	X
Library and Internet Sources	X	X	X
Parts of a Book	X	X	X

X = skill taught at grade level, • = topic taught at grade level

Sentences

In this chapter students will learn about

- writing a complete sentence
- capital letters
- end marks
- telling sentences
- commanding sentences
- asking sentences
- exclaiming sentences

A Visual, Please

Is It a Complete Sentence?

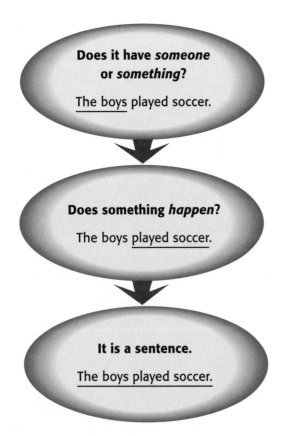

Does it have *someone* or *something*?

The <u>boys</u> played soccer.

Does something *happen*?

The boys <u>played soccer</u>.

It is a sentence.

The boys <u>played soccer</u>.

Grammar for Grown-ups

Strictly Sentences

The word *sentence* is derived from the Latin *sententia*, meaning "feeling" or "opinion." A sentence consists of several parts of speech organized into a pattern that expresses a complete thought. Every sentence has two basic parts: the subject, which is the explicit or implied person, place, or thing talked about; and the predicate, which is what the subject is, has, or does.

A declarative (telling) sentence makes a statement and ends with a period. An interrogative (asking) sentence asks a question and ends with a question mark. An imperative (commanding) sentence gives a command and ends with a period. An exclamatory (exclaiming) sentence expresses strong emotion and ends with an exclamation point.

Daily Edits

The Daily Edits provide students with daily practice in editing sentences. Prior to assigning the first Daily Edit, go over the Proofreading Marks chart on the inside back cover of the student book.

Begin each day's grammar lesson by writing on the board the Daily Edit. Help students correct the sentence. Then discuss the results as a class. Help students understand what corrections are necessary to make the sentence accurate and complete.

Consider leaving on the board the corrected sentences. Because each week's sentences form a story, there will be context clues to help students find and correct mistakes.

Common Errors

Or "Is This a Complete Sentence?"

Some developing writers write sentence fragments rather than complete sentences. This error occurs because young writers often forget that all sentences must express a complete thought.

ERROR: The cat.
CORRECT: The cat purrs.

ERROR: Raced down the street.
CORRECT: I raced down the street.

As students revise their writing, remind them to make sure each sentence is a complete thought or idea. Explain that a sentence must name something and show an action.

For Kids Who Are Ready

Or "The Parts of a Sentence"

For students who are ready to apply the finer points of grammar to their writing, discuss the following concept:

A sentence has two parts. The naming part (subject) of a sentence tells who or what the sentence is about. The action part (predicate) of a sentence tells what a person or a thing does.

SENTENCE: Talia has red mittens.
NAMING PART: Talia
ACTION PART: has red mittens.

SENTENCE: Sarah likes to sing.
NAMING PART: Sarah
ACTION PART: likes to sing.

Share with students the examples above. For extra practice, have students identify the naming parts and action parts of the sentences on page 13 of the student book.

Ask a Mentor

Real Situations, Real Solutions

Dear Grammar Geek,

Some of my students don't understand how to write complete sentences. How can I help them?

Help me,
Arlene F.

Dear Arlene,

Display the visual on page 6a. Review it often with students. Use other simple sentences to illustrate the concept.

Completing sentences around the world,
Grammar Geek

Dear Grammar Geezer,

Some of my students do not understand how to complete a sentence. What can I do to help them identify complete thoughts or ideas?

Fragmented,
Mae in Michigan

Dear Mae,

Write the following fragment on the board: The dogs. Ask your students the following questions:

Who is this sentence about? (The dogs) Can you tell what is being done? (no) How can we change the sentence so we answer these questions: Who is this about? What did they do?

Work with the class to fill in the missing information. Repeat the activity with other sentence fragments, such as Hopped on the rocks. The boys. and Ate my lunch. Then remind students that they should be able to answer the same questions with their own sentences.

Defragmenting lives,
Grammar Geezer

I THINK I'LL KEEP A DIARY

THE END OF PREHISTORY

David Cooney: www.CartoonStock.com

Personal Narratives

Genre Characteristics

At the end of this chapter, students will write a personal narrative. They will be guided through the writing process in the Writer's Workshop. The completed personal narrative will include the following:

- a topic about something that really happened to the writer
- a first-person point of view
- a beginning that tells what the story is about
- a middle that tells what happened
- an ending that finishes the story
- time order
- correct grammar, spelling, capitalization, and punctuation

Daily Story Starters

The Daily Story Starters for this chapter provide students with practice writing about themselves. This daily practice helps to prepare students for writing their personal narratives.

Begin each day by writing on the board the Daily Story Starter. Allow time for students to complete the sentence. Then discuss the results as a class. Because the purpose of this activity is to practice brainstorming, talk to students about their ideas and whether the ideas are appropriate for the genre.

Taking It Personally

Personal narratives are written to share significant events in writers' lives. They are personal to the core, and at their best they are revealing and relevant to others.

A personal narrative has a clear focus on a particular topic. The topic is always a true story or event that the writer experienced. First-person point of view indicates to the reader that the writer is telling the story about himself or herself. The ideas in the narrative help express the importance of the topic to the writer.

Effective personal narratives are well organized. Ideas are usually presented in order. The main idea is often clearly explained in the beginning, while the ending of a personal narrative gives a sense of resolution.

The writer of an effective personal narrative knows how to let his or her personality shine through with the use of humor, phrasing, dialog, or a combination of these characteristics. Personal narratives have an honest voice—one that is authentic and true. Throughout a personal narrative, the writing is correct in grammar, punctuation, capitalization, and spelling.

Teacher's Toolbox

Try the following ideas to help your students get the most out of the Writer's Workshop:

- Encourage students to keep a picture journal to record important or interesting personal experiences.

- Invite students to bring in pictures or drawings of favorite family events. Discuss how these events might make good personal narrative topics.

- Invite local officials or celebrities (such as the mayor, an entertainer, or the principal) to tell the class about an event they remember from their own childhood.

Reasons to Write

Share with your students the following times in which people write personal narratives. Talk about why it is important to become a good writer of personal narratives.

- a teacher writing about a classroom experience for a teaching journal

- a truck driver writing a description of her delivery

- a firefighter writing a report about a rescue operation

Literature Links

You can add the following titles to your classroom library to offer your students examples of well-written personal narratives:

My Name Is Yoon by Helen Recorvits

There's an Alligator Under My Bed by Mercer Mayer

Diary of a Spider by Doreen Cronin

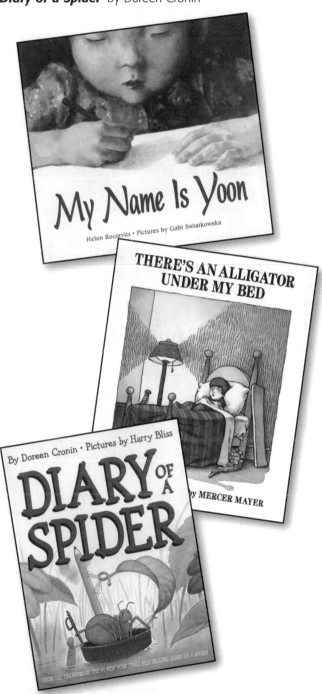

Name _____   Date _____

Personal Narrative

	Yes	No
My story is about me.	☐	☐
My story has a beginning, a middle, and an ending.	☐	☐
I used the words I, me, and my.	☐	☐
I used complete sentences.	☐	☐
I spelled words correctly.	☐	☐
I used capital letters correctly.	☐	☐
I used end marks correctly.	☐	☐

Voyages in English 1

Teacher's Scoring Rubric

Personal Narrative

0 = not evident
1 = minimal evidence of comprehension
2 = evidence of development toward comprehension
3 = strong evidence of comprehension
4 = outstanding evidence of comprehension

Ideas	Points
topic relates to a real event	

Organization	
has a logical sequence	
has a beginning	
has a middle	
has an ending	

Voice	
is written from the writer's point of view	

Word Choice	
uses appropriate words	
words are recognizable	

Sentence Fluency	
has correct sentence structure	

Conventions	
grammar	
spelling	
punctuation and capitalization	

Daily Voyages

Daily Edits

Monday	Tuesday	Wednesday	Thursday	Friday
leela sailed in a boat.	She sailed around Africa.	sometimes Leela got lost.	she sailed for months.	Leela saw ~~mny~~ *many* beautiful animals.
hank looks for special plants.	Hank studies plants ~~ina~~ *in a* lab.	Hank found a silver flower.	~~Ware~~ *Where* did he find it?	he found it on a mountain.
Fog floated ~~ovr~~ *over* the grass.	A bear growled outside.	I ran to the ~~windo.~~ *window*	i saw a dark shape.	It was just ~~mi~~ *my* dad!
My dog hid under the couch.	i put out a treat.	do you know what happened?	I ~~mad~~ *made* a ham sandwich.	my dog ~~cam~~ *came* out to share my sandwich.
a penguin sent me a postcard~~?~~.	He was ~~sik~~ *sick* of the cold.	he hopped on an iceberg.	The iceberg took him *to* Brazil.	the penguin ~~luved~~ *loved* the beach.

Daily Story Starters

Monday	Tuesday	Wednesday	Thursday	Friday
I once found a	For my last birthday I	I saw a flower at	I got wet when	I was surprised when
I once rode in a	I laughed when I saw	I was lucky when	I was with my friends when	It scared me when
I sang a song at	I traveled to	I got mad when	A new person I met was	I was excited when
It was loud when I	I once shared my	I saw a fish when	I once dressed up as	It was hot when
I helped make	I liked going to	Last Saturday I	My favorite meal was	It was fun when I

Chapter Adaptors

SPEAKING & LISTENING

Write on the board *who, what, when, where, why,* and *how.* Explain that news reporters use question words to find out information about someone or something. Share with students a fictitious event, such as the discovery of a living dinosaur or an interview with a space alien. Ask students to pretend that they are reporters covering the event. Have students write asking sentences about the situation. In the style of a press conference, improvise answers to students' questions. Help students make a short news article about the event.

SENTENCE SUPERHIGHWAY

Draw on the board a highway with four exit ramps. On the highway, write *Types of Sentences*. Label the ramps *Asking, Commanding, Exclaiming,* and *Telling.* Then draw a road sign at the beginning of each ramp with the corresponding questions: *Does it ask a question? Does it tell people to do something? Does it show excitement? Does it tell about something?* Say aloud a sentence and ask a volunteer to drive a toy car along the highway and to choose the correct exit ramp. Repeat with other volunteers and kinds of sentences.

SPEAKING & LISTENING

Remind students of their first day of school this year. Ask specific questions to prompt students to share specific details about that day. Tell students that whenever they share something that happened to them, they are sharing a personal narrative.

ENGLISH-LANGUAGE LEARNERS

Invite students to tell in complete sentences what they do at the park. Write on the board students' sentences. Erase one part of each sentence, such as the verb. Use pictures and pantomime to introduce new vocabulary. Have students write the new words in the sentences and read the sentences aloud.

RETEACHING

Display a colorful poster or picture. Have the class form two groups—an Asking Group and a Telling Group. Have a student in the Asking Group ask a question about the picture. Then have a student in the Telling Group answer the question with a complete idea. Remind students of the end mark that is needed for each sentence. After a few rounds, switch the groups and repeat the activity.

WRITING & EDITING

Make a poster to display in the classroom that includes the following peer-conferencing tips:
1. Always begin by saying what you liked about your partner's writing.
2. Be polite when talking about your partner's writing.
3. Listen to your partner's ideas.
4. Think about which of your partner's ideas you will use in your draft.

RETEACHING

Read aloud a popular short story. Ask students to tell the events that happened in the beginning, the middle, and the ending of the story. Remind students that a personal narrative must have all three parts in order to be complete.

CHAPTER

1

Sentences and Personal Narratives

HOO

Quotation Station

Writing is thinking on paper.

–William Zinsser author

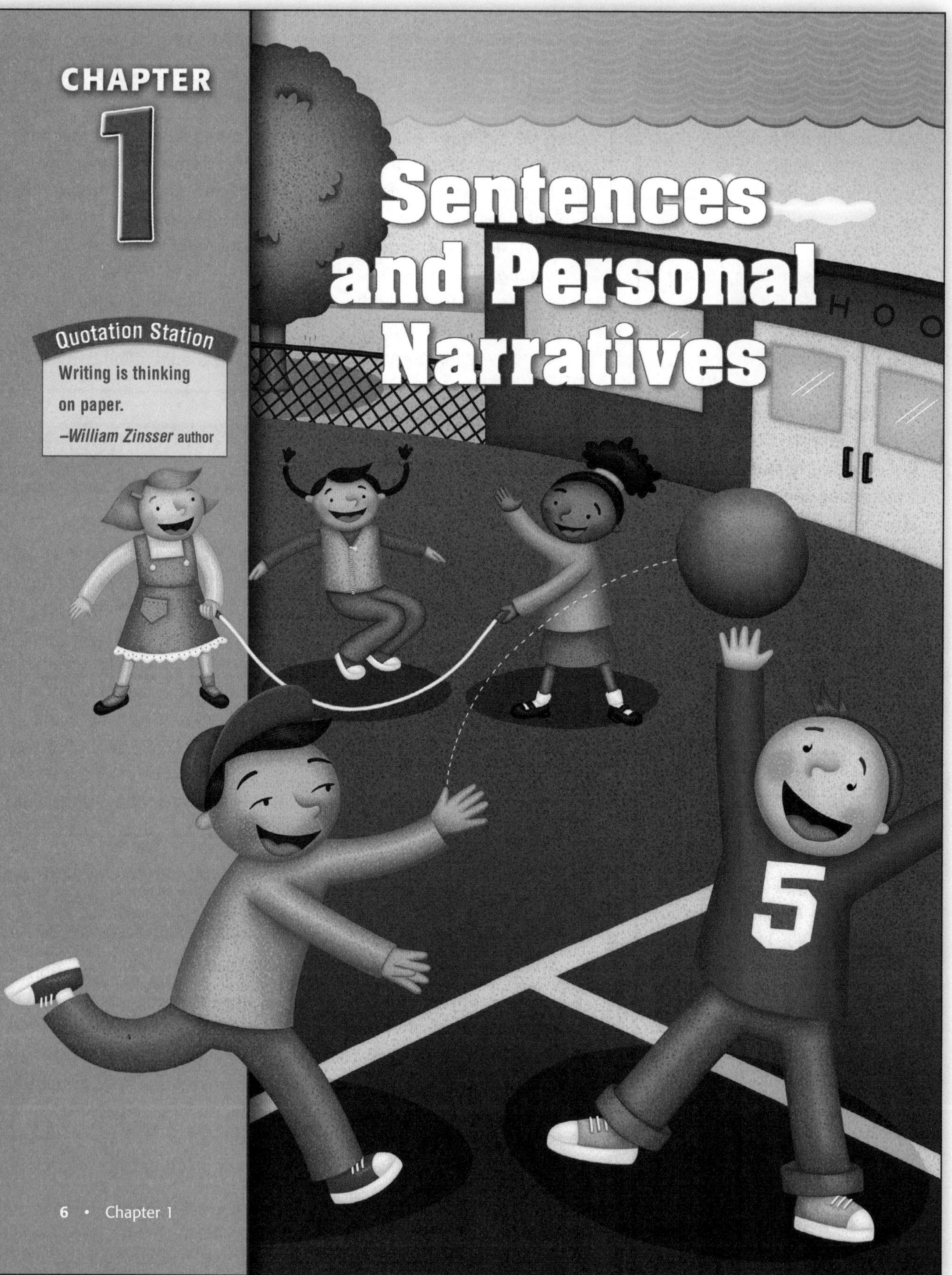

5

New at School

I was new at school. I did not know anyone. Then I heard a voice say hello to me. The boy said his name was Matt. He said he was new too. Now Matt is my best friend.

Name

Sentence Sense

A **sentence** is a group of words that tells a complete idea. The first word in a sentence always begins with a capital letter. A sentence always ends with an end mark.

This is not a complete sentence.

the pig

It only names something.

This is not a complete sentence.

oinked

It only shows an action.

This is a complete sentence.

The pig oinked.

It names something and shows an action.

● **Underline the group of words that is a sentence.**

1. <u>We colored the picture.</u>
   the picture

2. <u>The girl reads a story.</u>
   The girl

3. eat lunch
   <u>The children eat lunch.</u>

4. jumps rope
   <u>She jumps rope.</u>

5. <u>The birds make a nest.</u>
   The birds

6. plays soccer
   <u>Min plays soccer.</u>

7. <u>The puppy wags its tail.</u>
   The puppy

8. <u>The moon shines at night.</u>
   shines at night

9. Holden
   <u>Holden made a sandwich.</u>

10. <u>We climbed the hill.</u>
    climbed the hill

Name

Making Sentences

This is a sentence.

A frog hopped into the pond.

Write these words in the correct order to make sentences.

Lara   cookie   the   ate

1. *Lara ate the cookie* .

the   takes   Derrek   bus

2. *Derrek takes the bus* .

Mom   the   drives   car

3. *Mom drives the car* .

fish   a   Jody   caught

4. *Jody caught a fish* .

buzzed   around   Bees   me

5. *Bees buzzed around me* .

popsicles   I   like   cherry

6. *I like cherry popsicles* .

Name

Practice with Capital Letters

Does each sentence begin with a capital letter? Color yes or no.

		yes	no
1.	I went to an apple farm.	**yes**	**no**
2.	there were so many trees.	**yes**	no
3.	i picked lots of apples.	**yes**	no
4.	The apples were red.	yes	**no**
5.	then I went home.	**yes**	no
6.	I made an apple pie.	yes	**no**
7.	The pie tasted good.	yes	**no**
8.	apple pie is my favorite dessert.	**yes**	no

Name _____

Practice with Sentences

Complete each sentence. Use the word bank.

| Joel | need | Dogs | People | walk | owns |

1. *People* have many kinds of pets.

2. Mary Jane *owns* a dog.

3. *Dogs* are friendly animals.

4. Pets *need* food and water.

5. I *walk* my dog every day.

6. *Joel* loves his cat.

Name _____

Completing Sentences

Complete the sentences. Match the words in the first list to the words in the second list.

1. Zebras   make honey.

2. Fish   spin webs.

3. Bats   have stripes.

4. Giraffes   have humps on their backs.

5. Bees   live underwater.

6. Worms   have long necks.

7. Spiders   sleep upside-down.

8. Camels   crawl underground.

Name

Telling Sentences

A **telling sentence** tells about something. A telling sentence ends with a period (.).

We played a game.

● **Put a period at the end of each telling sentence.**

1. My cat can run fast ⊙

2. The bus stops at the corner ⊙

3. The police officer helps us ⊙

4. Our team won the game ⊙

5. Rosa chased the puppy ⊙

6. The funny rabbit hops ⊙

7. Toby saw the lion ⊙

8. We swim in the pool ⊙

9. This is my new bike ⊙

10. Tristen flew a kite ⊙

A little black dot that you can see,
Period is my name.
A telling sentence ends with me.
I play a telling game.

Sentences • **13**

Name

Making Telling Sentences

Complete each telling sentence. Use the correct word from the word bank. Put a period at the end of each sentence.

opened	carry	fixed	rides
plays	lie	ate	flew

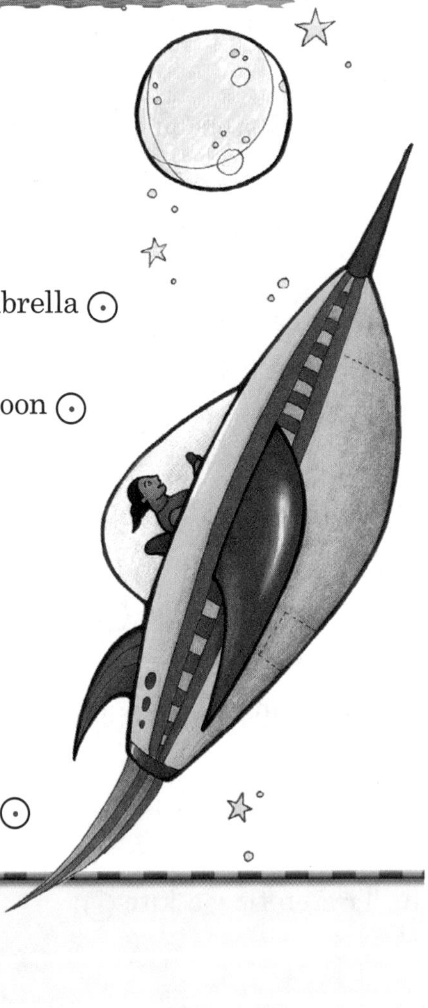

1. Carmen *rides* a bike ⊙

2. Snakes *lie* in the sun ⊙

3. On rainy days I *carry* my umbrella ⊙

4. The spaceship *flew* to the moon ⊙

5. Devon *plays* baseball ⊙

6. Rudy *opened* the door ⊙

7. Dad *fixed* a broken toy ⊙

8. The monkey *ate* a banana ⊙

Writer's Corner

Write a telling sentence about a bike.

Name

Asking Sentences

Some sentences ask a question. An **asking sentence** ends with a question mark (**?**).

Where is the library?

● **Put a question mark at the end of each asking sentence.**

1. What is the name of your teacher **?**

2. What did you say **?**

3. Which book did you read **?**

4. How many legs does a spider have **?**

5. When is your birthday **?**

6. What games do you play **?**

7. Is your coat blue **?**

8. Can you a ride a bike **?**

9. Where do you live **?**

10. Do you like peas **?**

I am a squiggle on your page
with a little dot below.
At the end of each asking sentence,
please place me just so.

Sentences • 15

Name

Making Asking Sentences

An asking sentence often begins with a **question word**.
Look at the question words in the honey pot.

**Write the correct question word for each sentence.
Sample answers shown.**

1. *Who* makes honey?

2. *What* does honey taste like?

3. *How* is honey made?

4. *Where* is the beehive?

5. *Where* is the honey jar?

6. *What* happened to the honey?

7. *Why* is the honey jar empty?

8. *When* can we eat the honey?

9. *Who* takes care of the bees?

10. *When* can we have more honey?

Who   When
Where   Why
What   How

Name

Find the Asking Sentences

Underline each asking sentence. Then add a question mark.
Add a period to each telling sentence.

1. Where are the children **?**
   The children are at the zoo **.**

2. The seals eat fish**.**
   What do the seals eat **?**

3. Where are the seals **?**
   The seals are in the water **.**

4. The zookeeper has a pail of fish **.**
   Who has a pail of fish **?**

5. The children like the seals **.**
   Who likes the seals **?**

6. Who feeds the seals **?**
   The zookeeper feeds the seals **.**

7. What do the seals do **?**
   The seals bark and swim **.**

8. The children smile and laugh **.**
   What do the children do **?**

Writer's Corner

Write an asking sentence about a book.

Name _____

Asking and Telling Sentences

Match the asking sentence in the first list to the telling sentence in the second list.

1. How many planets are there?

2. What is the largest animal?

3. What lays eggs?

4. What has a long trunk?

5. What month is hot?

6. What animal has a shell?

7. What planet has rings?

The whale is the largest animal.

July is a hot month.

An elephant has a long trunk.

There are nine planets.

A hen lays eggs.

The planet Saturn has rings.

A turtle has a shell.

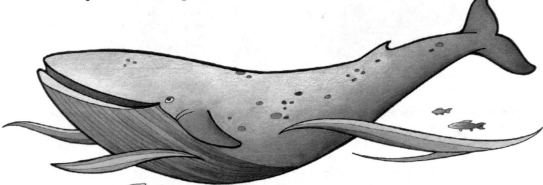

Name _____

Writing Telling Sentences

Use each word in a telling sentence. Put a period at the end of each sentence. **Answers will vary.**

hear

1. We hear the music.

look

2. We looked at the tree.

come

3. Please come to our house.

play

4. We can play outside today.

catch

5. We can catch the ball.

dance

6. The kids danced at the dancing floor.

Name _____

Writing Asking Sentences

Use each word in an asking sentence. Put a question mark at the end of each sentence. **Answers will vary.**

book

1. *Where is my book?*

school

2.

crossing guard

3.

umbrella

4.

car

5.

street

6.

Name

Commanding Sentences

Some sentences tell people what to do. These sentences are called **commanding sentences**. A commanding sentence ends with a period (.).

Tie your shoe.

Put a period at the end of each commanding sentence.

1. Come here, please .

2. Write your name on the chalkboard .

3. Go to the front of the bus .

4. Please feed the goldfish .

5. Open the door slowly .

6. Stop at the corner .

7. Eat slowly .

8. Walk quickly in the fire drill .

9. Please close the door .

10. Put the book away .

Commanding Sentence is my name.
Giving directions is my aim.
I help you know the things to do
at home, at play, and in school too!

Name _____

Find the Commanding Sentences

Underline each commanding sentence. Then add the correct end mark to each sentence.

1. Underline Follow the leader .
   Where are we going ?

2. Watch your step, please .
   When does the parade start ?

3. How big is the elephant ?
   Eat your ice cream quickly .

4. Look at the giant drum .
   The balloons are colorful .

5. Hold on to your balloon .
   The band plays a song .

6. The man plays the drum .
   Stop here, please .

7. The clowns make me laugh .
   Tell me a joke .

8. Dance with me .
   The tuba is shiny .

Writer's Corner

Write a commanding sentence about a door.

Name _____

Exclaiming Sentences

Some sentences show surprise or excitement. These sentences are called **exclaiming sentences**. An exclaiming sentence ends with an exclamation point (!).

It is so hot today!

Put an exclamation point at the end of each sentence.

1. Lydia caught a huge fish !

2. Look at the giant rainbow !

4. Here comes the train !

5. That is a funny bird !

3. The stars are very bright tonight !

6. The music is too loud !

7. The birthday cake is delicious !

8. The water is too cold !

9. I did it !

10. The snow is so deep !

My name is Exclamation Point.
Now if you are very wise,
you will put me at the end
of each sentence of surprise.

Name

Find the Exclaiming Sentences

Underline each exclaiming sentence.
Then add the correct end mark to each sentence.

1. The dolphin is in the water .
   <u>Orgo is here</u> !

2. How do dolphins jump ?
   <u>Orgo swims so fast</u> !

3. <u>That was a loud splash</u> !
   What is she doing ?

4. <u>She is a very brave trainer</u> !
   Orgo does tricks for the trainer .

5. Who got splashed ?
   <u>I am all wet</u> !

6. <u>Orgo is a wonderful dolphin</u> !
   Orgo jumps and spins .

7. <u>Hurrah for Orgo</u> !
   Everyone claps for Orgo .

8. I enjoyed watching Orgo .
   <u>It was so much fun to see Orgo</u> !

Writer's Corner

Write an exclaiming sentence about thunder.

Name

Scrambled Sentences

Unscramble these words to make sentences.
Remember, a sentence always begins with
a capital letter. A sentence ends with
a period(.), a question mark(?),
or an exclamation point(!).

| the | you | piano | can | play |

1. Can you play the piano?

| with | come | me |

2. Come with me.

| your | address | is | what |

3. What is your address?

| for | out | look | car | the |

4. Look out for the car!

| am | years | six | old | I |

5. I am six years old.

| the | scissors | with | be | careful |

6. Be careful with the scissors.

Name

Sentences to Complete

Complete each sentence. Put a period (**.**), a question mark (**?**),
or an exclamation point (**!**) at the end of each sentence. **Sample answers shown.**

1. What is your favorite *color?*

2. The boys can jump *rope.*

3. That is a scary *monster!*

4. Please button your *coat.*

5. How do you play *checkers?*

6. Those flowers are so *beautiful!*

7. Please wash your *hands.*

8. Iris likes to *sing.*

Name

More Sentences to Complete

Complete each sentence. Put a period (.), a question mark (?), or an exclamation point (!) at the end of each sentence. **Answers will vary.**

HELLO
my name is

1. My name is

2. This soup is too

3. Where is the

4. Comb your

5. I like to

6. When do you

7. Zip up your

8. It is really

Name _____

Show What You Know

Read each sentence. Write **t** for telling, **a** for asking, **c** for commanding, or **e** for exclaiming.

1. What day of the week is it? __a__

2. Go to the store, Kerry. __c__

3. Brenda is going camping. __t__

4. Catch the football. __c__

5. Andy will be so surprised! __e__

6. Can elephants swim? __a__

7. The squirrel ran up the tree. __t__

8. Will you tell a story? __a__

9. I saw a falling star! __e__

10. This is a great show! __e__

Name

Show What You Know

Read each sentence. Put a period (.), a question mark (?),
or an exclamation point (!) at the end of each sentence.

1. The noisy train went up the hill [.]

2. Did the train go up the hill [?]

3. This is such a noisy train [!]

4. We had so much fun at the party [!]

5. Who went to the birthday party [?]

6. Colleen likes vanilla ice cream [.]

7. Clean your room, please [.]

8. Here comes the rain [!]

9. Hold your umbrella tightly [.]

10. Is the sun shining [?]

What Is a Personal Narrative?

We use sentences to write stories.

A good story has a beginning, a middle, and an ending.

The **beginning** tells what the story is about.

I went to the beach today.

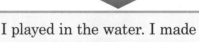

The **middle** tells what happened.

I played in the water. I made a sandcastle.

The **ending** finishes the story.

Then the sun went down. I went home.

Draw a line to match the **beginning**, the **middle**, or the **ending** to each part of the story.

Beginning My mom drove me to school. The rest of the day was better.

Middle I woke up late this morning.

Ending I could not find my shoes. Then I missed the bus.

Plan a Story

Think about a day you remember well.
Draw pictures for the beginning,
the middle, and the ending.
Write a sentence for each picture.

What a day! First, I _____

_____

_____

Then, I _____

_____

_____

_____

It was the _____ day ever.

I, Me, and *My*

A personal narrative is a special story. It is a story about you.

Use words that show the story is about you.

Use the words **I**, **me**, and **my**.

○ **Color the words about you.**

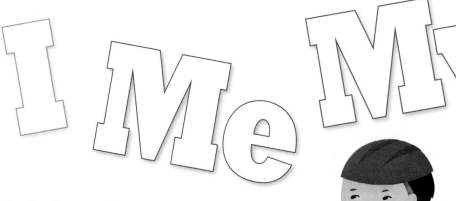

○ **Circle the words about you in this story.**

(I) had a birthday party. Everyone came.

Grandma gave (me) a skateboard.

(My) brother made (me) a cake. The cake

even had (my) name on it. It was a

great day. (I) had so much fun!

Finish a Story

Remember, you are the star of your personal narrative.

Finish this story about your first day of school. Use **I**, **me**, and **my**. Use your own words and words from the word bank. Use capital letters and the correct end marks.

friend	I	special	book	my
fun	lunch	me	recess	

On my first day of school I

My teacher

It was a day I will not forget.

Writer's Workshop

PREWRITING

Pick a Topic

A personal narrative is a story about you. The topic can be anything that happened to you.

when I learned
to kick a football

when I met my
friend Matt

when my dog
ate my dinner

Luis needs to pick a topic for a personal narrative. Look at his notes.

Write a story about you. It should be a real story that happened to you. Jot down ideas in your notebook. Think about when

• **you learned something new**

• **you made a new friend**

• **something silly happened to you**

Write down as many ideas as you can. Then circle the idea you like best. This will be your topic.

PREWRITING

Plan Your Story

Now Luis must plan his personal narrative. He draws pictures to help him plan his story. He draws pictures of the beginning, the middle, and the ending of his story.

Beginning

Middle

Ending

Think about your story. What pictures come to mind? Draw them in your notebook. Write **beginning** next to the beginning pictures. Write **middle** next to the middle pictures. Write **ending** next to the ending pictures.

Writer's Workshop

DRAFTING

When you write your story, you are drafting.
This is Luis's draft.

> I was new at school. I did not know anyone. Then I heard a voice say hello to me. The boy. He said he was new too.

Look at your pictures. Make sure they are in the right order.
Then write sentences to go with your pictures.

Write your draft in your notebook. Use your pictures and sentences
to help you. Use the word bank if you need help.

I	looked	friend	decided
me	forgot	silly	wanted
my	gave	learned	kind

I don't have an ending!

EDITING

When you check your draft, you are editing. Luis uses the Editing Checklist to check his draft.

Editing Checklist

☐ Do I have a beginning?

☐ Do I have a middle?

☐ Do I have an ending?

☐ Is my story about me?

say hello to me. The boy. He said he was new too. ∧ *Now Matt is my best friend.*

Look at the mistake Luis finds. How does he fix it?

Look at your draft. Then look at the checklist. Put an **X** in the box if you can answer yes to the question. You might ask a friend to read your story. A friend can help you spot mistakes.

REVISING

Luis revises his story. He adds changes that will make it better.

Copy your story. Add your changes and fix any mistakes.

Writer's Workshop

PROOFREADING

When you check your words and sentences, you are proofreading. Luis uses the Proofreading Checklist to check his draft.

Proofreading Checklist
- ☐ Are all the words spelled correctly?
- ☐ Did I use capital letters?
- ☐ Did I use the right end marks?
- ☐ Are the sentences complete?

> said his name was Matt
> say hello to me. The boy ∧ He said
> he was new too. Now Matt is my
> best friend.

Look at the mistake Luis finds. How does he fix it?

Read your story again. Use the checklist to check your draft. Put an **X** next to the questions if you can answer yes. If you cannot answer yes, make changes to your draft. Use these proofreading marks to make your changes.

Proofreading Marks		
Symbol	**Meaning**	**Example**
∧	add	We ∧ books. (read)
℘	take out	~~the~~ the park
⊙	add period	She is smart ⊙
≡	capital letter	carl jones
/	lowercase letter	He likes Soccer.

PUBLISHING

When you share your work with others, you are publishing it.
How will Luis publish his draft?

Are you ready to share your work? Copy it onto a sheet of paper.
Print neatly. Be sure to copy it exactly. Leave room to draw a picture.

You can share your story in many ways.
How will you share yours?

I want to read my story to my mom!

Mail it to a friend.

Read it to someone special.

Make a class book.

Give it to your parents.

Give it as a gift.

> New at School
> I was new at school. I did not know anyone. Then I heard a voice say hello to me. The boy said his name was Matt. He said was new too. Now Matt is my best friend.

Decide with your class how to share your story. Come up with new and fun ways.

Remember to keep thinking of new story ideas!

Nouns

In this chapter students will learn about

- nouns
- proper nouns, including days of the week and months of the year
- common nouns
- singular nouns and plural nouns
- compound words

A Visual, Please

Types of Proper Nouns

Commonly Used Proper Nouns	
names of days	Monday
names of months	July
names of holidays	Thanksgiving
family names used as names	Dad
titles of respect	Mrs.

Grammar for Grown-ups

What Are You Talking About?

The word *noun* comes from the Latin word *nomen,* meaning "name." A noun is a word that names a person, a place, a thing, or an idea.

Nouns can be categorized in several ways. Common nouns name general people, places, things, or ideas *(girl, park, car, freedom).* Proper nouns name particular people, places, things, or ideas *(Katie, John Hancock Center, Ford Escort, New Deal).*

A singular noun names one person, place, thing, or idea. A plural noun names more than one person, place, thing, or idea. Add -s to form the plural of most nouns *(cars).* Add -es to form the plural of nouns ending in *s, x, z, ch,* or *sh (buses, boxes, quizzes, inches, brushes).* If a noun ends in a consonant and *y,* change *y* to *i* and add -es *(cities).* Some nouns have irregular plural forms *(women, geese)* or don't change form from singular to plural *(sheep, moose).*

Daily Edits

The Daily Edits for this chapter provide students with daily practice editing sentences. Students should pay special attention to the use and capitalization of nouns.

Begin each day's grammar lesson by writing on the board the Daily Edit. Help students correct the sentence. Then discuss the results as a class. Help students understand what corrections are necessary to make the sentence accurate and complete.

Consider leaving on the board the corrected sentences. Because each week's sentences form a story, there will be context clues to help students find and correct mistakes.

Common Errors

Otherwise Known as "Where Has My Capital Gone?"

Some developing writers make mistakes when capitalizing proper nouns that are multiple words. They often capitalize only the first word of the proper noun, forgetting that the whole phrase is the special name and that every important word should be capitalized.

ERROR: Statue of liberty
CORRECT: Statue of Liberty

ERROR: New york
CORRECT: New York

Remind students to pay special attention to proper nouns as they revise their writing. Students should be able to determine when words in special names are capitalized. Have students work together to check and change any errors.

For Kids Who Are Ready

Or "To Whom Does It Belong?"

Some students may be ready to learn about possessives. Tell these students that *possession* means "ownership." Demonstrate how to show possession by using an apostrophe and *s*.

Mandy has a doll. It is **Mandy's** doll.

The elephant has a tail. It is the **elephant's** tail.

Explain that in each example, both sentences show possession, but the second sentence is shorter. Guide students to understand that when a noun is singular, an apostrophe and *s* are used to show that someone or something owns something.

Ask a Mentor

Real Situations, Real Solutions

Dear Grammar Geek,

Are there specific proper noun categories that a first grader should know?

I like lists,
Gretchen

Dear Gretchen,

Display and review the visual on page 40a. Your students might find it helpful when deciding which words to treat as proper nouns.

A fellow list liker,
Grammar Geek

Dear Grammar Geezer,

What do you do if a sentence begins with a noun that is a number? Do you begin the sentence with a numeral or with a word?

It doesn't add up,
Jing Mei Q.

Dear Jing Mei,

Remember that every sentence must begin with a capital letter. A numeral is not a letter, so don't begin a sentence with a numeral. Spell out the number word or revise the sentence so that the number is not used as the first word.

Grammar's number-one fan,
Grammar Geezer

Friendly Letters

Noel Ford: www.CartoonStock.com

"Hey—Cool! I've never seen a 'dear John' email before."

Genre Characteristics

At the end of this chapter, students will write a friendly letter. They will be guided through the writing process in the Writer's Workshop. The completed friendly letter will include the following:

- the date the letter was written
- a greeting that names the recipient
- a body that shares the writer's message
- a closing followed by the writer's name
- correct grammar, spelling, capitalization, and punctuation

Daily Story Starters

The Daily Story Starters for this chapter provide students with practice generating messages for friendly letters. This daily practice helps to prepare students for writing their friendly letters.

Begin each day by writing on the board the Daily Story Starter. Because the audience, or recipient, of a letter often determines the message, help students choose an audience before composing their sentences. Allow time for students to complete their sentences. Help students determine whether their messages are appropriate for the audiences and purposes of their letters. Discuss the results as a class.

Taking It Personally

Friendly letters, or personal letters, are perhaps the most common form of writing for most people. As a genre, friendly letters are unique in almost every way.

While many genres speak to a wide audience, the audience for a friendly letter is usually one person or a small group of people. The purpose of a friendly letter is variable. It might be to share a story or a message, to say thank you, or to ask a favor. Whatever the purpose, ideas in friendly letters reflect a writer's own experience and often share sentiments that forge a personal connection between the writer and reader.

Effective friendly letters follow a standard form that includes the date, a greeting that usually begins with *Dear* and the person's name, a body, a closing, and a signature. The body of a friendly letter shares ideas in a natural voice, often using informal language.

Effective friendly letters have a variety of sentence types for emphasis and impact. These sentences are correct in grammar, spelling, capitalization, and punctuation.

Teacher's Toolbox

Try the following ideas to help your students get the most out of the Writer's Workshop:

- Have students share personal letters, e-mails, or cards with personal messages that they have received.

- Consider taking the class on a field trip to the local post office.

- Create a bulletin-board display of personal letters that you have received, including both e-mails and those sent through the Postal Service.

Reasons to Write

Share with your students the following times at which people write friendly letters. Talk about why it is important to become good writers of letters.

- sharing news about an addition to the family or a new pet

- thanking someone for help he or she gave

- asking a friend to come to a party

Literature Links

You can add the following titles to your classroom library to offer your students examples of letters:

Corduroy Writes a Letter by Alison Inches

Yours Truly, Goldilocks by Alma Flor Ada

The Jolly Postman by Janet and Allan Ahlberg

Friendly Letter

	Yes	No
My letter shares a story or a message, says thank you, or asks a favor.	☐	☐
My letter has all the necessary parts.	☐	☐
I used nouns correctly.	☐	☐
I used complete sentences.	☐	☐
I spelled words correctly.	☐	☐
I used capital letters correctly.	☐	☐
I used end marks correctly.	☐	☐

Voyages in English 1

Teacher's Scoring Rubric

Friendly Letter

0 = not evident
1 = minimal evidence of comprehension
2 = evidence of development toward comprehension
3 = strong evidence of comprehension
4 = outstanding evidence of comprehension

Ideas	Points
communicates a coherent message, such as a story, an expression of gratitude, or a request	
Organization	
has a date	
has a greeting	
has a body	
has a closing	
has a signature	
Voice	
is written in a natural voice	
Word Choice	
uses nouns correctly	
uses appropriate words	
words are recognizable	
Sentence Fluency	
has correct sentence structure	
Conventions	
grammar	
spelling	
punctuation and capitalization	

Voyages in English 1

Daily Voyages

Daily Edits

Monday	Tuesday	Wednesday	Thursday	Friday
May I borrow your robot?	My robot *is* broken.	what happened to Robbie Robot?	he ate a whole pizza.	I bet his stomach *hurts* hurtz!
what is the problem?	I poured *water* wadder in the pail.	the Water disappeared!	Look down here.	I see a Hole in the Pail.
Watch out for that Dragon!	Some *dragons* dragoons breathe Fire.	give him your ice cream.	*Dragons* Dragon's love Ice Cream.	now he cannot breathe fire.
Seven Doctors went on a *trip* treip.	They spent six Days in china.	They went to russia in may.	They saw many *places* playses.	The *doctors* docters helped many people.
mrs. gold watched *snowflakes* snow flakes outside.	She fell *asleep* aslep in mr. Gold's chair.	Something woke Mrs. Gold.	she heard *someone* some one talking.	Mr. Gold was *talking* talken to a Snowman.

Daily Story Starters

Monday	Tuesday	Wednesday	Thursday	Friday
This week I made	Today I learned	Thank you for helping me	May I borrow	I want to show you
Thank you for telling me	Can you help me	I like to practice	Thank you for giving me	Will you come to
I heard a joke about	Don't forget to	Can you teach me to	Say hello to	Thank you for making me
I enjoyed your	Yesterday I played	Will you send me	Thank you for taking me	Can you tell me
May I use your	Thank you for sharing your	My favorite toy is	My teacher gave me	My friend is

Chapter Adaptors

SPEAKING & LISTENING

Draw a large picnic basket on the board and write *sandwich* inside the basket. Say: *I'm going on a picnic and I'm bringing a sandwich.* Then have a volunteer repeat the sentence and add another person or thing. *(Example: I'm going on a picnic and I'm bringing a sandwich and a drink.)* Write each new noun inside the basket. Continue until there are five or six nouns in the sentence. Have students identify each noun as a person or thing. Then repeat with other students.

ENGLISH-LANGUAGE LEARNERS

Some English-language learners may feel more comfortable with their speaking ability than with their writing ability. Tell students that a friendly letter is like a phone conversation because in both a message is shared. Role-play with students a short phone conversation in which a student shares a story or message, says thank you, or asks a favor. Then help students write down what they have said, using letter format. Guide students to include all the parts of a friendly letter when writing.

WRITING & EDITING

Explain to students that one way to check writing for misspelled words is to read backward from right to left, one word at a time. Tell students that they should point to each word and check the spelling, moving backward through the letter.

RETEACHING

Write on the board common nouns that name larger categories of people, places, and things. *(Examples: athlete, state, building)* Invite volunteers to name well-known examples for each common noun. Write students' responses on the board. Help students understand how proper nouns name specific examples of common nouns.

LETTER MAN

Ask students to draw a person on a sheet of paper, complete with head, face, arms, legs, and feet. Then guide students to label the person with the parts of a letter. *(head/Date, mouth/Greeting, body/Body, legs/Closing, feet/Your Name)* Invite volunteers to share their drawings.

WISH YOU WERE HERE

Have students make a post card from a fantastic place. *(Examples: outer space, land of dinosaurs)* Ask students to draw a picture of their imaginary place on one side of a sheet of paper. Then have them write on the other side a short letter to a friend or family member telling about the place they are visiting. Remind students to include all the necessary parts of a friendly letter. Invite students to share their post cards with the class.

RETEACHING

Draw on the board a three-column chart. Label the columns *People, Places,* and *Things.* Invite the class to name features of the school that are nouns. Write each suggestion in the appropriate column. *(Examples: principal under People, office under Places, chalk under Things)* When the chart has several nouns under each column, review each item. Remind students that a noun names any person, place, or thing.

CHAPTER 2

Nouns and Friendly Letters

Quotation Station

With a walking stick you reach many lands. You reach many more with words.

—Finnish proverb

May 10, 2008

Dear Mike,

My birthday is on Friday.
I am having a party at Big
Pond Park. We will play games.
We will have ice cream too.
Can you come?

Your friend,
Ana

Nouns and Friendly Letters • 41

Name

Nouns

A **noun** can name a person. A noun can name a place. A noun can name a thing.

| **person** | **place** | **thing** |
| *friend* | *farm* | *pencil* |

Write the nouns that name people, places, and things.
Use the word bank.

| yard | brother | circus |
| fork | girl | ball |

people	**places**	**things**
1. *girl*	1. *circus*	1. *fork*
2. *brother*	2. *yard*	2. *ball*

A noun names a person, a place, or a thing—
a friend, the park, or a bell that rings,
a boy, a building, a bat, or a ball.
Nouns are words that name them all.

Name

Proper Nouns

A **proper noun** can name a special person. A proper noun can name a special place. A proper noun can name a special thing. A proper noun always begins with a capital letter.

person

Kevin Hartnet   *Sara Perez*   *Brian Walsh*

place

New York   *Eagle Lake*   *Grand Canyon*

thing

Bouncing Boats   *Cuddly Caterpillar*   *Lazy Daisy*

Underline each proper noun.

1. They are going to Eagle Lake.

2. Sara Perez is in my class.

3. She saw the Bouncing Boats ride in the park.

4. The Cuddly Caterpillar is a fun ride.

5. New York is a big city.

6. Anton got roller skates for his birthday.

7. Brian Walsh won the contest.

8. Marta rode a mule into the Grand Canyon.

9. Kevin Hartnet took his sister on the Lazy Daisy ride.

I am a capital letter.
My size is big, you see.
A sentence or a proper noun always begins with me.

Nouns • 43

Name

Proper Nouns Name Special People

Mrs. Clancy   **Rita and Tom**   **Beth**   **Jon**   **Mr. Jackson**   **James**

A proper noun can name a special person.
A person's name begins with a capital letter.

Write the correct name for each person.

1. Beth

2. Mrs. Clancy

3. Jon

4. James

5. Mr. Jackson

6. Rita and Tom

Name

Proper Nouns Name Special Places

A proper noun can name a special place. A proper noun begins with a capital letter.

Match the number in the story with the special place in the picture. Write the correct proper noun.

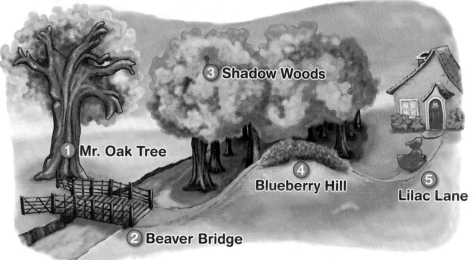

One day Red Riding Hood went to visit Grandmother. She walked on the

path toward 1. *Mr. Oak Tree* . Next she

crossed 2. *Beaver Bridge* . She saw a frisky

squirrel in 3. *Shadow Woods* . She climbed

over 4. *Blueberry Hill* . At last she saw

Grandmother's house on 5. *Lilac Lane* .

Name

Proper Nouns Name Special Things

A proper noun can name a special thing. A proper noun begins with a capital letter.

Write the proper noun for each ride. Then color the rides.

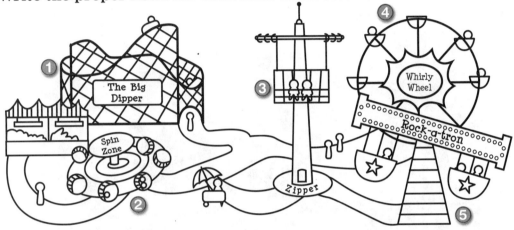

1. *The Big Dipper*

2. *Spin Zone*

3. *Zipper*

4. *Whirly Wheel*

5. *Rock-a-tron*

Writer's Corner

Write a sentence about a special thing. Use a proper noun.

Name

Common Nouns

A **common noun** can name any person. A common noun can name any place. A common noun can name any thing.

people	**places**	**things**
doctor	*town*	*coat*
writer	*store*	*toy*

Each underlined word is a common noun.
Is it a person, place, or thing? Circle the answer.

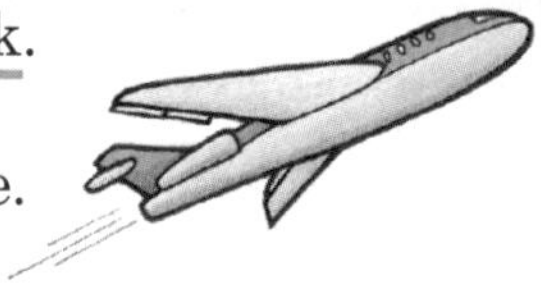

1. I live in a small <u>town</u>.   person (place) thing

2. This comic <u>book</u> is fun to read.   person place (thing)

3. The <u>baby</u> smiled at me.   (person) place thing

4. I fly my kite at the <u>park</u>.   person (place) thing

5. The <u>pilot</u> flew the plane.   (person) place thing

6. Tony went to the <u>library</u>.   person (place) thing

7. The yellow <u>crayon</u> is broken.   person place (thing)

8. Pete walked to <u>school</u>.   person (place) thing

9. My <u>bike</u> has a flat tire.   person place (thing)

10. Our <u>teacher</u> gave us homework.   (person) place thing

11. My <u>grandmother</u> walked us to school.   (person) place thing

12. Brady found a <u>frog</u> in the garden.   person place (thing)

Nouns • 47

Name _____

Common Nouns Name People

A common noun can name any person.

Write the common nouns that name the people in the pictures. Use the word bank.

| farmer | judge | nurse | pilot | firefighter | baby |

1. *nurse*
2. *pilot*
3. *judge*
4. *baby*
5. *farmer*
6. *firefighter*

Writer's Corner

Write a sentence about a person. Use a common noun.

Name

Common Nouns Name Places

A common noun can name any place.

Write the common nouns that name the places in the story. Use the word bank. Then color the places.

| library | seashore | school | jungle | zoo |

Brian went to 1. _____. He went to the 2. _____

to get some books. Brian saw a book about a 3. _____

He looked at another book about the 4. _____

Brian borrowed a book about the 5. _____

1. *school*

2. *library*

3. *zoo*

4. *seashore*

5. *jungle*

Name

Common Nouns Name Things

A common noun can name any thing.

Write the common nouns to complete the story. Use the word bank.

spoons	chairs	table	dishes	bed	coat

Goldilocks went for a walk. She came to a little house and went

inside. She saw a *table* and three *chairs* .

There were three *dishes* and three *spoons*

on the table. She was cold, so she put on a little green

coat . Then Goldilocks was tired. She went to find

a *bed* to take a nap. The three bears came home and

were surprised to find Goldilocks in their house.

Writer's Corner

Write a sentence about something you see every day.
Use a common noun.

Name _____

The Days of the Week

Days of the week are proper nouns. Each day of the week begins with a capital letter.

Trace each word. Then write it on the line.

Sunday   *Sunday* _____

Monday   *Monday* _____

Tuesday   *Tuesday* _____

Wednesday   *Wednesday* _____

Thursday   *Thursday* _____

Friday   *Friday* _____

Saturday   *Saturday* _____

Nouns • 51

Name

The Months of the Year

Months of the year are proper nouns. Each month of the year begins with a capital letter.

● **Trace each word. Then write it on the line.**

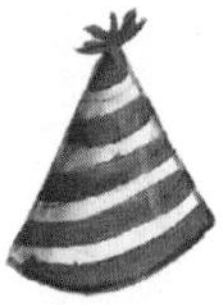

January   *January* _____

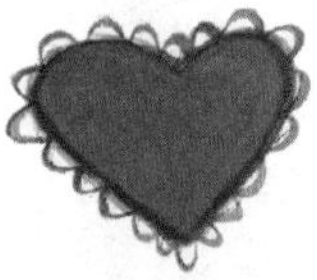

February   *February* _____

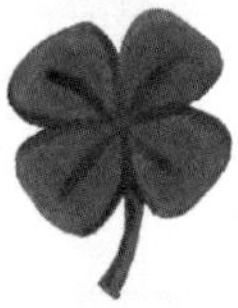

March   *March* _____

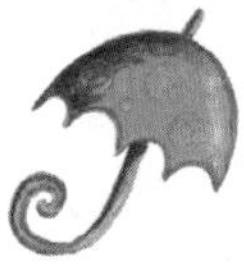

April   *April* _____

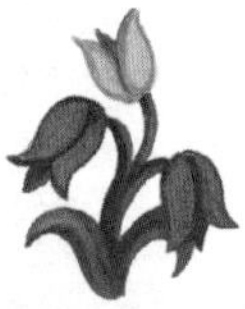

May   *May* _____

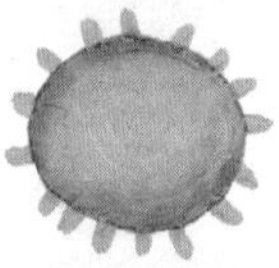

June   *June* _____

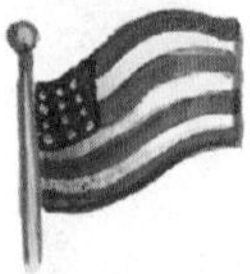

July   *July* _____

Name

The Months of the Year

Trace each word. Then write it on the line.

August   *August* — — — — — — — — — — —

September   *September* — — — — — — — —

October   *October* — — — — — — — — — —

November   *November* — — — — — — — —

December   *December* — — — — — — — —

30 days has September,
April, June, and November.
All the rest have 31
except for February, which has 28,
and 29 in a leap year, which is great!

Nouns • **53**

Name _____

Days and Months Review

Answer the questions. Remember, each day of the week and each month of the year begins with a capital letter.

Monday	**Tuesday**	**Wednesday**	**Thursday**
Friday	**Saturday**	**Sunday**	
January	**February**	**March**	**April**
May	**June**	**July**	**August**
September	**October**	**November**	**December**

1. What is your favorite day of the week? **Answers will vary.**

2. In what month is your birthday? **Answers will vary.**

3. In what month do we celebrate Thanksgiving? **November**

4. What day comes after Tuesday? **Wednesday**

5. What is the last month of the year? **December**

6. What month is very hot? **June, July, or August**

7. In some places, it snows during which month? **December, January, or February**

8. On what day do we start the school week? **Monday**

Name

Proper Nouns and Common Nouns Review

Circle each proper noun. Underline each common noun.

1. (Jodi) was on the <u>swing</u>.

2. There is a <u>sandbox</u> in (Hill Park.)

3. (Uncle Al) plays <u>baseball</u>.

4. (Doctor Kotarba) helped the sick <u>boy</u>.

5. Our <u>babysitter</u> lives on (Jay Street.)

6. The <u>market</u> is close to (Taylor School.)

7. (Maria) likes to camp in (July.)

9. (Kate) and (Rob) were on the <u>seesaw</u>.

8. (Mitch) went to the <u>playground</u>.

10. <u>Snow</u> falls in (January.)

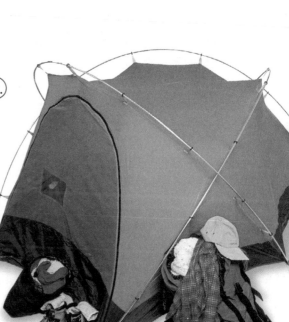

Nouns • 55

Name _____

More Proper Nouns
and Common Nouns Review

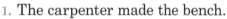

Circle each proper noun. Underline each common noun.

1. The <u>carpenter</u> made the <u>bench</u>.

2. (Mr. Jung) went to (Cedarville.)

3. <u>Students</u> go to <u>school</u> on (Mondays.)

4. My <u>cousin</u> lives in (Florida.)

5. (Thanksgiving) is in (November.)

6. (Kai) likes <u>popcorn</u>.

7. (Evan) wore a funny <u>costume</u>.

8. (March) is a windy <u>month</u>.

9. <u>Friends</u> play together on (Saturdays.)

10. On (Thursday) our <u>class</u> will visit (Lincoln Zoo.)

Name

Compound Words

A **compound word** is a word that is made by putting two words together.

sail + boat = sailboat

Put the words together to make compound words. Write each compound word.

1. work

book   *workbook*

bench   *workbench*

2. snow

ball   *snowball*

flake   *snowflake*

3. sun

set   *sunset*

rise   *sunrise*

4. school

yard   *schoolyard*

bag   *schoolbag*

5. rain

coat   *raincoat*

water   *rainwater*

Nouns • **57**

Name _____

Practice with Compound Words

Circle each compound word. Write the two words that make up each compound word.

1. Here is a (cupcake) for you.　*cup*　*cake*

2. Shawn's (necktie) is blue.　*neck*　*tie*

3. My brother works in a (supermarket.)　*super*　*market*

4. My (raincoat) is yellow.　*rain*　*coat*

5. There are many cars on the (highway.)　*high*　*way*

6. When is your (birthday?)　*birth*　*day*

7. We drove to the (airport.)　*air*　*port*

8. A (tugboat) is pulling the ship.　*tug*　*boat*

9. The (cowgirl) wore shiny boots.　*cow*　*girl*

> When you join two words together, you make a compound word. *Butterfly, snowball,* and *bluebird* are compound words that you have heard.

Writer's Corner

Write a sentence about winter. Use a compound word.

Name

One and More Than One

To make most nouns name more than one, add the letter **s**.

Write each noun. Draw a picture to show more than one.

1. one flag   two   *flags*

2. one ball   four   *balls*

3. one heart   three   *hearts*

4. one star   five   *stars*

5. one dog   three   *dogs*

6. one car   two   *cars*

Name

Practice with One and More Than One

Underline the correct noun in each sentence.

1. One (<u>ball</u> balls) is red.

2. Five (ball <u>balls</u>) are green.

3. Six (kite <u>kites</u>) are flying.

4. There are three (boat <u>boats</u>) on the lake.

5. A (<u>kitten</u> kittens) slept in a box.

6. The pool has two (slide <u>slides</u>).

7. Some (bird <u>birds</u>) are in the nest.

8. I borrowed three (book <u>books</u>) from the library.

9. Joshua gave me a shiny (<u>dime</u> dimes).

10. Spiders have eight (leg <u>legs</u>).

Name _____

More Practice with
One and More Than One

Underline the correct noun in each sentence.

1. The (<u>train</u>   trains) is on the track.

2. Three (car   <u>cars</u>) stopped at the light.

3. One (<u>lamp</u>   lamps) is missing from the shelf.

4. There are six (apple   <u>apples</u>) on the table.

5. Five (bike   <u>bikes</u>) stood in the window.

6. My brother sleeps eight (hour   <u>hours</u>) a day.

7. A (<u>chair</u>   chairs) was on the porch.

8. Four (frog   <u>frogs</u>) hopped into the pond.

9. There are two (bat   <u>bats</u>) against the fence.

10. Marissa holds a (<u>balloon</u>   balloons).

Name

Show What You Know

Circle each proper noun. Underline each common noun.

1. (Polly) opened the door.

2. Throw the football, (Keenan.)

3. (August) is a hot month.

4. The parade is on (Wednesday.)

5. (Mr. Ricardo) is a carpenter.

6. (Abraham Lincoln) was the tallest president.

7. Did your family move on (Thursday?)

8. The (Busy Bee) is my favorite ride.

9. Oranges grow in (California.)

10. (Paul) has a new bike.

Name _____

Show What You Know

Ⓐ Underline each compound word.

1. There is a letter in the <u>mailbox</u>.

2. Jack and Paula like <u>baseball</u>.

3. My little sister plays with her <u>dollhouse</u>.

4. The <u>bluebirds</u> fly very high.

5. The pretty <u>seashell</u> was cracked.

Ⓑ Underline each noun that names more than one.

1. The <u>airplanes</u> landed on the field.

2. Sheena has three <u>dolls</u>.

3. Five <u>trucks</u> came down the street.

4. I had two <u>crackers</u> in my lunch.

5. Ed has six <u>rocks</u> in his collection.

Get Ready to Write

What Is a Friendly Letter?

Friendly letters are letters to people we know. Here are some things to write in a friendly letter.

Share a story or a message.

> Dear Aunt Marlo,
> Today I went to swimming class. I learned to float!
> I will show you when I see you.

Say thank you.

> Dear Uncle Tim,
> Thank you for the football. I love it! I practice every day.

Ask a favor.

> Dear Mrs. Jensen,
> Mom said you have a puppy. May I play with him?

Look at each reason to write. Match it to the correct sentence.

1. Say thank you.   Will you help me make a kite?

2. Ask a favor.   I had fun playing with you.

3. Share a story or   Thank you for the
   a message.   birthday gift.

Parts of a Friendly Letter

Here are the different parts of a friendly letter.

Date ———
when you write the letter

Greeting ———
who the letter is for

Body ———
what you say in the letter

Closing ———
how you say goodbye

Your Name ———
write your name here

June 2, 2008

Dear Mom,

Look out! There is a
big alligator in the garage.
Do not go in. I already
told Dad.

Your son,

Harry

Draw a line to match each question to the answer.

1. Who wrote the letter? •   • Harry's mom

2. When did Harry write his letter? •   • June 2, 2008

3. Who is the letter for? •   • Your son,

4. How did Harry say goodbye? •   • Harry

Complete a Friendly Letter

Complete the friendly letter. Use the word bank.

| Your friend, | April 1, 2007 | Dear Luis, | Min |

> April 1, 2007
>
> Dear Luis,
>
> Here is a riddle for you.
> I am in a band. When
> someone taps me, I make
> a thumping sound. What
> am I?
>
> Your friend,
> Min

Finish a Friendly Letter

Finish this letter to a friend. Say thank you for something.

Date

Greeting *Dear* _____,

Body *Thank you for*

Closing *Your friend,*

Your Name

Writer's Workshop

PREWRITING

Pick a Topic

Ana is writing a friendly letter. She writes some ideas for letters in her notebook. Then she circles the idea she likes best.

Write a friendly letter. You might write to

a friend.   **a teacher.**   **a family member.**

Remember, friendly letters say different things. You might

share a story or a message.

say thank you.

ask a favor.

Think about a letter you can write. Jot down your ideas in your notebook. Write as many ideas as you can.

Look at your ideas. Then circle the one you like best.

Invite Mike to my birthday party.

Thank Cousin Kristin for visiting.

Ask Uncle Ted to help me build a tree house.

PREWRITING

Plan Your Letter

Ana plans her letter. She uses a chart to help her. Here is Ana's chart.

Today's date: May 10, 2008
My letter is for: Mike
What I want to say: Invite Mike to my birthday party
How I will say goodbye: Your friend,
My name: Ana

Plan your letter. Fill in the chart below.
Use your notebook if you need extra room.

Today's date:
My letter is for:
What I want to say:
How I will say goodbye:
My name:

Writer's Workshop

DRAFTING

Ana uses her chart to write her letter. Here is Ana's letter.

> May 10, 2008
>
> Dear Mike,
> My birthday is on friday. I am
> having a party at Big Pond Park.
> We will play games. We will have ice
> cream too. Can you come?
>
> Ana

Look at the chart you made. What other ideas do you have?
Write your ideas in your notebook.

As you write, remember that you can

share a story or a message. **say thank you.** **ask a favor.**

Then write your letter in your notebook. Use your chart as you write.
Use the word bank if you need help.

Dear_____ ,	Grandma	Your son,	Your daughter,
Love,	Grandpa	Your friend,	Uncle

EDITING

Ana reads her letter. Editing will make it even better. Ana uses the Editing Checklist.

> Can you come?   ∧Your friend,
> Ana

Look at the mistake Ana finds. How does she fix it?

Read your letter. Does it say what you want it to say? Can you answer yes to the questions in the Editing Checklist? Mark any changes that will make it better. Make it a letter that you would like to get.

Ask a family member to read your letter. He or she can help you make sure your letter is complete. Remember, you can always make more changes later.

I don't have a closing!

REVISING

Ana copies her letter. She includes the changes she marked. Ana knows that revising will make her letter better.

Copy your letter. Add anything that you forgot. Make your letter better than it was before.

Writer's Workshop

PROOFREADING

Ana proofreads her letter. She uses the Proofreading Checklist as she reads. Ana marks her letter when she wants to change something.

Proofreading Checklist

☐ Are all the words spelled correctly?

☐ Did I use capital letters?

☐ Did I use the right end marks?

☐ Did I use nouns correctly?

Dear Mike,
My birthday is on friday. I am having a party at Big Pond Park. We will play

Look at the mistake Ana finds. How does she fix it?

Read your letter again. Use the Proofreading Checklist as you read. Put an **X** next to the question if you can answer yes.

If you see a mistake, fix it. Use the proofreading marks chart at the back of your book.

PUBLISHING

When writers share their work, they are publishing it. Ana is almost ready to publish her letter. She copies it neatly onto a sheet of paper. She leaves room to draw a picture.

Get ready to publish your letter. Copy it onto a sheet of paper. Print as neatly as you can.

Sharing letters is fun. It is fun to write them. It is fun to read them too. How will you share your letter?

Read it to the class.

Put it on the class bulletin board.

Mail it to a friend or family member.

Give it to your parents.

Make a class book of letters.

Decide as a class how you will share your work. And keep writing letters!

Verbs

In this chapter students will learn about

- action verbs
- verbs ending in *s*
- verbs that do not end in *s*
- irregular verbs *has* and *have*
- regular verbs in the past tense
- irregular verbs *eat* and *ate*
- irregular verbs *give* and *gave*
- irregular verbs *see* and *saw*
- irregular verbs *write* and *wrote*
- being verbs

A Visual, Please

Interesting Irregular Verbs

Present Tense	Past Tense
eat	ate
give	gave
see	saw
write	wrote
go	went
do	did

Grammar for Grown-ups

Meaningful Words

Verb comes from the Latin *verbum,* meaning "word." A verb is a word that is used to describe an action—*Joe jumps*—or a state of being—*I am tired.* Every sentence must have a verb; without a verb the words form an incomplete thought. The main verb in a sentence tells what the subject does or is.

A verb has four principle parts: present *(run),* present participle *(running),* past *(ran),* and past participle *(run).*

A verb has tenses, including simple present *(send),* past *(sent),* and future *(will send);* present progressive *(am planning),* past progressive *(was planning),* and future progressive *(will be planning);* and present perfect *(have played),* past perfect *(had played),* and future perfect *(will have played).*

Regular verbs form the past and the past participle by adding *-d* or *-ed (boil, boiled, boiled).* The past and the past participle of irregular verbs do not follow any standard rules *(do, did, done).*

In a sentence the verb and the subject must agree. In the present tense *-s* or *-es* is added to the verb when the subject is a singular noun or the pronoun *he, she,* or *it*: *The girl talks. The girls talk.*

Daily Edits

The Daily Edits for this chapter provide students with daily practice editing sentences. Students should pay special attention to the use of verbs, including verb tenses, within each sentence.

Common Errors

Otherwise Known as "To -s or Not To -s?"

Many young writers incorrectly add *-s* to verbs that tell what more than one person or thing does.

ERROR: Jason and Allison walks home.
CORRECT: Jason and Allison walk home.

ERROR: The kittens nibbles the string.
CORRECT: The kittens nibble the string.

To help students avoid this common error, post the following rule at the top of a poster and display it in the classroom: *If the noun tells about one person or thing, add the letter* s *to the verb. If the noun tells about more than one person or thing, do not add the letter* s *to the verb.* Invite students to add to the poster correct examples of the rule, such as the following: *Marc throws the ball. The nurses give stickers.* Remind students to follow the rule in their own writing.

For Kids Who Are Ready

Also Known as "Double It"

For students who are ready, introduce verbs that end in a consonant preceded by a vowel, such as *skip, hop,* and *clap.*

The stone **skipped** across the lake.

Brad **hopped** with the rabbits.

We **clapped** when the play was over.

To help students remember this rule, write the following at the top of a poster and display it for students: *When a verb ends in a consonant after a vowel, double the consonant when adding the letters* ed. Invite students to write on the poster other verbs that follow this rule, such as *trimmed, dipped, begged, jogged,* and *mopped.*

Ask a Mentor

Real Situations, Real Solutions

Dear Grammar Geek,

Some of my students have trouble with irregular verbs in the past tense. Eat and ate almost caused a riot! Is there a way I can help my students identify common verbs with unusual past forms?
Wanting to show some good examples,
Mrs. R.

Dear Mrs. R.,

Display the visual on page 74a and review it with students. As students are exposed to other irregular verbs—such as *chose, bring, broke,* and *knew*—add them to the chart.

You are a good example,
Grammar Geek

Dear Grammar Geezer,

My students often tell or write stories that mix past and present tense verbs. How can I help them to be consistent?
Disliking change,
Kit in Cleveland

Dear Kit,

Revision is the key to eliminating the problem. Have students read their stories just for verb usage. Explain that if they begin a story in one tense, they should stick with it throughout. Be vigilant as students share stories orally, and help them to choose consistent tenses when they speak. Remember that the way students speak will often transfer to the way that they write.

Get ready for a welcome change,
Grammar Geezer

How-to Articles

Adey Bryant: www.CartoonStock.com

Genre Characteristics

At the end of this chapter, students will write a how-to article. They will be guided through the writing process in the Writer's Workshop. The completed how-to article will include the following:

- a topic that explains how to make or to do something
- a body that lists required steps
- steps listed in logical order
- correct grammar, spelling, capitalization, and punctuation

Daily Story Starters

The Daily Story Starters for this chapter provide students with practice generating topics for how-to articles. This daily practice helps to prepare students for writing their how-to articles.

Allow time for students to complete the day's sentence. Then discuss the results with the class. Help students determine whether their topics are appropriate for a how-to article. Talk with students about what topics can be easily and clearly covered in a how-to article. Discuss with students who the audience for their how-to articles will be.

How Do You Do That?

How-to writing can offer guidance and direction for accomplishing a task or goal, such as childproofing your home. How-to writing can also provide step-by-step instructions for doing or making something, such as putting together an outdoor grill or making chili.

Effective how-to writing provides a comprehensive, yet concise, explanation of the topic. Ideas are detailed so the reader clearly understands each step of the process. Unimportant or unnecessary information is left out.

An effective how-to writer considers the audience. If the instructions are for children, for example, the language and ideas are appropriate for that age group. A how-to writer also considers the knowledge, background, and experience of the audience.

A how-to article includes an informative introduction, clearly stating the purpose of the piece and what is being taught. The body describes the materials needed and the steps required to accomplish the task or goal in logical order. Finally the piece presents a conclusion that summarizes what was taught, draws a conclusion, or makes a prediction.

Clear, concise steps are essential to effective how-to writing. The steps are presented in the order in which they should be completed. Information can be presented as numbered steps or as logical, sequential paragraphs, depending on the topic. It should be easy to follow from one step to the next through the use of numbers, letters, order words, or anything else that clarifies the order of the process. Throughout an effective how-to article, the writing is correct in grammar, punctuation, capitalization, and spelling.

Teacher's Toolbox

Try the following ideas to help your students get the most out of the Writer's Workshop:

- Guide students to find how-to articles in textbooks, such as science, reading, and social studies. Talk about how these textbooks use forms of how-to writing.

- Provide students with a variety of games that include directions. Help students go over the directions. Then allow groups to play the games. When they have finished, talk about whether the games could have been successfully played without reading the directions.

- Make a bulletin-board display of how-to pamphlets, brochures, recipe cards, and craft articles.

Reasons to Write

Discuss with students why it is important for the following people to become effective how-to writers:

- video game creators

- teachers

- scientists

Literature Links

You can add the following titles to your classroom library to offer your students examples of how-to articles:

The Usborne Book of Masks by Ray Gibson

Easy Art Fun: Do-It-Yourself Crafts for Beginning Readers by Jill Frankel Hauser

My First Book of How Things Are Made by George Jones

How-to Article

	Yes	No
My article tells how to make or do something.	☐	☐
My article lists what someone will need.	☐	☐
My article tells the steps in order.	☐	☐
I used verbs correctly.	☐	☐
I used complete sentences.	☐	☐
I spelled words correctly.	☐	☐
I used capital letters correctly.	☐	☐
I used end marks correctly.	☐	☐

Voyages in English 1

Teacher's Scoring Rubric

How-to Article

0 = not evident
1 = minimal evidence of comprehension
2 = evidence of development toward comprehension
3 = strong evidence of comprehension
4 = outstanding evidence of comprehension

Ideas	Points
has a topic that tells how to make or to do something	
Organization	
has a complete list of the necessary materials	
has logical steps organized in list form	
has instructions expressed in step-by-step order	
Voice	
is written in a natural voice	
Word Choice	
uses verbs correctly	
uses appropriate words	
words are recognizable	
Sentence Fluency	
has correct sentence structure	
Conventions	
grammar	
spelling	
punctuation and capitalization	

Voyages in English 1

Daily Voyages

Daily Edits

Monday	Tuesday	Wednesday	Thursday	Friday
Uncle walter sent me a walrus.	The Walrus did funny tricks.	i gave him a Grape.	The warus (walrus) ate all my grapes.	I sent him back to my uncle?
John live (lives) on a sailboat.	Whales visits (visit) him for lunch.	They talk about wavs (waves) and fish.	The wals (whales) ask John about texas.	They wishs (wish) they could viset (visit) Texas.
Jacob have (has) a bird in his tree.	What kind of Bird is it?	the bird is a gyant (giant) vulture.	Does jacob have a broome (broom)?	he kan (can) scare the bird away.
A Famous Writer came to town.	Pearl asked hym (him) to sign her book.	the writer gived (gave) her a strange look.	pearl brought the wrong book!	He sign (signed) Pearl's book anyway.
Did yous (you) eat a bananana (banana)?	Paula eated (ate) a banana today.	Bananas am (are) good to eat.	Paulas (Paula's) banana were (was) green.	Green bananas is (are) not good to eat.

Daily Story Starters

Monday	Tuesday	Wednesday	Thursday	Friday
It was fun to make	One time I baked a	Once I planted	I taught someone how to	It was fun when I built
I often like to	I know how to cook	I learned how to make	I can do	Last summer I learned how to
My favorite snack to make is	The prettiest thing I made was	In the winter I like to make	My friends want to know how I	My friend taught me to
A relative taught me to	At school I made	My hobby is	A strange thing I made was	My favorite game is
Outside I like to play	I can take care of	One chore I have is	I can draw a	I know how to decorate

Chapter Adaptors

SPEAKING & LISTENING

Ask students to say action verbs and to write their verbs on the board. Then read aloud a story that uses several action verbs, substituting in order the verbs on the board for the action verbs in the story. Pause before reading each verb and ask students which ending the verb should have. *(s, ed, or no ending)*

ENGLISH-LANGUAGE LEARNERS

Write verbs with no endings and endings students have studied, each on a separate note card. *(Examples: wave, runs, painted)* Have students choose one note card from a box. Ask students to write a sentence using the verb they chose. Have partners go over each other's work.

RETEACHING

Write on separate note cards the steps needed to complete simple tasks. *(Example: steps for building a snowman)* Shuffle each set of cards and have small groups work together to arrange the cards in the correct order. Then ask students to draw each step.

VERB ADVENTURE

Make a game board with a particular scene or theme. *(Examples: a forest, a castle)* Mark the board with *Start* and *Finish* lines. For each space on the board, write an action verb that students can pantomime. *(Examples: write, jump, swim)* Play the game with four or five students at a time. Give students game pieces. Have students take turns rolling a die and moving their game piece the appropriate number of spaces. Tell students that when they land on a space, they must act out the action verb. The first player to cross the finish line is the winner.

ACTION ART

Write on the board a list of action verbs. Give students craft stems and ask them to choose a verb. Then tell students to use the craft stems to make a figure performing the action. When students have finished, invite volunteers to share their work. Collect students' artwork and mount it on a large poster board. Have students label their figure on the poster with the appropriate action verb. Display the poster board in the classroom.

WRITING & EDITING

Tell students that one way to be sure that all the steps in the draft of a how-to article are included is to have a friend or family member act out the steps, one by one. Ask students to take notes about any steps that were hard to follow. Encourage students to add details where necessary to make their how-to articles clearer and more complete.

RETEACHING

Give partners a large sheet of paper with one line drawn vertically down the center. Tell students to choose an animal. *(Example: a bear)* Ask students to draw one of that animal on one half of the paper, and more than one of that animal on the other half. Have students write under each picture a sentence that describes what that animal or animals are doing. Tell students to use in one sentence a verb that adds -*s* and to use in the other sentence a verb that does not add -*s*. *(Examples: The bear growls. The bears growl.)* Invite students to share their drawings and sentences.

CHAPTER 3

Verbs and How-to Articles

Make a Snow Angel

Have you ever made a snow angel? Snow angels are easy to make. You need warm clothes and a snowy patch of ground.

1. Lie in the snow.
2. Move your arms and legs from side to side.
3. Stand up carefully.

Verbs and How-to Articles • **75**

Name

Action Verbs

A **verb** is a word that can show action.

*The dog **barks**.*

Underline the action verb in each sentence.

1. Josh <u>hikes</u> at camp.

2. The children <u>sing</u> "Happy Birthday."

3. Elena <u>eats</u> dinner at six.

4. Tim and Maya <u>dance</u>.

5. Peggy <u>jumps</u> rope with her friends.

6. Elephants <u>squirt</u> water.

7. Lou <u>swims</u> in the pool.

8. The dog <u>runs</u> in the yard.

9. Andrea <u>draws</u> pictures.

10. We <u>carry</u> the books.

Run and *jump* and *play* and *sing—*
these are action words.
When you want to show what happens,
use an action verb.

Name _____

Verbs Ending in *s*

Add the letter **s** to a verb when the verb tells what **one** person or thing does.

*The frog hop**s**.*

Underline the correct verb in each sentence.

1. That bear (<u>likes</u> like) honey.

2. Jack (walk <u>walks</u>) to school.

3. Rita (<u>throws</u> throw) the ball.

4. The bus (rumble <u>rumbles</u>) down the street.

5. Mom (wave <u>waves</u>) to the children.

6. Our ball (bounce <u>bounces</u>) off the sidewalk.

7. The moon (<u>shines</u> shine) at night.

8. Maren (<u>plays</u> play) with the puppy.

9. The corn (pop <u>pops</u>) in the bag.

10. Mr. Park (<u>plants</u> plant) carrots in his garden.

Name _____

Practice with Verbs Ending in *s*

Add the letter **s** to the verb in each sentence. Read the sentence out loud.

1. The football player wear**s** a uniform.

2. Ava eat**s** lunch at noon.

3. The cow moo**s** in the field.

4. Kate drive**s** the car.

5. The duck swim**s** in the pond.

6. Kurt learn**s** about rain forests.

7. Lucas want**s** more green beans.

8. Maria clap**s** her hands.

Writer's Corner

Write a sentence about a spider. Use an action verb.

Name

Verbs Not Ending in *s*

Do not add the letter **s** to a verb when the verb tells what **more than one** person or thing does.

*The girls **play**.*

Underline the correct verb in each sentence.

1. My friends (<u>like</u> likes) pizza.

2. The lions (<u>hunt</u> hunts) for food.

3. Amelia and Charlie (shakes <u>shake</u>) hands.

4. The boys (<u>cook</u> cooks) dinner.

5. Jay and Tim (smells <u>smell</u>) the pie in the oven.

6. Her cousins (<u>live</u> lives) in Texas.

7. Dogs (chews <u>chew</u>) on bones.

8. Rabbits (<u>nibble</u> nibbles) carrots.

9. Josie and Helen (drinks <u>drink</u>) milk.

10. The firefighters (<u>talk</u> talks) about safety.

Verbs • **79**

Name _____

Practice with Verbs Not Ending in *s*

Underline the correct verb in each sentence.

1. Cats (<u>lick</u> licks) their paws.

2. Farmers (grows <u>grow</u>) vegetables.

3. Flags (<u>wave</u> waves) in the breeze.

4. The kids (jumps <u>jump</u>) into the water.

5. The girls (<u>play</u> plays) soccer.

6. My brothers (waters <u>water</u>) the plants.

7. Stars (<u>shine</u> shines) in the sky.

8. The sleds (races <u>race</u>) down the hill.

9. The windows (<u>rattle</u> rattles) when the wind blows.

10. Horns (beeps <u>beep</u>) loudly on the street.

80 • Chapter 3

Name _____

Action Verbs Review

Complete each sentence with the correct verb. Use the word bank.

swim	runs	works	rides
hike	jump	open	dances

1. My dog *runs* after butterflies.

2. The children *open* their gifts.

3. Sue *rides* her bike.

4. Tom and Ben *hike* in the woods.

5. Gerry *dances* in ballet class.

6. Fish *swim* in the pond.

7. Carmen and Stevie *jump* rope.

8. Alma *works* at her office.

Name

More Action Verbs Review

Complete each sentence with the correct verb. Add the letter **s** if the verb tells what one person or thing does. Use the word bank.

sing	**feed**	**wear**	**look**
make	**join**	**buy**	**honk**

1. Dad *honks* the car horn.

2. Daniel *looks* at the butterflies.

3. Kim and Kumi *sing* a happy song.

4. Jen *buys* a new skateboard.

5. Justin and John *wear* funny hats.

6. We *feed* the dog every morning.

7. Many students *join* clubs at school.

8. He *makes* a clay pot in art class.

Name _____

Has and *Have*

Use **has** when the noun names **one**. Use **have** when the noun or nouns name **more than one**.

*The girl **has** red hair.*   *The girls **have** red hair.*

Underline the correct verb in each sentence.

1. A bird (<u>has</u> have) wings.

2. The potatoes (has <u>have</u>) butter on them.

3. Kiki (<u>has</u> have) a hockey stick.

4. The twins (has <u>have</u>) a chest for their toys.

5. My uncle (<u>has</u> have) a new puppy.

6. The plants (has <u>have</u>) pretty flowers.

7. Nancy (<u>has</u> have) a new pencil box.

8. The kittens (has <u>have</u>) whiskers.

9. This truck (<u>has</u> have) a special horn.

10. These camels (has <u>have</u>) two humps on their backs.

Name

Practice with *Has* and *Have*

Complete each sentence with the correct verb. Use **has** or **have**.

1. Chris *has* six fireflies in his jar.

2. These buckets *have* water in them.

3. My pencil *has* a sharp point.

4. Marta *has* a new dress.

5. Buses *have* loud motors.

6. A fox *has* soft fur.

7. Jill's shoes *have* new shoelaces.

8. These grapes *have* no seeds.

Writer's Corner

Write a sentence about something a friend owns. Use *has* or *have*.

Name

Verbs Ending in *ed*

Some verbs tell what happened **in the past**. Add the letters **ed** to most verbs to make them tell what happened in the past.

*The cows moo**ed** this morning.*

Complete each sentence with a verb that tells what happened in the past. Use the word bank.

| buttoned | talked | walked | climbed |
| splashed | cleaned | watched | painted |

> If it happened in the past, be sure to add -ed. Add it to an action verb, like *cooked* and *jumped*, you see.

1. Marni *cleaned* her room last week.

2. Kara *walked* her dog last night.

3. They *watched* the movie last Tuesday.

4. The child *buttoned* his coat yesterday.

5. Gary *climbed* the mountain last year.

6. My dad *painted* the picture last month.

7. James *talked* to Tori on the phone yesterday.

8. The baby *splashed* in the bathtub this morning.

Verbs • **85**

Name

Practice with Verbs Ending in *ed*

Write the correct verb to complete the story. Use the word bank. Be sure to add the letters **ed**.

clean	play	brush	walk
talk	finish	wash	dust

Yesterday Casey woke up early. She *washed* her face and *brushed* her teeth. After Casey *finished* her breakfast, she *cleaned* her room. Then she *dusted* the piano. All of her chores were done. Casey *talked* with Courtney on the phone. Finally Casey *walked* to the park and *played* with her friends.

Writer's Corner

Write a sentence about something you did yesterday. Use a verb that tells what happened in the past.

Name _____

Eat and *Ate*

Some verbs **do not** use the letters **ed** to tell about something that happened in the past.

Use **ate** instead of **eat** to tell about something that happened in the past.

Complete each sentence with eat or ate.

1. We will *eat* rice and beans.

2. Julian *ate* a sandwich yesterday.

3. They like to *eat* hot dogs.

4. Carolyn *ate* pasta last Monday.

5. Our class *ate* pizza at the picnic last summer.

6. Jackie *ate* turnips last Thanksgiving.

7. Harry *ate* five carrot sticks yesterday.

8. Pam and Nancy will *eat* cake for dessert.

Verbs • **87**

Name _____

Give and Gave

Use **gave** instead of **give** to tell about something that happened in the past.

● **Complete each sentence with give or gave.**

1. The judge *gave* me a blue ribbon at the fair last year.

2. The carpenters will *give* us nails.

3. Kathy *gave* Ken a picture yesterday.

4. The coaches will *give* us our uniforms.

5. Mr. Hex likes to *give* books to the library.

6. Uncle Tom *gave* me apples last Tuesday.

7. Larry and Riley will *give* the kitten milk.

8. My parents *gave* the dog a bath last night.

Name

See and Saw

Use **saw** instead of **see** to tell about something that happened in the past.

Complete each sentence with see or saw.

1. They like to *see* the animals at the zoo.

2. Carol and Tasha will *see* their aunt today.

3. My friends *saw* a movie last week.

4. Caleb *saw* a play last Friday.

5. The hiker *saw* a big mountain on her trip.

6. Cady *saw* some snowflakes last winter.

7. We will *see* colorful kites at the park.

8. Olivia *saw* the TV show last night.

Verbs • **89**

Name _____

Write and Wrote

Use **wrote** instead of **write** to tell about something that happened in the past.

● **Complete each sentence with write or wrote.**

1. We like to *write* funny poems.

2. Thomas *wrote* a report for class last month.

3. Lauren *wrote* in her journal yesterday.

4. Evan and Daniel like to *write* for the newspaper.

5. My teacher *wrote* a skit for our class this morning.

6. Malcolm *wrote* me a letter last spring.

7. Brad and Janet like to *write* songs.

8. Karen and Raul will *write* a shopping list.

Name

Being Verbs

Some verbs show action. *Sing, dance, laugh,* and *skip* are action verbs.
Some verbs **do not** show action. These verbs are called **being verbs**.

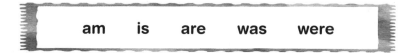

| am | is | are | was | were |

**Underline the being verb in each sentence.
Use the word bank for help.**

1. Violets <u>are</u> spring flowers.

2. A monkey <u>is</u> a funny animal.

3. Many elephants <u>were</u> in the parade.

4. The girls <u>are</u> at the movies.

5. My pet snake <u>was</u> in the yard.

6. There <u>were</u> bugs on the leaves.

7. I <u>am</u> six years old.

8. The apple <u>is</u> bright red.

Am, is, are, was, and *were*—
these are being words.
When you do not show action,
use a being verb.

Verbs • 91

Name

Am, Is, and Are

Use **am** after **I**.
Use **is** when the noun names **one**.
Use **are** when the noun or nouns name **more than one**.

Underline the correct verb in each sentence.

1. I (<u>am</u> is are) the winner of the contest.

2. One snowball (am <u>is</u> are) on the ground.

3. Three birds (am is <u>are</u>) in the tree.

4. The dog (am <u>is</u> are) shaggy and brown.

5. The baseball cards (am is <u>are</u>) new.

6. One turtle (am <u>is</u> are) on the rock.

7. The peaches (am is <u>are</u>) in the basket.

8. I (<u>am</u> is are) in the band.

9. The soft drinks (am is <u>are</u>) in the cooler.

10. The sky (am <u>is</u> are) blue.

 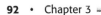

Name _____

Practice with *Am*, *Is*, and *Are*

Write am after I. Write is when the noun names one.
Write are when the noun or nouns name more than one.

1. One big tree _is_ in the yard.

2. I _am_ at the library.

3. Two pigs _are_ in the pen.

4. A cat _is_ on the porch.

5. The book _is_ on the shelf.

6. Five boats _are_ on the lake.

7. Three dresses _are_ in the closet.

8. One penny _is_ in the jar.

9. I _am_ taking piano lessons.

10. Many winter coats _are_ for sale.

Verbs • 93

Name

Was and *Were*

Use **was** when the noun names **one**. Use **were** when the noun or nouns name **more than one**.

● **Underline the correct verb in each sentence.**

1. A big truck (<u>was</u> were) on the road.

2. Two dogs (was <u>were</u>) in the yard.

3. The radios (was <u>were</u>) too loud.

4. Monkeys (was <u>were</u>) at the zoo.

5. The movie (<u>was</u> were) funny.

6. The papers (was <u>were</u>) on the windowsill.

7. Our car (<u>was</u> were) bright blue.

8. His paintbrushes (was <u>were</u>) still wet.

9. My sister (<u>was</u> were) the winner.

10. The puppy (<u>was</u> were) sound asleep.

Name

Practice with *Was* and *Were*

Write **was** if the noun names one. Write **were** if the noun or nouns name more than one.

1. The book *was* on the table.

2. Many toys *were* in the box.

3. The marbles *were* in the bag.

4. The baseball bats *were* in the gym.

5. A watch *was* in his pocket.

6. My gloves *were* wet with snow.

7. His shirt *was* light blue.

8. The pancakes *were* on the griddle.

9. The sled *was* in the basement.

10. Darla *was* in the tree house.

Writer's Corner

Write a sentence about a toy. Use a being verb.

Verbs • 95

Name _____

Show What You Know

A Underline the correct verb in each sentence.

1. Our puppy (play <u>plays</u>) with a ball.

2. We (<u>swim</u> swims) in the lake.

3. Mrs. Lu (cook <u>cooks</u>) good meals.

4. That bell (ring <u>rings</u>) every day.

5. Our teacher (sing <u>sings</u>) us a song.

6. The birds (<u>flap</u> flaps) their wings.

B Underline the correct verb in each sentence.

1. Joseph (<u>has</u> have) many marbles.

2. They (has <u>have</u>) two snakes.

3. The girls (has <u>have</u>) a pet rabbit.

4. Teresa (<u>has</u> have) a shiny bike.

5. Those trees (has <u>have</u>) pretty leaves.

6. Ben (<u>has</u> have) a surprise for us.

Name

Show What You Know

A Add the letters **ed** to the correct verb in each sentence. Use the word bank.

| watch | walk | visit | pick | brush |

1. Sally *walked* home from school yesterday.

2. My friend *picked* flowers last Thursday.

3. Taye *watched* the airplane take off last night.

4. Trevor *brushed* his teeth this morning.

5. My aunt *visited* from Ohio last year.

B Underline the correct verb in each sentence.

1. We (eat <u>ate</u>) tacos yesterday.

2. Jamal (<u>gave</u> give) her flowers last week.

3. They (<u>saw</u> see) a movie last night.

4. Seth (write <u>wrote</u>) a letter yesterday.

C Underline the correct verb in each sentence.

1. The books (am is <u>are</u>) on the shelf.

2. Mike's painting (am <u>is</u> are) on the wall.

3. A cup (<u>was</u> were) on the table.

4. I (<u>am</u> is are) in the first grade.

5. The piggy banks (was <u>were</u>) full.

Get Ready to Write

What Is a How-to Article?

What do you know how to make? What do you know how to do? A how-to article tells how to make something or do something.

Underline the ideas that tell how to make or do something.

how to play checkers   spring and summer

elephants and other big animals   how to climb a tree

how to fly a kite   stories about dinosaurs

how to skateboard

how to bake cookies

Order in a How-to Article

A how-to article tells what to do in step-by-step order.

Put these steps in the right order. Use the numbers 1, 2, and 3.

A

| 3 | Sit down. |

| 1 | Go into the classroom. |

| 2 | Find your seat. |

B

| 2 | Put toothpaste on your toothbrush. |

| 1 | Take the cap off the toothpaste. |

| 3 | Brush your teeth. |

C

| 2 | Pull up the covers. |

| 3 | Go to sleep. |

| 1 | Get into bed. |

How-to Articles • 99

Steps in a How-to Article

Write the steps in order. Use the pictures for help.

| Drop in strawberries.   Put cereal in a bowl.   Add the milk. |

A healthy breakfast is easy to make.

1. Put cereal in a bowl.

2. Add the milk.

3. Drop in strawberries.

| Put on your shoes.   Tie your shoes.   Put on your socks. |

Get ready for school fast!

1. Put on your socks.

2. Put on your shoes.

3. Tie your shoes.

100 • Chapter 3

Plan a How-to Article

Plan a how-to article. Think about something you know how to make or do. Draw each step.

How to _____

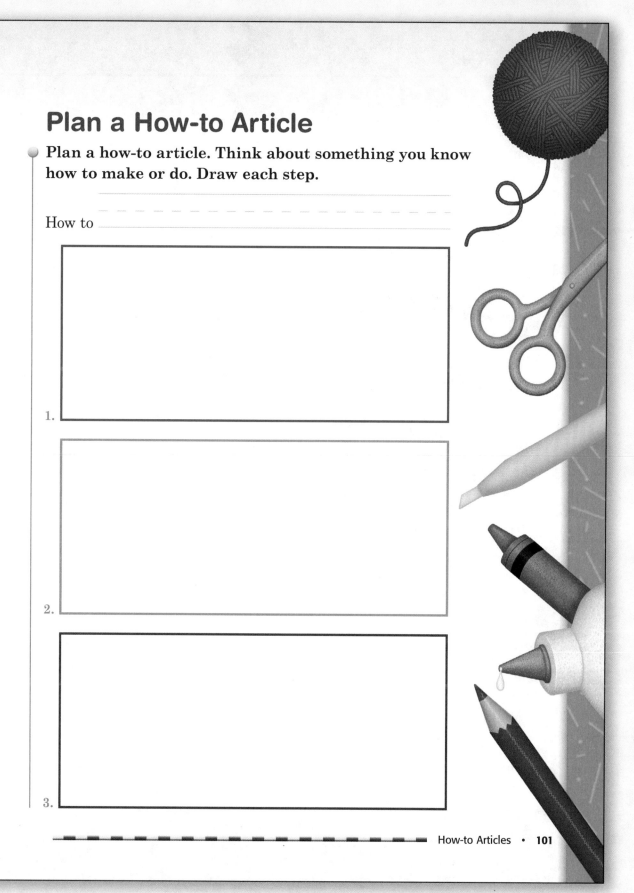

1.

2.

3.

Writer's Workshop

PREWRITING

Pick a Topic

A how-to article tells how to make or do something. The topic can be anything you know how to make or do.

tie my shoe

make a snow angel

make my bed

build a sandcastle

Kyle needs to pick a topic for his how-to article. Look at Kyle's notes.

Pick a topic for a how-to article. What do you know how to make? What do you know how to do? Do you know how to

care for a pet?

make a paper airplane?

plant a flower?

make a snack?

Draw or write your ideas in your notebook. Be sure to label them.

Which topic would other people like to learn about? Write your topic on the line below.

My topic is:

_____

How to _____

PREWRITING

Plan Your How-to Article

Now Kyle must plan his how-to article. First he lists what he needs.
Then Kyle draws pictures of each step.

> ### WHAT YOU NEED
>
> warm clothes   snowy patch of ground

1.

2.

3.

Make a plan. List what you will need in your notebook.
Then draw pictures of the steps.

Writer's Workshop

DRAFTING

This is Kyle's draft.

Have you ever made a snow angel?

Snow angels is easy to make. You need

warm clothes and a snowy patch

of ground.

1. Stand up carefully.

2. Move your arms and legs from side to side.

3. Lie in the snow.

Look at your plan. Think about sentences that might go with your pictures.

Write your how-to article in your notebook. First tell your readers what they will make or do. Next tell them what they will need. Don't leave anything out. Then list each step. Be sure to use your plan as you write.

EDITING

Kyle uses the Editing Checklist to check his draft.

1. Stand up carefully. ↪ 1. Lie in the snow.

2. Move your arms and legs from side to side.

3. Lie in the snow. ↪ 3. Stand up carefully.

Look at the mistake Kyle finds. How does he fix it?

My steps are not in order.

Read your how-to article. What else can you add? Use the Editing Checklist. Mark any changes that will make it better. Make your how-to article one that you would like to read.

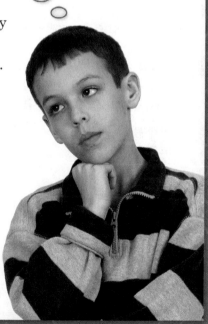

REVISING

Kyle copies his draft. He includes the changes he marked. Kyle knows that revising will make his how-to article better.

Copy your draft. Fix any mistakes you marked.

Writer's Workshop

PROOFREADING

Kyle uses this Proofreading Checklist to check his draft.

Proofreading Checklist

☐ Are all the words spelled correctly?

☐ Did I use capital letters?

☐ Did I use the right end marks?

☐ Are all the verbs used correctly?

Have you ever made a snow angel?
Snow angels is ~~is~~ are easy to make. You need warm clothes and a snowy patch

Look at the mistake Kyle finds. How does he fix it?

Read your how-to article again. Use the checklist to check your draft. Check for one thing at a time. Fix any mistakes you see. Use the proofreading marks chart at the back of this book.

PUBLISHING

Look at how Kyle publishes his draft. Remember, when you share your work, you are publishing.

Get ready to share your work. Copy your how-to article onto a sheet of paper. Print neatly. Copy all of your changes. Draw a picture to go with your how-to article.

How will you publish your work? Decide with your class. Use one of these ideas or come up with your own.

Put it in a class How-to Book.

Make a poster.

Read it to the class.

Give it to a friend who wants to learn something new.

Make a Snow Angel

Make a Snow Angel
Have you ever made a snow angel? Snow angels are easy to make. You need warm clothes and a snowy patch of ground.
1. Lie in the snow.
2. Move your arms and legs from side to side.
3. Stand up carefully.

How-to Articles • 107

Pronouns and Adjectives

In this chapter students will learn about

- pronouns
- the pronoun *it*
- the pronouns *he* and *she*
- the pronouns *I* and *me*
- the pronouns *we* and *they*
- adjectives
- color words
- number words
- size words and shape words
- feeling words
- sensory words
- adjectives that compare

A Visual, Please

Adding Adjectives for Clarity and Interest

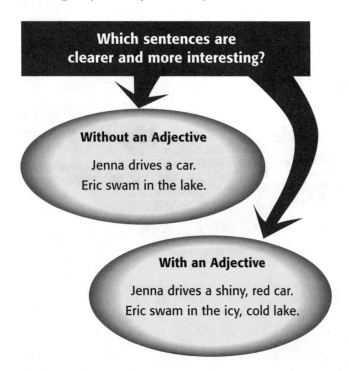

Which sentences are clearer and more interesting?

Without an Adjective

Jenna drives a car.
Eric swam in the lake.

With an Adjective

Jenna drives a shiny, red car.
Eric swam in the icy, cold lake.

Grammar for Grown-ups

Standing In

Pronoun comes from the Latin prefix *pro-,* meaning "for," and the Latin root *nomen,* meaning "name." Pronouns are words used in place of nouns. Some pronouns have the qualities of person, gender, number, and case.

Pronouns indicate person. Pronouns in the first person identify the speaker. Pronouns in the second person identify the person spoken to. Pronouns in the third person identify the person or thing spoken about. Third person singular pronouns reflect gender.

The three cases of personal pronouns are subject *(I, you, he, she, it, we, they),* possessive *(mine, yours, his, hers, its, ours, theirs),* and object *(me, you, him, her, it, us, them).* A subject pronoun must always agree with its verb: *She cries, they cry.*

Tell Me All About It

Adjective comes from the Latin word *adjectivum,* meaning "something that is added." An adjective modifies the meaning of a noun or a pronoun.

Adjectives can be used to count *(three, sixty, fourth)* or to describe *(sandy, clear, red).* They can come before the words they modify *(bright sun, salty tears),* or they can come after linking verbs as subject complements: *She is smart. The roses are red.*

Daily Edits

The Daily Edits for this chapter provide students with daily practice editing sentences. Students should pay special attention to their use of pronouns and adjectives in each sentence.

Common Errors

Otherwise Known as "Am I I or am I me?"

Many speakers and writers make the common error of placing *I* and *me* in the wrong part of a sentence.

ERROR: Jack and me drew pictures.
CORRECT: Jack and I drew pictures.

ERROR: Sydney is going with I.
CORRECT: Sydney is going with me.

To help students avoid this common error, make a poster with the following sentence: *I like me.* Guide students to identify *like* as the action verb of the sentence. Explain that in sentences *I* comes before the verb and *me* comes after the verb. Guide students to say example sentences that use *I* and *me,* and write them on the poster. Display the poster throughout the year and encourage students to refer to it when trying to decide whether to use *I* or *me* in a sentence.

For Kids Who Are Ready

Or, The Proper Thing to Do

Some students might more quickly understand how to use adjectives. For students who are ready, introduce the following concept:

A proper adjective is an adjective that is formed from a proper noun. Proper adjectives are always capitalized. Some examples of proper adjectives are *African, Spanish,* and *Chinese.*

Tell students that words ending in *-an, -ish,* or *-ese* that describe a culture are often proper adjectives. Talk with students about other examples of proper adjectives that describe culture.

Ask a Mentor

Real Situations, Real Solutions

Dear Grammar Geek,

How can I get my students to see that adjectives can make their writing more interesting and clear? Can't think of anything interesting,
Iris in Inglewood

Dear Iris,

Create a poster using the visual on page 108a. Display the poster and ask your students the following: Which sentences are more interesting? Which are clearer? Which sentences help you imagine what is happening? Each day, invite a volunteer to add two sentences to the visual, one without an adjective and one with an adjective.

Hope you find that very interesting, Iris,
Grammar Geek

Dear Grammar Geezer,

Some of my students are adding more and most when adding -er and -est to adjectives. Yesterday Carlos told Morgan that his house was "the most biggest on the block." What should I do?

Needing a little help,
Mrs. Neems

Dear Mrs. Neems,

Gently explain that for one adjective, the endings -er and -est are never used at the same time with more or most. For example, The baby is most happiest in the morning is incorrect. Remove the most and you've got yourself a correct sentence. Consistently correct these errors in students' speech and remind them to check for this error in their writing.

Hope that helps,
Grammar Geezer

Adey Bryant: www.CartoonStock.com

"When you described it as a remote house
in the country…….."

Descriptions

Talk with students about what topic is suggested by the completed sentence. Help students determine when a topic is a good topic for a description. Allow students to compare sentences in order to demonstrate the varied ways the same topic can be described.

Genre Characteristics

At the end of this chapter, students will write a description. They will be guided through the writing process in the Writer's Workshop. The completed description will include the following:

- a beginning that names the topic
- a middle that describes a person, a place, a thing, or an event
- vivid adjectives
- sensory words
- correct grammar, spelling, capitalization, and punctuation

Describe It for Me

An effective description is like a photograph—an image that seems almost real. Whether it is part of a longer piece of writing or complete in itself, its focus on the topic is sharp and distinct, so the reader always knows exactly what is being described. Its content is illustrative, developing and printing a picture in the reader's mind.

The writer of an effective description captures the reader's attention with an informative beginning, keeps the reader engaged in a middle with logical connections, and crafts a summarizing ending that leaves a lingering impression. Rich sensory details make the piece both satisfying and informative. The language is always appropriate to the audience.

The description may be organized using time order, spatial order, or order of importance. A description is well constructed, and the sentences flow from one to the other in a logical progressive order. These sentences are correct in grammar, capitalization, spelling, and punctuation.

Daily Story Starters

Some Daily Story Starters for this chapter provide students with practice brainstorming topics for descriptions, real or imaginary. Other Daily Story Starters provide students with practice writing sentences that describe the familiar or imaginary. This daily practice helps students understand how to choose topics and also broadens students' understanding of how descriptions are useful in all kinds of writing.

Begin each day by writing on the board the Daily Story Starter. Allow time for students to complete the sentence. Then discuss the results as a class.

Teacher's Toolbox

Try the following ideas to help your students get the most out of the Writer's Workshop:

- Encourage students to keep a journal or picture journal to write or draw their impressions of interesting people, places, things, or events.

- Add to your classroom library literature rich in descriptive language.

- Create a bulletin-board display of descriptive marketing materials, such as descriptions of appealing vacation spots, toys, or food.

Reasons to Write

Share with students the following list of people who write descriptions. Discuss why it is important to become a good writer of descriptions.

- scientists who study volcanoes

- movie or book reviewers

- travel writers

Literature Links

You can add to your classroom library the following titles to offer your students examples of descriptions:

Henry and Mudge: The First Book by Cynthia Rylant

I Went Walking by Sue Williams

Frog and Toad All Year by Arnold Lobel

Description

	Yes	No
My description tells about a person, a place, a thing, or an event.	☐	☐
My description has a beginning that tells the topic.	☐	☐
My description uses sensory words.	☐	☐
I used pronouns and adjectives correctly.	☐	☐
I used complete sentences.	☐	☐
I spelled words correctly.	☐	☐
I used capital letters correctly.	☐	☐
I used end marks correctly.	☐	☐

Voyages in English 1

Teacher's Scoring Rubric

Description

    0 = not evident
    1 = minimal evidence of comprehension
    2 = evidence of development toward comprehension
    3 = strong evidence of comprehension
    4 = outstanding evidence of comprehension

Ideas	Points
is about a person, a place, a thing, or an event	
Organization	
has a beginning that names the topic	
describes the topic in a logical sequence	
Voice	
is written in a natural voice	
Word Choice	
uses pronouns and adjectives correctly	
uses sensory words	
words are recognizable	
Sentence Fluency	
has correct sentence structure	
Conventions	
grammar	
spelling	
punctuation and capitalization	

Voyages in English 1

Daily Voyages

Daily Edits

Monday	Tuesday	Wednesday	Thursday	Friday
I eat pumpkin pie last saturday. *(ate; saturday)*	The piy was soft and sweet. *(pie)*	my aunt fell asleep in her chare. *(chair)*	I eated her pece of pie. *(ate; piece)*	She was not hapy with with me. *(happy)*
My Mother gived me clay. *(gave)*	I shared my clay with robert.	I and Robert made lians. *(and I; lions)*	his lion ate lion. *(my)*	His took home all the Clay. *(He)*
Krista and me play chekkers. *(I; checkers)*	We do not No how to play. *(know)*	we bild towers with checkers. *(build)*	Krista gave the ruls. *(me; rules)*	Towers is more fun than Rules. *(are)*
Max dad sails on a ship huge. *(Max's; huge)*	It have flags and manny sailors. *(has; many)*	max's mom wave at the gray ship. *(waves)*	Max hold his moms hand. *(holds; mom's)*	Max fells sad on the way home. *(feels)*
I and my friends race our pets. *(My friends and)*	Lydia's hamster are slow. *(is)*	Me turtle is slow than the hamster. *(My; slower)*	Arturo's snael is the slower of all. *(snail; slowest)*	This is the longast race evar. *(longest; ever)*

Daily Story Starters

Monday	Tuesday	Wednesday	Thursday	Friday
The desert is	My perfect bike would be	My favorite fruit is	Gardens are	My perfect day would be
My friend wears	I like the smell of	Rain drops are	My favorite toy is	In space it is
On cold days I	The beach is	I like to read at	My favorite treat is	Someone took me to
I have an interesting	My favorite room is	Space creatures wear	Inside a volcano is	My perfect pet would be
On sunny days I	I dream of going to	Inside a cloud is	My favorite pillow is	On Halloween I

Chapter Adaptors

SPEAKING & LISTENING

Think of an animal and describe it to students without saying what it is. Have students guess the animal. Then discuss with students words that helped them guess the animal. Repeat the activity with different animals.

ENGLISH-LANGUAGE LEARNERS

Write color words on the board. Point at a color word and invite English-language learners to name something that is that color. Have students answer in adjective-noun form. *(Example: yellow sun)* Write their responses on the board. Point out that adjectives in English are usually placed before nouns. Invite volunteers to use the phrases on the board in sentences. Repeat with other color words.

RETEACHING

Write the following sentences on the board: *Jen likes cats. She saw Steven's cat. It has gray fur. He found the cat in the barn.* Read aloud each sentence and ask students to identify the pronouns. Underline each pronoun and talk with students about which word is replaced.

ADJECTIVE ADVENTURE

Select several objects from around the classroom. *(Examples: a globe, a plant)* Display them in front of the class. Allow students time to examine the objects. Ask students to think of adjectives that describe each object. Invite volunteers to share their adjectives in complete sentences. *(Examples: The globe is round. The plant is green.)* Encourage other students to offer additional sentences for the objects, using new adjectives.

PRONOUN RACE

Make a game board with four rows and four columns. Number the squares in each column from 1 to 4. Give each of four students a game piece. Tell students to each place their game piece in a #1 square. Say a sentence that has a proper noun. *(Example: Mary sang a song.)* Ask the first student to replace the proper noun with a pronoun. *(She sang a song.)* If the student answers correctly, he or she moves the game piece to the #2 square. Then say for each student a new sentence. Continue until one student reaches the #4 square.

WRITING & EDITING

After students finish their five-senses charts in the Writer's Workshop, have them exchange their charts with partners. Encourage students to look over their partner's chart and to suggest additional sensory words that are appropriate for the topic. Remind students that they do not have to use their partner's suggestions in their drafts.

RETEACHING

Show students an object such as an apple. Remind students that a description uses sensory words to tell how something looks, sounds, smells, tastes, or feels. Write the following questions on the board: *What does it look like? What does it sound like? What does it smell like? How does it taste? How does it feel?* Talk with students about how they might answer each question. Help students create a five-senses chart in their notebook for the object. Repeat with other objects. Point out that not all objects can be described using all five senses but that the best descriptions use as many of the senses as possible.

CHAPTER 4

Pronouns, Adjectives, and Descriptions

108 • Chapter 4

Winter

I love to play in the snow.
Sophie and I dig long tunnels.
I can hear snowflakes fall
if I am really quiet. I taste
cold snowflakes on my tongue.
I can see my breath. The snow
crunches under my boots.
We are like explorers at the
South Pole.

Pronouns, Adjectives, and Descriptions • **109**

Name

Pronouns

A **pronoun** is a word that takes the place of a noun.

Read the pronouns on
the balloons. Underline
the pronoun in
each sentence.

1. <u>We</u> are at the zoo.

2. <u>I</u> see a clown.

3. <u>He</u> has balloons.

4. The clown gives <u>me</u> a balloon.

5. Raj ties <u>it</u> on my wrist.

6. <u>She</u> wants a balloon.

7. <u>We</u> like the balloons.

8. <u>They</u> have many balloons.

9. <u>I</u> like the red balloons the best.

10. <u>He</u> will give Eli another balloon.

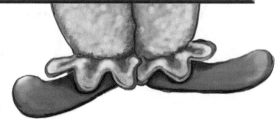

I, me, she, he, it, we, and *they*—
these pronouns might
come your way.
They stand for nouns;
they take their place,
like *he* for Jim or *it* for vase.

110 • Chapter 4

Name

The Pronoun *It*

The pronoun **it** takes the place of a thing.

Give the robot to Maya.

*Give **it** to Maya.*

**Color the robot and read the story.
Write it on the lines.**

Maya and Morgan had a robot

named R.E. They liked *it* very much.

The robot could walk and talk.

It could answer the phone and

vacuum the rug. Maya and Morgan oiled R.E.'s hinges and took

care of *it* . Sometimes they walked with *it* to the store.

R.E. could shop. *It* could buy good food. The children liked

to play with *it* .

Writer's Corner

If R.E. were at your house, what could it do for you?
Write a sentence using *it*.

Name

The Pronouns *He* and *She*

The pronoun **he** takes the place of a boy or a man.

The pronoun **she** takes the place of a girl or a woman.

> ***Karl*** *likes green beans.*   ***He*** *likes green beans.*
> ***Leah*** *can play chess.*   ***She*** *can play chess.*

Underline the correct pronoun in each sentence pair.

1. Uncle Albert is good at sports. (<u>He</u> She) plays soccer with me.

2. John rakes leaves. (<u>He</u> She) enjoys the different colors.

3. Carrie has a jump rope. (He <u>She</u>) knows many games.

4. Ann has a CD player. (He <u>She</u>) likes to play songs.

5. My aunt knits sweaters. (He <u>She</u>) made one for me.

6. Steven has a bicycle. (<u>He</u> She) can ride fast.

7. Elsa lives nearby. (He <u>She</u>) often visits us.

8. Elena is at the zoo. (He <u>She</u>) is watching the animals.

9. Jamal likes to swim. (<u>He</u> She) enjoys the ocean.

10. Julia is at the carnival. (He <u>She</u>) eats a pretzel.

112 • Chapter 4

Name

The Pronoun *I*

The word **I** is a pronoun. It takes the place of your name.
Use **I** before the action verb in a sentence.

*Jack and **I** paint pictures.*

● **Write the pronoun I in each sentence.**

1. *I* can write my address.

2. Jack and *I* ride the roller coaster.

3. Gretchen and *I* made a pie.

4. *I* want to go with you.

5. Rory and *I* ate popcorn.

6. My sister and *I* brought lunch.

7. Kate and *I* helped the magician.

8. *I* can share with you.

Pronouns and Adjectives • 113

Name _____

The Pronoun *Me*

The word **me** is a pronoun. It takes the place of your name. Use **me** after the action verb in a sentence.

*Jack paints **me** a picture.*

Write the pronoun me in each sentence.

1. Dad calls *me* for dinner.

2. Please read *me* a story.

3. Pass *me* the milk.

4. Sally plays *me* a song.

5. Gwen helps *me* carry the books.

6. Tina lends *me* her crayons.

7. Mom gave Tim and *me* raisins.

8. Grandpa shows Todd and *me* how to play checkers.

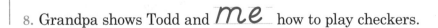

114 • Chapter 4

Name

The Pronouns *I* and *Me*

Circle the action verb in each sentence. Then underline the correct pronoun. Remember, **I** is used before the action verb. **Me** is used after the action verb.

1. (I Me) go to the beach.

2. Kim asks (I me) for a towel.

3. (I Me) use a bucket and shovel.

4. (I Me) make a sandcastle.

5. Sue and (I me) play in the sand.

6. Tom finds (I me) a turtle.

7. David and (I me) like the beach.

8. Juan splashes Nick and (I me).

9. Grace and (I me) swim.

10. Ed gives (I me) seashells.

Pronouns and Adjectives • 115

Name

Practice with *I* and *Me*

Write three sentences with **I**. Write three sentences with **me**. Use the word bank if you need help.

swings	slide	park
sandbox	giggle	friend

1.

2.

3.

1.

2.

3.

Writer's Corner

Write a sentence about a hobby you have or a sport you play.
Use *I* or *me*.

Name

The Pronouns *We* and *They*

Use **we** when telling about yourself and other people.

> *Laz* and *I* sing songs.   *We* sing songs.

Use **they** when telling only about other people.

> *Laz* and *Lily* jump rope.   *They* jump rope.

Underline the correct pronoun in each sentence pair.

1. Judy and I play with the toys.
   (<u>We</u> They) play with the toys.

2. Mom and Dad go bowling.
   (We <u>They</u>) go bowling.

3. My grandparents take walks.
   (We <u>They</u>) take walks.

4. Rye and I read a poem.
   (<u>We</u> They) read a poem.

5. Barb and I play checkers.
   (<u>We</u> They) play checkers.

6. Shawn and Jason rode the train.
   (We <u>They</u>) rode the train.

7. Keenan and Devon saw the lake.
   (We <u>They</u>) saw the lake.

8. Marya and I ate grapes.
   (<u>We</u> They) ate grapes.

9. Stefan and Kim made tacos.
   (We <u>They</u>) made tacos.

10. Fred and I danced.
    (<u>We</u> They) danced.

Pronouns and Adjectives • 117

Name

Pronouns Review

Underline the correct pronoun in each sentence.

1. (He She) is my uncle.

2. (I Me) am very tall.

3. (We They) do their chores.

4. Lyn saw (I me) at the circus.

5. (It They) is crawling up the wall.

6. (We They) do our homework.

7. (He She) is my sister.

8. Rayna and (I me) play hockey.

9. Is (he she) your grandma?

10. My brother walks (I me) to school.

118 • Chapter 4

Name

Adjectives

An **adjective** can tell about a person. An adjective can tell about a place. An adjective can tell about a thing.

*The dog has a **long** tail.*

The adjective **long** tells about the dog's tail.

Draw a line to match each picture to the correct adjective.

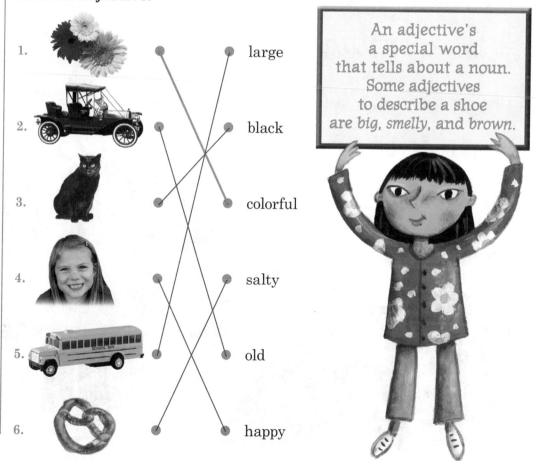

1.   large

2.   black

3.   colorful

4.   salty

5.   old

6.   happy

An adjective's a special word that tells about a noun. Some adjectives to describe a shoe are *big*, *smelly*, and *brown*.

Pronouns and Adjectives • **119**

Name

Color Words

Some adjectives tell about colors. These are **color words**.

*Tina has a **red** umbrella.*

The adjective **red** tells the color of the umbrella.

○ **Look at the picture. Complete each sentence with the correct adjective. Use the word bank.**

green

yellow

brown

purple

blue

orange

1. Grandpa wears a *yellow* apron.

2. We dig in the *brown* dirt.

3. Grandpa and I plant *purple* flowers.

4. We use an *orange* shovel.

5. The *green* grass tickles my feet.

6. The *blue* sky is bright.

Name

Number Words

Some adjectives tell how many. These are **number words**.
*There are **five** birds in the trees.*

The adjective **five** tells how many birds.

one

two

nine

six

four

three

○ **Look at the picture. Complete each sentence
with the correct adjective. Use the word bank.**

1. There are *nine* flowers in the field.

2. There is *one* large fountain.

3. There are *four* statues on the fountain.

4. There are *six* trees.

5. There are *three* girls playing.

6. There are *two* ducks in the fountain.

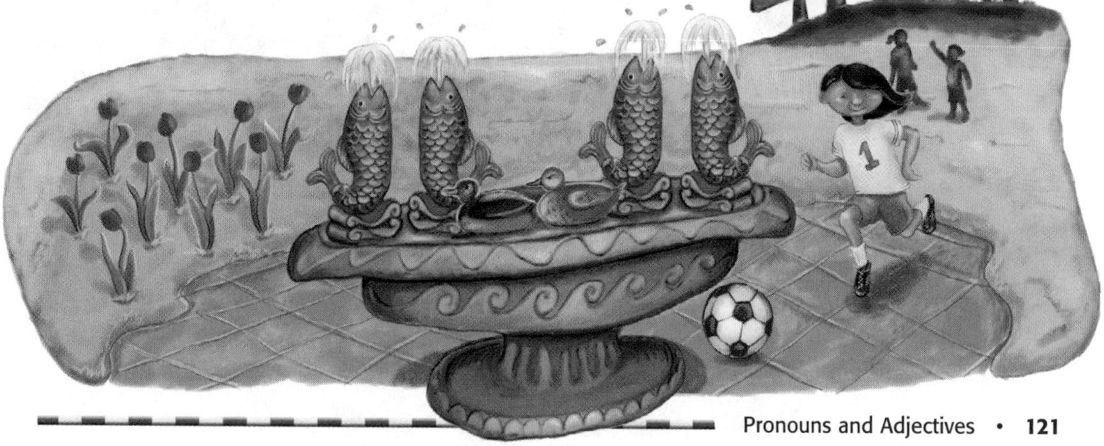

Name

Size Words and Shape Words

Some adjectives tell about sizes and shapes. These are **size** and **shape words**.

> *Kelly pets the **little** kitten.*

The adjective **little** tells about the kitten's size.

Look at the picture. Underline the correct adjective in each sentence.

1. The (tall short) man holds a box.
2. The (round square) box he holds is a gift.
3. The (tall short) woman is happy.
4. The (large small) clock tower is very old.
5. A group of (big little) children play ball.
6. The (round square) ball bounces.
7. A (big little) dog runs by.
8. There is a (large small) tree next to the bench.

Writer's Corner

Write a sentence about the library. Use a size word or shape word.

Name _____

Feeling Words

Some adjectives tell about feelings. These are **feeling words**.

*Tara feels **excited** to see Aunt Rose.*

The adjective **excited** tells about the way Tara feels.

Complete each sentence with the correct adjective. Use the word bank. Sample answers shown.

happy	sad	angry	sorry
afraid	hungry	tired	silly

1. Jen feels *sorry* she broke the lamp.

2. Rocket ships make Daniel feel *happy*.

3. Tonya and Jeff are *afraid* of spiders.

4. I feel *sad* we lost the soccer game.

5. Acting like a monkey is *silly*.

6. I feel *hungry* before lunchtime.

7. At bedtime Kevin feels *tired*.

8. Meg feels *angry* she missed the bus.

Pronouns and Adjectives • **123**

Name

Sensory Words

People have five senses. They are **sight**, **sound**, **smell**, **taste**, and **touch**. Some adjectives tell about how things look, sound, smell, taste, or feel. These are **sensory words.**

Match each sensory word to the correct part of the body. Write the letter on the line.

1. loud _____ **B**

2. rough _____ **E**

3. shiny _____ **A**

4. spicy _____ **D**

5. smoky _____ **C**

6. purple _____ **A**

7. stinky _____ **C**

8. squeaky _____ **B**

9. smooth _____ **E**

10. salty _____ **D**

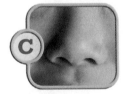

Sound, smell, taste, touch, and sight— sensory words make descriptions clear and bright.

Name

Practice with Sensory Words

Write the correct sensory word in each sentence.
Use the word bank.

| wet | soft | screechy | hot |
| red | sour | sweet | crunchy |

1. We pet the rabbit's *soft* _____ fur.

2. Sara chews a *crunchy* _____ carrot.

3. I tasted the *sour* _____ lemon.

4. She wears *sweet* _____ perfume.

5. The *hot* _____ sun melted the ice cream.

6. There is a *red* _____ fire hydrant at the corner.

7. Max and I hear the *screechy* _____ train whistle.

8. Nora and I got *wet* _____ from the lawn sprinkler.

Writer's Corner

Write a sentence about a food you like. Use a sensory word.

_____

_____

Pronouns and Adjectives • 125

Name

Adjectives Ending in *er* and *est*

Some adjectives compare things. To compare two things, add the letters **er** to the end of the adjective. To compare three or more things, add the letters **est** to the end of the adjective.

A worm is long. *A snake is long**er**.* *An alligator is long**est** of all.*

○ **Add the letters er or est to each adjective.**

1. fast   *faster*   *fastest*

2. tall   *taller*   *tallest*

3. slow   *slower*   *slowest*

4. deep   *deeper*   *deepest*

5. small   *smaller*   *smallest*

Name

Practice with Adjectives

Circle the adjective that tells about each underlined person, place, or thing.

1. We drink the (cold) lemonade.

2. I can help the (young) girl.

3. My sister is a (fast) runner.

4. Dad holds the (new) baby.

5. Luis is a (smart) boy.

6. The (happy) principal walks into the school.

7. The (nice) police officer rides a horse.

8. I wave at the (busy) mail carrier.

9. The (little) girl has a (red) bicycle.

10. The (tired) man sat in the (large) chair.

Pronouns and Adjectives • **127**

Name

More Practice with Adjectives

Circle the adjective that tells about each underlined person, place, or thing.

1. We played in the (wet) sand.

2. Brian works in his (colorful) garden.

3. Our class visited the (old) farm.

4. Look at the bird in the (tiny) nest.

5. The (red) house is on the corner.

6. The (noisy) team plays catch.

7. We go to a (big) school with (friendly) students.

8. We can see the (yellow) birds in the (large) tree.

9. Sara put the (small) book on the (round) table.

10. The (little) children swim in the (new) pool.

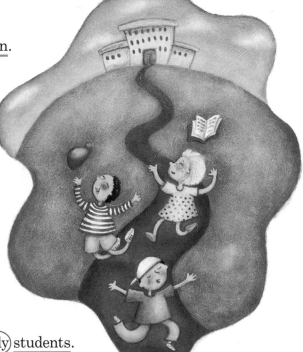

Name _____

Adjectives Review

Write the correct adjective for each sentence.
Use the word bank. **Sample answers shown.**

seven	excited	old	little
slower	red	rough	cold

1. The *old* slipper has a hole.

2. Trisha rode in the *red* wagon.

3. Here is a glass of *cold* milk.

4. Anna feels *excited* that she won the art contest.

5. Dad uses *rough* sandpaper.

6. There are *seven* candles on the cake.

7. Lions are *slower* than cheetahs.

8. The *little* mouse ran under the table.

Pronouns and Adjectives • **129**

Name

Show What You Know

A **Underline the correct pronoun in each sentence.**

1. Jeremy ate breakfast. (He She) ate breakfast.

2. We planted the flower. We planted (it they).

3. Clara is a carpenter. (He She) is a carpenter.

4. Kate and Carson are our neighbors. (We They) are our neighbors.

5. Simon and I built a tower. (We They) built a tower.

B **Underline the correct pronoun in each sentence.**

1. Please lend (I me) the toy.

2. Mike gave (I me) a penny.

3. (I Me) like to ice skate.

4. Damon and (I me) water ski in the summer.

5. My brother and (I me) played a game.

Name

Show What You Know

Underline the correct adjective in each sentence.

1. The (round square) oranges are in the basket.

2. Jordan feels (tired afraid) during the thunderstorm.

3. Ants are (bigger smaller) than hamsters.

4. The (short tall) girl cannot reach the top shelf.

5. I bite into a shiny (purple red) apple.

6. There are (six square) petals on the flower.

7. Olivia eats (buttery flat) popcorn at the movies.

8. My cousin laughs when she feels (sorry happy).

9. A cat's tail is (longer shorter) than a pig's tail.

10. An alligator's tail is the (longer longest) of all three.

What Is a Description?

A **description** tells about something or someone. It tells about a person, a place, a thing, or an event. The **beginning** tells the topic.

A description also uses words that have to do with our senses.

sight	sound	smell	taste	touch
big car	*loud roar*	*smoky fire*	*juicy orange*	*hot stove*

Read each item. Which sense would you use?

1. quiet whisper   *sound*

2. red flower   *sight*

3. prickly cactus   *touch*

4. stinky garbage   *smell*

5. sour pickles   *taste*

132 • Chapter 4

Use Sensory Words to Describe

Sensory words tell how things look, sound, smell, taste, or feel. They help to describe things. Use sensory words to make your description more real for the reader.

Write the correct sensory word in each sentence. Use the word bank.

bumpy	cool	sweet
curly	buzzing	

1. I feel a *cool* breeze outside.

2. Did you hear that *buzzing* bee?

3. We rode our bikes down a *bumpy* road.

4. He has *curly* hair.

5. Emma smells the *sweet* roses.

Descriptions • 133

Complete a Description

Write the correct word to complete each description.
Use the word banks.

small	tall	noisy

1. The park on Pioneer Road is my favorite place. It has a

   small pond and *tall* trees. The *noisy*

   ducks quack and swim. The park is a really fun place.

gray	long	loud

2. My cat Homer is the best cat in the world! He has

   gray fur. His *long* whiskers tickle me.

   When I hear his *loud* meow, I know he is hungry.

popping	fluffy	crispy

3. I love Saturday morning breakfast. The bacon makes a

   popping sound. The *fluffy*

   scrambled eggs are cooking. The *crispy*

   toast is hot.

Finish a Description

Finish these descriptions. Tell how these things look, sound, smell, taste, or feel. Use the word banks if you need help. **Answers will vary.**

wet   tickles   splash   raindrops

A Rainy Day

A rainy day can be fun.

campfire   smoky   hot   gooey

Toasting Marshmallows

I love toasting marshmallows.

Descriptions • 135

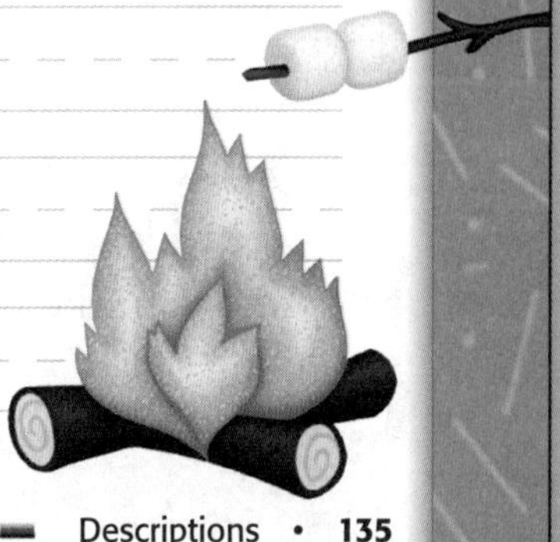

Writer's Workshop

PREWRITING

Pick a Topic

Nora is writing a description. She writes some topic ideas in her notebook. Then she circles the topic she will write about.

the skating rink

my new bike

Uncle Joe

playing in the snow

Write a description. Write or draw your topic ideas in your notebook. Your topic can be about

a person
    someone you know

a place
    somewhere you like to go

a thing
    something you have

an event
    something you like to do

Look at each idea. What can you write about it? Think about your ideas. Then choose the one you like best.

136 • Chapter 4

PREWRITING

Plan Your Description

Nora plans her description. She uses a chart to help her think of words. Here is her chart.

MY TOPIC: PLAYING IN THE SNOW	
Sight	long tunnels, snowflakes, my breath
Sound	snowflakes falling, snow crunching under my boots
Smell	
Taste	snowflakes on my tongue
Touch	cold

Plan your description. Fill in the chart below. Use your notebook if you need extra room.

MY TOPIC: _____	
Sight	
Sound	
Smell	
Taste	
Touch	

Writer's Workshop

DRAFTING

Nora uses her chart to write. This is Nora's draft.

> Sophie and me dig long tunnels. I can hear snowflakes fall if I am really quiet. I taste cold snowflakes on my tongue. I can see my breath. The snow crunches under my boots. We are like explorers at the South Pole.

Look at the chart you made. Add to your chart if you need to. Add any words that will make your description better.

Write your description in your notebook. Tell your topic in the **beginning**. Use your chart as you write. Use sensory words that show what you see, hear, smell, taste, and feel.

138 • Chapter 4

EDITING

Nora reads her draft. Editing it will make it even better. She uses the Editing Checklist.

Editing Checklist

☐ Do I describe a person, a place, a thing, or an event?

☐ Do I have a beginning that tells the topic?

☐ Do I use words that show what I see, hear, smell, taste, and feel?

I love to play in the snow.
∧Sophie and me dig long tunnels.

I forgot to tell my topic!

Look at the mistake Nora finds. How does she fix it?

Read your draft. Can you answer yes to the questions in the checklist? Mark any changes on your paper. Add any words that will make your description great. Be sure to add sensory words.

REVISING

Nora copies her draft. She includes the changes she marked. She knows that revising will make her paper better.

Copy your draft. Fix any mistakes you marked. Make your description better than it was before.

Descriptions • 139

Writer's Workshop

PROOFREADING

Nora proofreads her description. She looks at this checklist as she reads. She marks her paper when she finds something to change.

Proofreading Checklist

☐ Are all the words spelled correctly?

☐ Did I use capital letters?

☐ Did I use the right end marks?

☐ Are pronouns and adjectives used correctly?

> I love to play in the snow.
>
> Sophie and ~~me~~ ^I dig long tunnels.
>
> I can hear snowflakes fall if

Look at the mistake Nora finds. How does she fix it?

Read your description again. Use the Proofreading Checklist as you read. Put an **X** next to the question if you can answer yes.

Fix any mistakes you see. Use the proofreading marks at the back of your book.

Try reading your description out loud. Listen carefully. Does it sound the way you want it to sound?

PUBLISHING

When you publish, you share your work with others. Nora is almost ready to publish her work. She writes her description neatly onto a sheet of paper. She copies everything exactly. Nora is finally ready to publish her description.

Copy your description. Print as neatly as you can.

How will you publish your work? Decide with your class. Use one of these ideas or one of your own.

Mail it to someone special.

Frame it.

Put it on a bulletin board.

Hang it up.

Read it to the class.

Make a book of People, Places, Things, and Events.

Contractions

In this chapter students will learn about

- contractions
- contractions with *not*
- the contractions *I'm* and *I'll*
- contractions with *is* and *are*

A Visual, Please

Contraction Equations

it's = it + is

BUT

its = its
(not a contraction)

Grammar for Grown-ups

Contractions That Care

A contraction is formed when two words are combined and one or more letters are omitted. An apostrophe is used to represent the missing letter or letters. In writing, contractions are a way of representing oral language. They help improve the flow of writing and keep it from becoming stilted.

It is a commonly accepted practice to use contractions in informal writing, such as personal narratives or friendly letters. It is better, however, not to use them in more formal expository pieces. Avoiding contractions when writing research reports, for example, may help students distinguish between a formal and an informal tone.

Among the most commonly seen contractions are those formed with *not*. In these cases the contraction is formed with a verb and *not (can't, don't, aren't).* Some contractions are formed using a subject pronoun and a form of *be*. These include contractions with *am, is,* and *are (I'm, she's, he's, we're, you're).* Contractions may also use a form of *have*, which include contractions with *has* and *had (she's, he's, we've, they've, he'd, she'd, we'd).*

Daily Edits

The Daily Edits for this chapter provide students with daily practice editing sentences. Students should pay special attention to the use of contractions.

Common Errors

Or "A Case of Apostrophe Apathy"

Some developing writers, when forming contractions, mistakenly leave out the apostrophe.

ERROR: Nadine and Erica dont like apples.
CORRECT: Nadine and Erica don't like apples.

ERROR: My brother couldnt open the jar.
CORRECT: My brother couldn't open the jar.

To help students avoid this common error, remind them of the purpose and importance of an apostrophe. Point out that in a contraction, an apostrophe replaces a letter or letters that are left out. As students revise their writing, remind them to check for missing apostrophes.

For Kids Who Are Ready

Otherwise Known as "Would You Join Us?"

For students who are already comfortable with the contractions taught in this chapter, introduce contractions with *would*.

Tell students that contractions with *would* are formed in the same way as other contractions they have learned. In contractions with *would*, the apostrophe replaces the *woul*.

EXAMPLES: we + would = we'd
she + would = she'd
he + would = he'd
I + would = I'd
they + would = they'd

Share the above examples with students. Encourage them to practice using contractions with *would* in sentences.

Ask a Mentor

Real Situations, Real Solutions

Dear Grammar Geek,

My students frequently misuse its and it's in their writing. How can I help them?

It's the pits,
Beatrice

Dear Beatrice,

Display the visual on page 142a. When they are unsure about using a contraction, have students ask themselves whether the two words that make up the contraction can be substituted in the sentence. If they can, the contraction is being used correctly.

It's going to get easier,
Grammar Geek

Dear Grammar Geezer,

Some of my students use the contraction ain't in their writing and speech. How can I make them see that ain't isn't a word?

Ain't this a pickle,
Mark from Maine

Dear Mark,

This is a pickle! But it's nothing a simple explanation can't solve. Remind students that contractions are made up of two words, and write on the board the following examples: didn't = did + not, isn't = is + not, aren't = are + not, ain't = ? Then ask students to name the two words that make up the contraction ain't. The silence should prove your point! Tell students that because ain't can't be separated into two words, it isn't a real contraction. Work with the class to come up with contractions that should be used instead of ain't, such as isn't and aren't.

Let's make ain't extinct,
Grammar Geezer

Andrew Toos: www.CartoonStock.com

HA, I PUBLISHED MY BOOK!

HA, I REVIEWED HIS BOOK!

Book Reports

Read and Report

Expository writing is writing that informs. One of the most common forms of expository writing is the report. For students, perhaps the most common report is the book report. An effective book report begins with a thought-provoking book and an enthusiastic reader. Fiction, rather than nonfiction, is often best for classroom book reports. A well-written book report goes beyond recalling character, setting, plot, and theme—it also shows the conclusions that the reader has drawn and judgments the reader has made.

Effective book reports are logically organized. The writer provides general information about the story in the beginning, often describing the main characters and the setting. The middle briefly summarizes main events in time order. The ending discusses the report writer's opinion of the book, often sharing insights or recommendations to potential readers.

Effective book reports are written in a confident, lively voice. They use exact words that make a book's plot understandable. Sentences that express the writer's opinion are strategically placed for impact. Effective book reports are correct in grammar, spelling, capitalization, and punctuation.

Genre Characteristics

At the end of this chapter, students will write a book report. They will be guided through the writing process in the Writer's Workshop. The completed book report will include the following:

- a beginning that names the title, author, and main characters
- a middle that describes what happens in the book
- an ending that gives the writer's opinion
- correct grammar, spelling, capitalization, and punctuation

Daily Story Starters

The Daily Story Starters for this chapter provide students with practice brainstorming topics for book reports. By responding to a variety of prompts, students will learn how to generate multiple topic ideas for book reports.

Begin each day by writing on the board the Daily Story Starter. Allow time for students to complete the sentence. Then discuss the results as a class. Because the purpose of this activity is to help students think of book types and titles, talk to students about their ideas and whether the ideas are appropriate for their book reports.

Teacher's Toolbox

Try the following ideas to help your students get the most out of the Writer's Workshop:

- Add to your classroom library a variety of quality fiction.

- Create a bulletin-board display of popular book jackets that can be opened so that the inside flaps can be read. Inside each jacket, provide a two- or three-sentence summary of the book.

- As students consider possible books for their reports, encourage them to ask themselves the following questions: *Do I feel strongly about the book, whether I like it or dislike it? Do I know enough about the characters and what happens in the book to write a good report?*

Reasons to Write

Share with students the following list of people who write reports. Discuss why it is important to become a good report writer.

- doctors
- newspaper reporters
- presidents

Literature Links

You can add to your classroom library the following titles to offer your students good topics for book reports:

Babe: The Gallant Pig by Dick King-Smith

If You Give a Pig a Party by Laura Numeroff

Chang's Paper Pony by Eleanor Coerr

Book Report

	Yes	No
My report is about a book I have read.	☐	☐
My beginning tells the title, author, and characters.	☐	☐
My middle tells what happens.	☐	☐
My ending tells how I feel about the book.	☐	☐
I used contractions correctly.	☐	☐
I used complete sentences.	☐	☐
I spelled words correctly.	☐	☐
I used capital letters correctly.	☐	☐
I used end marks correctly.	☐	☐

Voyages in English 1

© Loyola Press

Teacher's Scoring Rubric

Book Report

0 = not evident
1 = minimal evidence of comprehension
2 = evidence of development toward comprehension
3 = strong evidence of comprehension
4 = outstanding evidence of comprehension

Ideas	Points
is about a book that the student has read	
Organization	
has a beginning that tells the title, author, and characters	
has a middle that tells what happens	
has an ending that expresses the student's opinion of the book	
Voice	
is written in a natural voice	
Word Choice	
uses contractions correctly	
words are recognizable	
Sentence Fluency	
has correct sentence structure	
Conventions	
grammar	
spelling	
punctuation and capitalization	

Voyages in English 1

Daily Voyages

Daily Edits

Monday	Tuesday	Wednesday	Thursday	Friday
Jim ~~gived~~ [gave] rob a new scarecrow.	Rob put the ~~skarecrow~~ [scarecrow] in his field.	the crows stayed ~~awy~~ [away].	The ~~Corn~~ was ~~saf~~ [safe] from crows.	Rob ~~missd~~ [missed] the ~~preddy~~ [pretty] black crows.
I want [to] teach my dog a ~~trik~~ [trick].	He can shake hands [with] me.	He can cook ~~nooodles~~ [noodles] and beans.	I want ~~hime~~ [him] to drive me to ~~School~~.	I ~~don'nt~~ [don't] like to take the bus.
I went ~~roler~~ [roller] skating by the ~~Pond~~.	I ~~didn'~~t [didn't] see the ducks crossing the path.	I ~~couldnt~~ [couldn't] stop in time.	I quickly ~~turnd~~ [turned] off ~~they~~ [the] path.	the ducks watched me swim that ~~Day~~.
the knight charges up the mountain.	His horse ~~gallop~~ [gallops] up the ~~rokky~~ [rocky] path.	He is ~~all most~~ [almost] to the castle.	The knight ~~is'nt~~ [isn't] in ~~Danger~~.	~~Hes~~ [He's] just late for dinner.
Hannah ~~writed~~ [wrote] a story about a fairy.	The ~~Fairy~~ had a ~~brokken~~ [broken] wing.	A wizard found the ~~the~~ fairy and ~~helpd~~ [helped] it.	Now ~~theyre~~ [they're] good ~~freends~~ [friends].	Hannah wishes ~~thay~~ [they] were real.

Daily Story Starters

Monday	Tuesday	Wednesday	Thursday	Friday
A book I've read many times is	The best book someone read to me is	The funniest book is	The best book about outer space is	The smartest character in a book is
The best boy character is	My favorite girl character is	A book I didn't like is	The best fairy tale is	The last book I read was
My favorite animal character is	If I could be any character, I would be	I like books about	My favorite author is	A book that taught me something was
The best mystery book is	The best book about kids is	A good book with monsters is	A book about the past is	A sad book is
The best hero in a book is	The best adventure book is	A strange book I read was	The scariest book is	A book with good pictures is

Chapter Adaptors

SPEAKING & LISTENING

Say to a volunteer a sentence that has a contraction. Have the student identify the contraction and the two words that make up the contraction. Ask the student to tell where the apostrophe is placed in the contraction. Repeat until each student has had a turn.

RETEACHING

Cut out a large apostrophe. Write on the board a contraction without the apostrophe, leaving space between the letters. Invite a volunteer to place the apostrophe in the correct place on the board. Ask the volunteer to tell what letter or letters are replaced by the apostrophe. Erase the contraction and repeat with others.

BOOK-COVER MURAL

Have each student draw a cover for a book he or she recently read. Ask students to include the title and the author. Then have students write below their drawings a sentence that tells what they liked about the book. Have students attach their drawings to a wall in the classroom to make a mural of book covers.

RETEACHING

Have students each choose a book for a book report. Allow time for students to free write about their books. Tell students to write any words that come to mind when they think of the book. Encourage students to write not only about the characters and what happens in the book, but also what they feel about the book. When students have finished, have them look over their free writing. Remind students to use their notes when they write their drafts.

ENGLISH-LANGUAGE LEARNERS

Invite English-language learners to discuss books written in their primary language. Ask students to talk about the characters, what happens, and what they feel about the books. Tell students that by talking about these books, they are giving an informal book report. Have students write in English one or two sentences about what they have discussed. Have students refer to their notes when they write their book reports about a book written in English.

WRITING & EDITING

Tell students that the beginning, the middle, and the ending of a book report each do a special job. Suggest that before students add new information, they check that they are adding it to the right part of the book report.

CONTRACTION ICE-CREAM CONES

Photocopy outlines of ice-cream cones and scoops of ice cream. Distribute one scoop and one cone to each student. Assign each student a word that can be used to make a contraction. (Examples: have, she, we, not, are) Have students color and write their word on the scoop. Allow students to decorate and write their names on the cones. Collect the scoops and put them in a box. Invite a volunteer to pick one scoop from the box and give a contraction using the word on the scoop. (Examples: haven't, she's, we're, weren't, aren't). Allow the student to attach the scoop to his or her cone if the correct answer is given. Repeat until every student has had a turn and made an ice-cream cone. Display the contraction cones around the classroom.

CHAPTER 5

Contractions and Book Reports

142 • Chapter 5

Good Knight and Great Book
by Dermot Gibson

Get Well, Good Knight is by Shelley Moore Thomas. It's about a Good Knight and three little dragons. The three little dragons are sick. The Good Knight wants to help them get well. He brings them all kinds of strange soup. The dragons don't like the soup at all! I like this book because the Good Knight is very funny and helpful.

Name

Contractions

A **contraction** is a short way of writing two words. When you write a contraction, you leave out a letter or letters and put in an **apostrophe**.

This is an apostrophe (').

● **Trace over each contraction.**

1. do not

don't

2. did not

didn't

3. does not

doesn't

4. could not

couldn't

5. is not

isn't

6. are not

aren't

7. has not

hasn't

8. have not

haven't

144 • Chapter 5

Name

More Contractions

A **contraction** is a short way of writing two words. When you write a contraction, you leave out a letter or letters and put in an **apostrophe** (').

● **Trace over each contraction.**

1. cannot

    can't

2. was not

    wasn't

3. were not

    weren't

4. I am

    I'm

5. I will

    I'll

6. it is

    it's

7. he is

    he's

8. she is

    she's

9. we are

    we're

10. they are

    they're

Name

The Contraction *Don't*

Some contractions are made with the word **not**. To make a contraction with **not**, drop the **o** and put in an apostrophe (').

A Trace over the words below.

do not   *don't*

Do not *cross the street.*   **Don't** *cross the street.*

B Underline the two words that make up each contraction. Write the contraction on the line.

1. Bicycles <u>do not</u> have motors.

   Bicycles *don't* have motors.

2. Dogs <u>do not</u> live in trees.

   Dogs *don't* live in trees.

3. These sleeping bags <u>do not</u> zip.

   These sleeping bags *don't* zip.

4. Kittens <u>do not</u> have wings.

   Kittens *don't* have wings.

5. Goats <u>do not</u> make webs.

   Goats *don't* make webs.

> A contraction is a way to write two words as one. Replace a letter or letters with an apostrophe, and it's already done.

146 • Chapter 5

Name _____

The Contraction *Didn't*

A Trace over the words below.

did not   *didn't*

We **did not** go fishing.   We **didn't** go fishing.

B Underline the two words that make up each contraction.
Write the contraction on the line.

1. Marty <u>did not</u> fly the kite.

   Marty *didn't* fly the kite.

2. You <u>did not</u> sail the boat.

   You *didn't* sail the boat.

3. Tony <u>did not</u> swing the bat.

   Tony *didn't* swing the bat.

4. Rose <u>did not</u> go to the movies.

   Rose *didn't* go to the movies.

5. The plane <u>did not</u> land on time.

   The plane *didn't* land on time.

6. The dog <u>did not</u> bark at the moon.

   The dog *didn't* bark at the moon.

Contractions • 147

Name _____

The Contraction *Doesn't*

A **Trace over the words below.**

does not   *doesn't*

*Ryan **does not** play ball.*   *Ryan **doesn't** play ball.*

B **Underline the two words that make up each contraction. Write the contraction on the line.**

1. The lid <u>does not</u> come off the jar.

   The lid *doesn't* come off the jar.

2. The last puzzle piece <u>does not</u> fit.

   The last puzzle piece *doesn't* fit.

3. Ivan <u>does not</u> take the bus.

   Ivan *doesn't* take the bus.

4. The tape <u>does not</u> stick to the paper.

   The tape *doesn't* stick to the paper.

5. The new curtain <u>does not</u> hang straight.

   The new curtain *doesn't* hang straight.

6. The peacock <u>does not</u> show its feathers.

   The peacock *doesn't* show its feathers.

Name

The Contraction *Couldn't*

A Trace over the words below.

could not   *couldn't*

We **could not** play outside.   We **couldn't** play outside.

B Underline the two words that make up each contraction.
Write the contraction on the line.

1. Paul could not catch.

   Paul *couldn't* catch.

2. Tiffany could not run.

   Tiffany *couldn't* run.

3. Teresa could not sing.

   Teresa *couldn't* sing.

4. Rich could not go.

   Rich *couldn't* go.

5. I could not swim.

   I *couldn't* swim.

6. Jo could not hop.

   Jo *couldn't* hop.

Writer's Corner

Write a sentence about something you couldn't do last year.

Contractions • **149**

Name _____

The Contraction *Isn't*

A Trace over the words below.

is not   isn't

*Erin **is not** here today.*   *Erin **isn't** here today.*

B Underline the two words that make up each contraction. Write the contraction on the line.

1. Today <u>is not</u> Saturday.

   Today *isn't* Saturday.

2. The game <u>is not</u> on TV.

   The game *isn't* on TV.

3. This mitt <u>is not</u> mine.

   This mitt *isn't* mine.

4. My computer <u>is not</u> on.

   My computer *isn't* on.

5. The river <u>is not</u> very deep.

   The river *isn't* very deep.

6. The duck <u>is not</u> in the water.

   The duck *isn't* in the water.

Writer's Corner

Pretend you live on the moon. Write a sentence using *isn't*.

Name _____

The Contraction *Aren't*

A Trace over the words below.

are not   aren't

They **are not** in first grade.   They **aren't** in first grade.

B Underline the two words that make up each contraction.
Write the contraction on the line.

1. The cars <u>are not</u> big.

   The cars *aren't* big.

2. Turtles <u>are not</u> fast.

   Turtles *aren't* fast.

3. The men <u>are not</u> here.

   The men *aren't* here.

4. The boats <u>are not</u> sailing.

   The boats *aren't* sailing.

5. We <u>are not</u> bowling.

   We *aren't* bowling.

6. They <u>are not</u> coming.

   They *aren't* coming.

Name _____

The Contraction *Hasn't*

A Trace over the words below.

has not   hasn't

He **has not** arrived.   He **hasn't** arrived.

B Underline the two words that make up each contraction.
Write the contraction on the line.

1. Andy <u>has not</u> lost a game.

   Andy *hasn't* lost a game.

2. Dion <u>has not</u> watered the plants.

   Dion *hasn't* watered the plants.

3. My dad <u>has not</u> set the clock.

   My dad *hasn't* set the clock.

4. Jill <u>has not</u> opened the door.

   Jill *hasn't* opened the door.

5. Staci <u>has not</u> seen the bike.

   Staci *hasn't* seen the bike.

6. The bird <u>has not</u> flown away.

   The bird *hasn't* flown away.

Name _____

The Contraction *Haven't*

A Trace over the words below.

have not   *haven't*

I **have not** read the book.   I **haven't** read the book.

B Underline the two words that make up each contraction. Write the contraction on the line.

1. Nan and Matt <u>have not</u> called yet.

   Nan and Matt *haven't* called yet.

2. They <u>have not</u> visited us lately.

   They *haven't* visited us lately.

3. We <u>have not</u> jumped rope.

   We *haven't* jumped rope.

4. The seals <u>have not</u> eaten the fish.

   The seals *haven't* eaten the fish.

5. The girls <u>have not</u> seen our cat.

   The girls *haven't* seen our cat.

6. We <u>have not</u> done our chores.

   We *haven't* done our chores.

Name _____

The Contraction *Can't*

A Trace over the words below.

cannot   can't

*She **cannot** sleep.*   *She **can't** sleep.*

B Underline the word that makes up each contraction.
Write the contraction on the line.

1. Gloria <u>cannot</u> climb.

   Gloria *can't* climb.

2. My aunt <u>cannot</u> cook.

   My aunt *can't* cook.

3. Pablo <u>cannot</u> drive.

   Pablo *can't* drive.

4. Morgan <u>cannot</u> draw.

   Morgan *can't* draw.

5. Robots <u>cannot</u> think.

   Robots *can't* think.

6. The boys <u>cannot</u> lift the box.

   The boys *can't* lift the box.

Writer's Corner

Write a sentence about something an animal can't do.

Name

The Contraction *Wasn't*

A Trace over the words below.

was not   *wasn't*

*Jake **was not** at the park.*   *Jake **wasn't** at the park.*

B Underline the two words that make up each contraction.
Write the contraction on the line.

1. I <u>was not</u> yelling.

   I *wasn't* yelling.

2. Kira <u>was not</u> in the play.

   Kira *wasn't* in the play.

3. Lucas <u>was not</u> dancing.

   Lucas *wasn't* dancing.

4. The dog <u>was not</u> on a leash.

   The dog *wasn't* on a leash.

5. The window <u>was not</u> closed.

   The window *wasn't* closed.

6. Courtney <u>was not</u> wearing a coat.

   Courtney *wasn't* wearing a coat.

Contractions • 155

Name

The Contraction *Weren't*

A Trace over the words below.

were not   weren't

They **were not** cleaning.   They **weren't** cleaning.

B Underline the two words that make up each contraction.
Write the contraction on the line.

1. We <u>were not</u> running in the house.

   We *weren't* running in the house.

2. Mom and Dad <u>were not</u> making dinner.

   Mom and Dad *weren't* making dinner.

3. They <u>were not</u> at the library.

   They *weren't* at the library.

4. Oscar and Dario <u>were not</u> helping.

   Oscar and Dario *weren't* helping.

5. My sisters <u>were not</u> raking the leaves.

   My sisters *weren't* raking the leaves.

6. The children <u>were not</u> splashing in the puddles.

   The children *weren't* splashing in the puddles.

Name

Contractions Review

Underline the contraction that is spelled correctly in each sentence.

1. We (<u>aren't</u> are'nt) going to the fair.

2. Carolyn (ca'nt <u>can't</u>) reach the apple on the branch.

3. They (do'nt <u>don't</u>) know the way to the library.

4. I (<u>didn't</u> did'nt) take the dog for a walk.

5. He (has'nt <u>hasn't</u>) read the book yet.

6. Henry (<u>doesn't</u> does'nt) understand the directions.

7. Joan and Darius (<u>couldn't</u> could'nt) leave on time.

8. This (is'nt <u>isn't</u>) the song we like.

9. I (<u>haven't</u> have'nt) seen that movie.

10. Chris (was'nt <u>wasn't</u>) at the party.

Name _____

The Contraction *I'm*

Some contractions are made with the word **am**. To make a contraction with **am**, drop the **a** and put in an apostrophe (').

(A) **Trace over the words below.**

I am   *I'm*

I am *seven years old.*   **I'm** *seven years old.*

(B) **Underline the two words that make up each contraction. Write the contraction on the line.**

1. I am riding my bike.

   I'm riding my bike.

2. I am roller-skating.

   I'm roller-skating.

3. I am playing the game.

   I'm playing the game.

4. I am wearing a new suit.

   I'm wearing a new suit.

5. I am drinking water.

   I'm drinking water.

6. I am writing to my grandpa.

   I'm writing to my grandpa.

Name

The Contraction *I'll*

Some contractions are made with the word **will**. To make a contraction with **will**, drop the **wi** and put in an apostrophe (').

A Trace over the words below.

I will take your picture.   **I'll** take your picture.

B Underline the two words that make up each contraction. Write the contraction on the line.

1. I will go to the dance tonight.

   I'll go to the dance tonight.

2. I will sing in the recital.

   I'll sing in the recital.

3. I will wear my blue sweater.

   I'll wear my blue sweater.

4. I will make a funny mask.

   I'll make a funny mask.

5. I will go to his house.

   I'll go to his house.

6. I will make a salad.

   I'll make a salad.

Writer's Corner

Write a sentence about what you will do this weekend. Use *I'll.*

Contractions • 159

Name

The Contraction *It's*

Some contractions are made with the word **is**. To make a contraction with **is**, drop the **i** and put in an apostrophe (').

A **Trace over the words below.**

it is   *it's*

It is *raining today.*   ***It's*** *raining today.*

B **Underline the two words that make up each contraction.
Write the contraction on the line.**

1. Lin says <u>it is</u> easy to juggle.

    Lin says *it's* easy to juggle.

2. <u>It is</u> the last day of school.

    It's the last day of school.

3. I hope <u>it is</u> almost ready.

    I hope *it's* almost ready.

4. <u>It is</u> hot outside.

    It's hot outside.

5. <u>It is</u> a beautiful day.

    It's a beautiful day.

6. <u>It is</u> a sad movie.

    It's a sad movie.

Name _____

The Contractions *He's* and *She's*

A Trace over the words below.

he is

He is my brother.

he's

He's my brother.

she is

She is my sister.

she's

She's my sister.

B Underline the two words that make up each contraction. Write the contraction on the line.

1. <u>She is</u> good at math.

   She's good at math.

2. I think <u>he is</u> nice.

   I think *he's* nice.

3. <u>He is</u> on the team.

   He's on the team.

4. <u>She is</u> not home.

   She's not home.

5. Bo says <u>he is</u> cold.

   Bo says *he's* cold.

6. <u>He is</u> in a band.

   He's in a band.

Name

The Contractions *We're* and *They're*

Some contractions are made with the word **are**. To make a contraction with **are**, drop the **a** and put in an apostrophe (').

A Trace over the words below.

we are

We are *making lunch.*

we're

We're *making lunch.*

they are

They are *setting the table.*

they're

They're *setting the table.*

B Underline the two words that make up each contraction. Write the contraction on the line.

1. We are making a pie.

   We're_____ making a pie.

2. They are washing dishes.

   They're washing dishes.

3. They are sitting inside.

   They're sitting inside.

4. We are driving to Canada.

   We're driving to Canada.

5. I heard they are leaving.

   I heard they're leaving.

6. Tell Cate we are ready.

   Tell Cate we're ready.

Name _____

Contractions Review

Underline the contraction that is spelled correctly in each sentence.

1. (<u>I'm</u> I'am) joining the soccer team.

2. Joanne thinks (h'is <u>he's</u>) at the store.

3. (<u>They're</u> Theyr'e) flying kites in the field.

4. (<u>I'll</u> Il'l) teach the dog a trick.

5. Amanda says (sh'es <u>she's</u>) going to the library.

6. (Wer'e <u>We're</u>) visiting our uncle in Montana.

7. I am sure (<u>we're</u> wer'e) invited to the party.

8. (Its' <u>It's</u>) very cold outside.

9. I hope (the'yre <u>they're</u>) coming with us.

10. The teacher says (<u>it's</u> its') a short test.

Name

Show What You Know

A Draw a line from the words in the first list to their contractions.

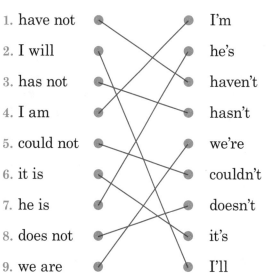

1. have not   I'm

2. I will   he's

3. has not   haven't

4. I am   hasn't

5. could not   we're

6. it is   couldn't

7. he is   doesn't

8. does not   it's

9. we are   I'll

B Draw a line from the words in the first list to their contractions.

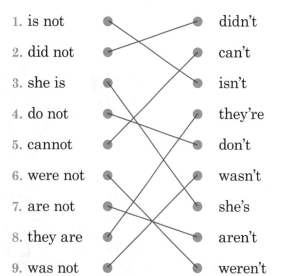

1. is not   didn't

2. did not   can't

3. she is   isn't

4. do not   they're

5. cannot   don't

6. were not   wasn't

7. are not   she's

8. they are   aren't

9. was not   weren't

Show What You Know

Write the contraction for the words in green.

1. *He's* _____ missing his shoe. **He is**

2. Maria *isn't* _____ busy now. **is not**

3. The farmer *didn't* _____ plant the seeds yet. **did not**

4. *We're* _____ going to the circus. **We are**

5. *I'm* _____ ready to go home. **I am**

6. He *doesn't* _____ know my name. **does not**

7. Jack *couldn't* watch the parade. **could not**

8. *It's* _____ going to snow tomorrow. **It is**

9. *I'll* _____ show Dennis the magic trick. **I will**

10. The men *aren't* _____ here yet. **are not**

Contractions • 165

Get Ready to Write

What Is a Book Report?

In a **book report** you tell about a book you have read. You share how you feel about the book too.

The **title** is the name of the book. Always underline the title of a book.

The **author** is the person who wrote the book.

A **character** is someone or something in the story.

● **Read the book report below. Then answer the questions.**

> <u>Anatole</u> is by Eve Titus. Anatole is a French mouse. He has to find food to feed his family. He gets an unusual job for a mouse. I like this book because it shows how smart a little mouse can be.

1. What is the title of the book? *Anatole*

2. Who is the author? *Eve Titus*

3. Who is a character in the book? *Anatole*

4. What happens in the story? *Anatole has to find food for his family. He gets an unusual job.*

5. How does the writer feel about the book? *The writer likes the book.*

166 • Chapter 5

Parts of a Book Report

A book report has a **beginning**, a **middle**, and an **ending**.

The **beginning** is where you tell the book's title, the author's name, and the characters in the story. Underline the book's title.

The **middle** is where you tell what happens in the story.

The **ending** is where you tell how you feel about the book.

● Draw a line to match each book report part to the correct sentences.

Beginning

Middle

Ending

Pip is sunbathing. He falls into a river and has a wild ride.

I really like this book. Pip has lots of silly adventures.

River Ride is by Nicola Taso. It's about Pip the snake.

● Draw a line to match each book report part to the correct sentences.

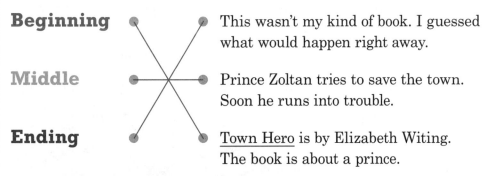

Beginning

Middle

Ending

This wasn't my kind of book. I guessed what would happen right away.

Prince Zoltan tries to save the town. Soon he runs into trouble.

Town Hero is by Elizabeth Witing. The book is about a prince.

Book Reports • 167

Complete a Book Report

Look at the book reports below. Write the missing information where it belongs. Use the word banks.

grandpa   Taro   Jason Zack   Monsters, Do Not Enter

1. *Monsters, Do Not Enter* is a book by *Jason Zack*. *Taro* is in first grade. He is afraid of monsters. So his *grandpa* teaches him some tricks to keep monsters away. Grandpa's tricks work! I like this book because Grandpa is so funny. I laughed the whole time.

Just a Tiny Fish   Beth Cole   Rudi

2. *Beth Cole* wrote the book *Just a Tiny Fish*. Rudi is a small fish in a big pond. One day the turtles decide to go on strike. Then the frogs decide they want to move. It's up to *Rudi* to save the day and the pond. This book is great. It shows that you don't have to be big or popular to do important things.

Plan a Book Report

Think about a book you've read. Fill in the chart below.

Title

Author

Characters

What happens

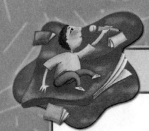

Writer's Workshop

PREWRITING

Pick a Topic

Dermot is writing a book report. First he needs to pick a topic. Dermot thinks about the books that he's read. He lists them in his notebook. Then he circles <u>Get Well, Good Knight</u>. He thinks his classmates would enjoy hearing about this book the most.

Loose Tooth

A Quiet Place

Get Well, Good Knight

Bintou's Braids

List in your notebook some books you've read. Then think about each book you've listed. Pick the book that you would like to write about. Circle the title. This will be the topic of your book report.

170 • Chapter 5

PREWRITING

Plan Your Book Report

Dermot plans his book report. He knows having a plan will help him to write. He draws this plan in his notebook. He fills in all the information about his book.

Title	<u>Get Well, Good Knight</u>
Author	Shelley Moore Thomas

Characters

The Good Knight

Three Little Dragons

What happens

The dragons are sick.

The Good Knight brings soup.

YUCK!

The soup tastes bad.

How I feel about this book

I liked this book.

The Good Knight is funny and helpful.

Make a plan like Dermot's in your notebook. Fill in your information on your chart. Read your book again if you need to.

Writer's Workshop

DRAFTING

Dermot writes his draft. He uses his plan as he writes.
He's careful to follow his plan.

> _Get Well, Good Knight_ is by Shelley Moore Thomas. The three little dragons are sick. The Good Knight wants to help them get well. He brings them all kinds of strange soup. The dragons do'nt like the soup at all! I liked this book because the Good Knight is very funny and helpful.

Write your draft in your notebook. Use the plan you made. Include anything from the book that will be helpful to your reader. Leave out anything that isn't important. Try to get all your ideas on paper. Remember that you can always make changes later.

EDITING

Dermot edits his book report. He knows that editing will make his report better.

Dermot uses this checklist as he reads. He looks at one question at a time.

Editing Checklist

☐ Do I have a beginning that tells the title, author, and characters?

☐ Do I have a middle that tells what happens?

☐ Do I have an ending that tells how I feel about the book?

> <u>Get Well, Good Knight</u> is by Shelley Moore
> It's about a Good Knight and three little dragons.
> Thomas.∧The three little dragons are sick.
>
> The Good Knight wants to help them get

I didn't tell about the characters!

Look at the mistake Dermot finds. How does he fix it?

Edit your book report. Use the Editing Checklist as you read. Look for one kind of mistake at a time. Make changes until you can say yes to all the questions.

REVISING

Dermot copies his draft. He includes all the changes he's marked. He knows that by revising, his book report will be even better.

Copy your draft. Fix any mistakes you marked. Make your book report better than it was before.

Book Reports • 173

Writer's Workshop

PROOFREADING

Dermot proofreads his book report to look for mistakes. He uses a proofreading checklist. He looks at one question at a time.

Proofreading Checklist

☐ Are all the words spelled correctly?

☐ Did I use capital letters?

☐ Did I use the right end marks?

☐ Are contractions used correctly?

well. He brings them all kinds of strange soup. The dragons don't like the soup at all!

Look at the mistake Dermot finds. How does he fix it?

Proofread your book report. Use the Proofreading Checklist. Look at one question at a time.

If you need to make a change, mark it on your draft. Use the proofreading marks at the back of this book. Make your book report the best it can be.

Ask someone who hasn't read the book to read your report. Is your report interesting to him or her? Is it easy to follow?

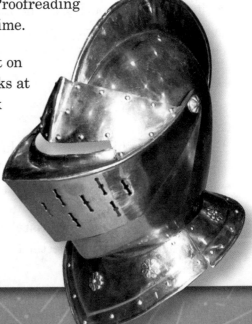

PUBLISHING

Dermot is excited to publish his book report. He knows that his friends will read it. He wants to share a great book report.

Make a copy of your book report. Write it neatly. Write a title for your book report at the top of your paper. Then write your name. Include all of your changes. This will be the book report that you share with your readers. Make it the best it can be.

How will you share your book report? Choose one of these ideas or come up with your own.

Put your report on the class bulletin board.

Dress up like a character and present your report.

Attach a drawing to your book report.

Make a class book of everyone's reports.

Make a poster ad for your book.

Word Study

In this chapter students will learn about

- synonyms
- antonyms
- homophones

A Visual, Please

Using Won *and* One

The **one** boat

that **won** the boat race

won by **one** minute

at a very fast pace!

Grammar for Grown-ups

Synonym Study

The word *synonym* comes from the Greek *syn* ("plus") and *onoma* ("name"). Synonyms are words with nearly the same meanings. Examples of synonyms include *quiet, silent; talk, speak; begin, start;* and *find, discover.* Students should take care when replacing a word with its synonym. Often a word may have a more exact meaning in the context of a sentence. For example, *long* and *extended* are synonyms, but a *long arm* and an *extended arm* mean two different things.

Antonym Analysis

The word *antonym* comes from the Greek *anti* ("against") and *onoma* ("name"). Antonyms are words that have opposite meanings. Words that have multiple meanings may have several antonyms, depending on the word's usage. Examples of antonyms include *strong, weak; light, heavy; always, never;* and *bright, dark.*

Regarding Homophones

The word *homophone* comes from the Greek *homoios* ("identical") and *phone* ("sound"). Homophones are words that sound the same, but have different spellings and meanings, such as *to, two,* and *too.* The word *homophone* is often confused with *homonym* or *homograph. Homograph,* which comes from the Greek *homoios* ("identical") and *graph* ("to write"), can more literally be interpreted as "the same letters." Homographs are words that are spelled the same but have different pronunciations and meanings, such as *tear* (a verb) and *tear* (a noun). Homonyms are words that have the same spelling and pronunciation but different meanings, such as *bark* (the sharp sound a dog makes) and *bark* (the tough covering of a tree). Homophones are sometimes called *homonyms.*

Daily Edits

The Daily Edits for this chapter provide students with daily practice editing sentences. Students should pay special attention to their use of homophones.

Common Errors

Or "Two Dogs to Walk Is Too Many"

Some developing writers misuse the homophones *too, to,* and *two.* To help students avoid this common error, write on the board the sentence *Two dogs to walk is too many.* Help students use the sentence to understand the usage of *two, to,* and *too.* Tell students to use the sentence to check *two, to,* and *too* in their own writing.

For Kids Who Are Ready

Otherwise Known as "The List Goes On"

For students who are already comfortable with synonym pairs, introduce the concept of words with more than one synonym.

EXAMPLES: **big:** large, huge, gigantic

happy: glad, cheerful, joyful

small: little, tiny, teeny

Share the above examples with students. Encourage them to use a thesaurus to find other synonyms for synonym pairs that they learn about in this chapter. Emphasize that because synonyms have varied meanings, students should check a dictionary to make sure they are using the word that best suits their purpose.

Ask a Mentor

Real Situations, Real Solutions

Dear Grammar Geek,

Homophones habitually hinder my students. How can I help without hindering their headway? Help!
Harriet

Dear Harriet,

Display the visual on page 176a. Because the differences between homophones cannot be heard when read aloud, students will benefit most from seeing homophones written in sentences. This will help students learn the definition of each homophone and pair it with its correct spelling. The more often students see a homophone in context, the more likely they will be able to use it correctly in their own writing.

You've won one battle,
Grammar Geek

Dear Grammar Geezer,

My students frequently use the same words over and over. How can I help them add variety to their vocabulary?

Variety is the spice of life—and writing,
Mr. Jennings

Dear Mr. Jennings,

Right you are! One of the easiest ways to expand students' vocabulary is by encouraging them to use synonyms in place of words they repeatedly use. Review common synonym pairs often and remind students that replacing words with synonyms can add variety to their speech and writing.

Let's spice it up,
Grammar Geezer

Research Reports

Adey Bryant: www.CartoonStock.com

"Miss Travers, bring me that report on absenteeism.... Miss Travers?...Miss Travers?..."

Genre Characteristics

At the end of this chapter, students will write a research report. They will be guided through the writing process in the Writer's Workshop. The completed research report will include the following:

- a beginning that states the topic
- a middle that includes important facts
- an ending that summarizes
- correct grammar, spelling, capitalization, and punctuation

Daily Story Starters

The Daily Story Starters for this chapter provide students with practice brainstorming topics for research reports. This daily practice helps students understand the variety of topics they can research.

Begin each day by writing on the board the Daily Story Starter. Allow time for students to complete the sentence. Then discuss the results as a class. Because the purpose of this activity is to generate topics for research reports, talk to students about their ideas and whether the ideas interest them and whether the topics are narrow enough for a research report.

Show What You Know

A research report is an expository piece that provides information about a specific topic. The information is derived from a variety of sources found by the writer. The writer then interprets, analyzes, and draws conclusions from the information to develop a topic sentence and supporting ideas.

The writer of a research report often completes a process such as the following: choose a topic, form a preliminary topic sentence, locate sources, take notes on note cards, draft, revise, edit, and publish.

Effective research reports include a beginning that states the topic, a middle that supports the topic, and an ending that summarizes the report. Throughout the piece, the writer uses formal language, a variety of sentence styles and lengths, and correct grammar, spelling, capitalization, and punctuation.

Chapter 7 of the student book provides lessons and activities that teach students how to use reference tools. You may find it helpful to teach Chapter 7 prior to or concurrently with Chapter 6 in order to prepare students to write their research reports.

Teacher's Toolbox

Try the following ideas to help your students get the most out of the Writer's Workshop:

- Add to your classroom library a variety of nonfiction works to spark topic ideas.

- Create a bulletin-board display of interesting articles and photographs from news, science, or nature magazines.

- Meet with students as they are considering topics. Discuss students' possible topics and guide them to pick an appropriate topic that isn't too broad.

- Consider displaying the student's Research Report scoring rubric in poster form or on an overhead projector during each writing session.

Reasons to Write

Share with students the following list of people who write research reports. Discuss why it is important to become a good research report writer.

- doctor
- teacher
- police officer

Literature Links

You can add to your classroom library the following titles to offer your students examples of well-crafted expository writing:

What's It Like to Be a Fish? by Wendy Pfeffer

The Magic School Bus Inside the Human Body by Joanna Cole

From Seed to Plant by Gail Gibbons

Research Report

	Yes	No
My beginning tells the topic sentence.	☐	☐
My middle tells important facts.	☐	☐
My ending sums up the report.	☐	☐
I used synonyms to replace words used over and over.	☐	☐
I used antonyms correctly.	☐	☐
I used homophones correctly.	☐	☐
I used complete sentences.	☐	☐
I spelled words correctly.	☐	☐
I used capital letters and end marks correctly.	☐	☐

Teacher's Scoring Rubric

Research Report

0 = not evident
1 = minimal evidence of comprehension
2 = evidence of development toward comprehension
3 = strong evidence of comprehension
4 = outstanding evidence of comprehension

	Points
Ideas	
is about a topic that can be researched	
Organization	
has a beginning that includes a topic sentence	
has a middle that tells relevant facts	
has an ending that sums up the report	
Voice	
is written in a natural voice	
Word Choice	
replaces overused words with synonyms	
uses antonyms correctly	
uses homophones correctly	
words are recognizable	
Sentence Fluency	
has correct sentence structure	
Conventions	
grammar	
spelling	
punctuation and capitalization	

Voyages in English 1

Daily Voyages

Daily Edits

Monday	Tuesday	Wednesday	Thursday	Friday
Jill ~~wented~~ (went) out into her yard.	she ~~decideed~~ (decided) to make mud pies.	Jill watered the ~~the~~ dirt to ~~mak~~ (make) mud.	she ~~aded~~ (added) sticks and rocks.	A ~~read~~ (red) button made a ~~chirry~~ (cherry) on top.
Daniel ~~bilt~~ (built) a tower of ~~blocs~~ (blocks).	He set ~~eash~~ (each) block ~~care fully~~ (carefully).	The ~~towor~~ (tower) grew as big as daniel.	He ~~new~~ (knew) he was out of Blocks.	He wished he could make ~~it~~ it ~~biger~~ (bigger).
Mackie ~~like~~ (likes) to dig in her ~~sandbocks~~ (sandbox).	She uses a ~~blew~~ (blue) shovel.	She found a ~~seeshell~~ (seashell) once.	~~Ones~~ (Once) she even found a ~~crayn~~ (crayon).	She ~~doesnt~~ (doesn't) ~~no~~ (know) where it came from.
Scarlett ~~red~~ (read) about a ~~famos~~ (famous) writer.	She decided ~~two~~ (to) ~~right~~ (write) stories.	Scarlett ~~new~~ (knew) she ~~were~~ (was) a good writer.	She ~~rote~~ (wrote) stories for many ~~year~~ (years).	Today she ~~are~~ (is) a famous Writer.
You are ~~allmost~~ (almost) done with daily edits.	~~Witch~~ (Which) story did you like best~~.~~?	~~we hopp~~ (We hope) you liked editing.	You ~~dided~~ (did) a terrific Job!	Keep on writing and sharing your ~~werk~~ (work).

Daily Story Starters

Monday	Tuesday	Wednesday	Thursday	Friday
A place I'd like to explore is	I've always wondered why	Who invented the	I like reading about	I want to know why
I took an interesting trip to	An amazing thing is	Why is it called	Something in nature I like is	A fact I'd like to share is
I've always wondered where	I want to know more about	What is it like in	I don't know a lot about	How do they make
An interesting animal is	I've always wondered how	I know a lot about	A country I want to visit is	Someone in history I like is
Something useful is	What is it like to be	Who discovered	Who was the first person to	Why do we celebrate

Chapter Adaptors

MAKE A SENTENCE SANDWICH

Distribute to students cut-out drawings of bread slices, lunchmeat slices, cheese slices, and tomato slices. Then write on the board *The brown dog runs.* Explain that in the sentence the verb is the "meat," the noun is the "cheese," and the adjective is the "tomato." Tell students that the top piece of bread is the capital letter of the first word, and that the bottom piece of bread is the end mark. Guide students to write on each cutout the correct part of the sentence and to assemble their sentence sandwiches. Repeat the activity with other sentences.

RETEACHING

Write on the board the lyrics to a popular nursery rhyme or song. Read each line and help students identify words that might be replaced with synonyms. *(Examples: Paddle, paddle, paddle your ship; Jack and Jill ran up the hill; Sparkle, sparkle tiny star)* Replace each word with a student synonym. When students have finished, have them read or sing as a class the new rhyme.

WRITING & EDITING

Have students write or edit their drafts in the school library. Point out that as they write their research reports, they may find that they are missing an important fact. Tell students that if they are not sure whether a fact is true, they can use reference tools to double-check the fact.

AUNT NYM SAYS

Remind students that antonyms are words that mean the opposite. Play a game similar to Simon Says with students. However, tell students that whatever "Aunt Nym" says, they should do the opposite. *(Example: If Aunt Nym says* Open your eyes, *students should close their eyes.)*

RETEACHING

Read aloud the following sentence pairs: *The wind blew in from the north. The sky is bright blue. I have two apples. Sally walks to school.* Ask students to name and spell the homophones. Then have students explain what each word means. Repeat with similar sentence pairs.

ENGLISH-LANGUAGE LEARNERS

Provide English-language learners with letter tiles from a word game. Give each student two piles, each with the letters necessary to spell out the words in a homophone pair. Say the word and help each student correctly spell the word one way and then the other. Talk about the meaning of each word. Say additional sentences that use each homophone and have students indicate which spelling of the word is correct. Repeat with additional homophones.

SPEAKING & LISTENING

Remind students that a research report tells about something real. Write on the board the following topic ideas: *the first flight to the moon, the day that creatures from outer space landed on Earth, the first human who could fly, the inventor of the airplane.* Talk about which topics would be appropriate for a research report and why.

CHAPTER

6

Word Study and Research Reports

Quotation Station

The secret of becoming a writer is to write, write, and keep on writing.

–Ken MacLeod
author

176

Ladybugs

A ladybug is a helpful and pretty bug. Ladybugs eat aphids. Aphids are bugs that can harm crops. That is why farmers like ladybugs too. Ladybugs are red with black spots. As a ladybug gets old, the spots fade. The next time you see a ladybug, remember that it is a useful bug.

177

Name

Synonyms

Synonyms are words that have almost the same meaning. Use a synonym instead of writing the same word over and over.

I feel **cold**. *I feel* **chilly**.

● **Draw a line to match each picture to the correct synonyms.**

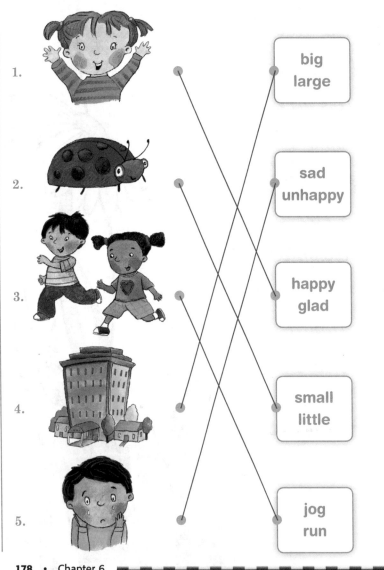

1.

2.

3.

4.

5.

big
large

sad
unhappy

happy
glad

small
little

jog
run

Name

More Synonyms

Synonyms are words that have almost the same meaning. Use a synonym instead of writing the same word over and over.

○ **Draw a line to match each word to the correct synonym.**

1.   kind   street

2.   look   grin

3.   road   pal

4.   friend   nice

5.   smile   peek

Synonyms, synonyms, we know quite a few.
Quick and *fast*, *shout* and *yell*, *glad* and *happy* too.
Synonyms, synonyms, how our list will grow.
Words that we call synonyms are jolly friends to know.

Word Study • **179**

Name _____

Working with Synonyms

Write the correct synonym in the boxes next to each sentence. Use the word bank.

street	pal	little	nice	glad
unhappy	grin	large	run	look

1. There was a big fish in the tank. `l a r g e`

2. Please put a smile on your face. `g r i n`

3. Our teacher is kind. `n i c e`

4. The road was covered with ice. `s t r e e t`

5. I jog with my dad every day. `r u n`

6. I took a peek in the oven. `l o o k`

7. The small toy was under her bed. `l i t t l e`

8. My brother is my friend. `p a l`

9. Are you happy to see Aunt Lara? `g l a d`

10. We were sad that the play was over. `u n h a p p y`

Name _____

Synonyms Review

Circle the correct synonym for each underlined word.

1. My <u>pal</u> is a very good dancer. ((friend) grin)

2. He is <u>unhappy</u> that he did not win the race. (little (sad))

3. Turn left on the next <u>street</u> to get to the bank. (peek (road))

4. The baby bird is very <u>little</u>. ((small) happy)

5. There was a <u>large</u> truck parked outside. (nice (big))

6. Marcus likes to <u>run</u> in the park on Sundays. (look (jog))

7. We are <u>glad</u> our class is taking a field trip. ((happy) large)

8. Please <u>look</u> in the toy chest for the game. (run (peek))

9. It was <u>nice</u> of you to help me. ((kind) pal)

10. The clown had a big <u>grin</u>. ((smile) small)

Writer's Corner

Write a sentence about the weather. Use a synonym for *hot*.

Name _____

More Synonyms Review

Complete each sentence with a synonym. **Sample answers shown.**

large	glad	little	road	sad
big	happy	small	street	unhappy
jog	look	kind	grin	pal
run	peek	nice	smile	friend

1. Rico is my *friend* .

2. I *smile/grin* when I am happy.

3. Soccer players *jog/run* every day.

4. The tired baby looks *sad/unhappy* .

5. Take a *look/peek* inside the tree house.

6. We were *glad/happy* to see the first snowfall.

7. The bus bounced down the bumpy *road/street* .

8. A *large/big* tractor pushed the dirt.

9. Mrs. Kim is a *kind/nice* neighbor.

10. A *little/small* kitten jumped into my lap.

Name

Antonyms

Antonyms are words that have opposite meanings.

*The rock is **hard**.   The pillow is **soft**.*

● **Draw a line to match each word to the correct antonym.**

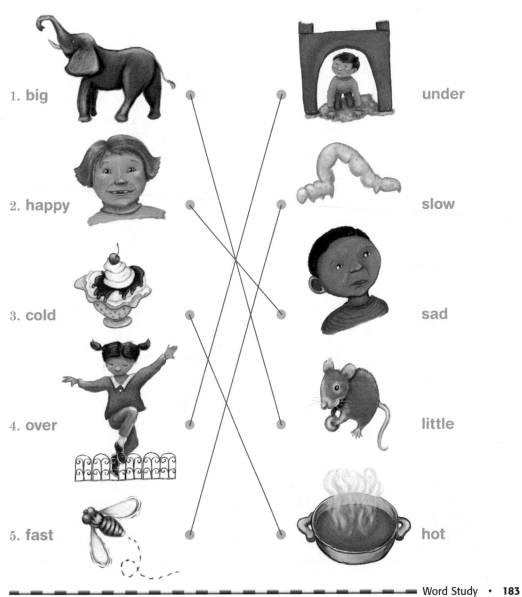

1. big   under

2. happy   slow

3. cold   sad

4. over   little

5. fast   hot

Name _____

More Antonyms

Antonyms are words that have opposite meanings.

● **Draw a line to match each word to the correct antonym.**

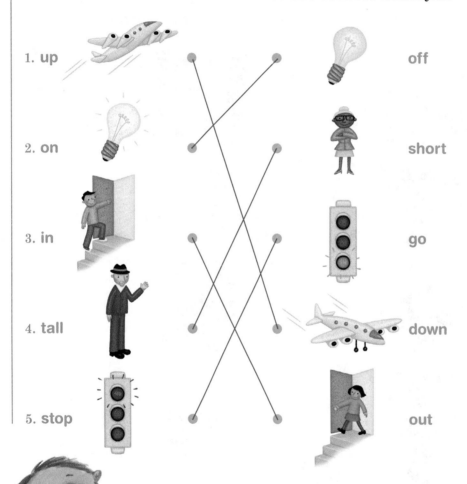

1. up

2. on

3. in

4. tall

5. stop

off

short

go

down

out

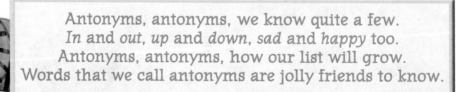

Antonyms, antonyms, we know quite a few.
In and *out*, *up* and *down*, *sad* and *happy* too.
Antonyms, antonyms, how our list will grow.
Words that we call antonyms are jolly friends to know.

184 • Chapter 6

Name

Working with Antonyms

Complete each sentence with the correct antonym for each underlined word. Use the word bank.

| cold | tall | stop | down | fast | off | in | happy |

1. The seesaw went up and *down* .

2. A rabbit is *fast* , but a turtle is slow.

3. I smile when I'm *happy* and frown when I'm sad.

4. The short monkey climbed a *tall* tree.

5. The door swings *in* and out.

6. Maggie pushed the button on and *off* .

7. This ice cube is *cold* , and the sun is hot.

8. The green light means go, and the red light means *stop* .

Name

Antonyms Review

Circle the correct antonym to complete each sentence.

1. In summertime the weather is (hot cold).

2. I can't lift that (little big) rock.

3. Maria went (down up) the slide.

4. The (tall short) man has long legs.

5. Please (go stop) at the corner before crossing the street.

6. A turtle is a very (fast slow) animal.

7. Water flows (under over) the bridge.

8. When the radio is (on off), I can hear music.

9. I drew a (sad happy) face with a big smile.

10. Close the gate or my dog will get (in out).

Writer's Corner

Write two sentences using the antonyms *open* and *shut*.

Name

More Antonyms Review

● **Circle the correct antonym to complete each sentence.**

1. The snowball feels (hot (cold)).

2. Jack is too ((short) tall) to reach the top shelf.

3. A cheetah is a very ((fast) slow) runner.

4. The bird is (out (in)) the tree.

5. At bedtime we turn (on (off)) the lights.

6. Jeff threw the ball ((up) down) into the air.

7. The race will start when I say ((go) stop).

8. We were (happy (sad)) when our favorite show ended.

9. The stars shine ((over) under) our heads.

10. The (big (little)) book fits in my pocket.

Word Study • 187

Name

Homophones

Homophones are words that sound alike but are spelled differently and have different meanings.

*I can **hear** the music over **here**.*

Read each pair of homophones. Then write each word.

	blew		blue	
1.	*blew*		*blue*	

	meat		meet	
2.	*meat*		*meet*	

	no		know	
3.	*no*		*know*	

	sale		sail	
4.	*sale*		*sail*	

	one		won	
5.	*one*		*won*	

Name

More Homophones

Homophones are words that sound alike but are spelled differently and have different meanings.

● **Read each pair of homophones. Then write each word.**

ate

1. ate

eight

eight

deer

2. deer

dear

dear

hear

3. hear

here

here

see

4. see

sea

sea

to

5. to

two

two

too

too

Name _____

The Homophones
Meat-Meet and *Blew-Blue*

Write the correct homophone for each sentence. Use the word banks.

1. The *meat* is cooked.

2. Please *meet* me at the game.

3. We will *meet* at the store.

4. Do you eat *meat* ?

meat

meet

5. My hat *blew* away in the wind.

6. The flag is red, white, and *blue* .

7. We *blew* some bubbles outside.

8. The sky today is bright *blue* .

blue

blew

> Homophones, homophones, we know quite a few.
> *Dear* and *deer*, *here* and *hear*, *to* and *two* and *too*.
> Homophones, homophones, how our list will grow.
> Words that we call homophones are jolly friends to know.

Name

The Homophones
No-Know and Ate-Eight

Write the correct homophone for each sentence. Use the word banks.

1. I don't *know* Geri.

2. There are *no* pears left.

3. I *know* this poem.

4. There are *no* leaves on the trees.

5. Our family has *eight* people.

6. The horse *ate* the carrot.

7. We *ate* breakfast together.

8. We went to school at *eight* o'clock.

know

no

eight

ate

Word Study • 191

Name _____

The Homophones
Sale-Sail and *One-Won*

Write the correct homophone for each sentence. Use the word banks.

1. There was one *sail* on the boat.

sail

2. The store had a big *sale* .

3. The *sail* on the tall ship was white.

sale

4. Is this hat on *sale* ?

5. May I please have *one* toy?

one

6. The hockey team *won* the game.

7. Shelby *won* the spelling bee.

won

8. You may take *one* apple.

Writer's Corner

Write two sentences using the homophones *knight* and *night*.

Name _____

The Homophones
Dear-Deer and *Hear-Here*

Write the correct homophone for each sentence. Use the word banks.

1. Erin is very *dear* to me.

2. Pedro saw a *deer* in the woods.

3. She is a *dear* friend.

4. I think *deer* are pretty animals.

5. They can't *hear* the music.

6. Please come over *here* .

7. We are meeting *here* after lunch.

8. I like to *hear* Mari play piano.

Word Study • 193

Name

The Homophones
See-Sea and *To-Two-Too*

Write the correct homophone for each sentence. Use the word banks.

1. The *sea* has many kinds of fish.

2. I use my eyes to *see*.

3. Jordan likes to swim in the *sea*.

4. Did you *see* the rainbow?

see

sea

5. Gail went *to* the store.

6. I saw *two* robins.

7. I'd like some soup *too*.

8. There were *two* bananas on the table.

to

too

two

194 • Chapter 6

Name

Homophones Review

Circle the correct homophone to complete each sentence.

1. The cook cut the (meet (meat)).

2. This rocket is going ((to) two too) the moon.

3. My gloves are (blew (blue)) and white.

4. Our pet rabbit (eight (ate)) all the carrots.

5. Who ((won) one) the baseball game?

6. Pat does not ((know) no) where Kevin lives.

7. My mom had a garage (sail (sale)).

8. The ((deer) dear) has a fluffy tail.

9. Our house is near the (see (sea)).

10. Did you ((hear) here) the bell ring?

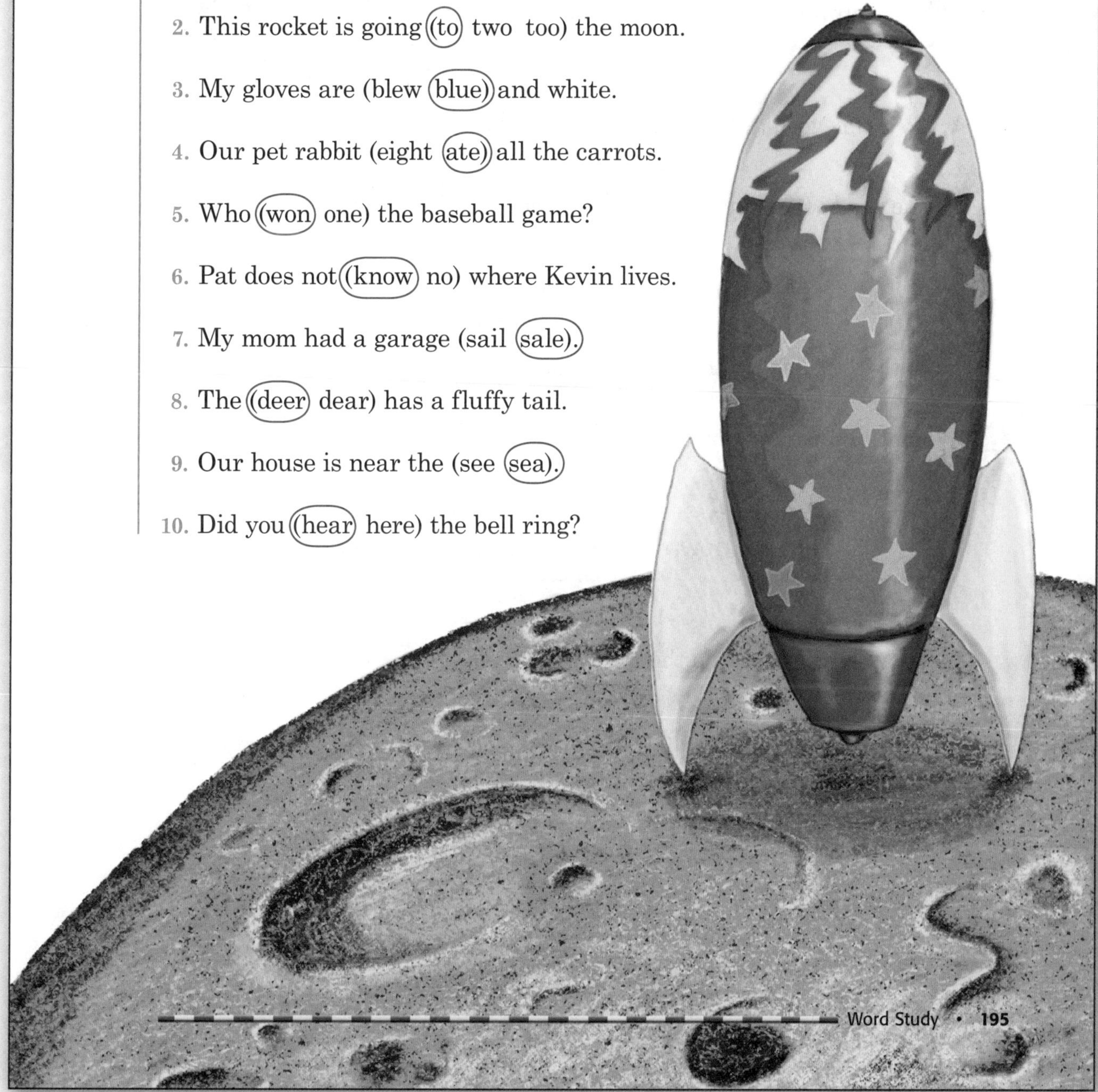

Word Study • 195

Name _____

Show What You Know

A Write the correct synonym for each underlined word.
Use the word bank.

| small | friend | look | street |

1. My <u>pal</u> is good at basketball. *friend*

2. The <u>road</u> was slippery after the storm. *street*

3. A <u>little</u> bee buzzed around the room. *small*

4. Katie took a <u>peek</u> around the corner. *look*

B Write the correct antonym for each underlined word.
Use the word bank.

| cold | down | out | over |

1. The train chugged <u>up</u> the mountain. *down*

2. We climbed <u>under</u> the fence. *over*

3. Please don't let the cat <u>in</u>. *out*

4. It's too <u>hot</u> outside. *cold*

Name _____

Show What You Know

Complete each sentence with the correct homophone.
Use the word banks.

1. I will *meet* you at the corner.

2. The number after seven is *eight*.

3. The wind *blew* my umbrella inside out.

4. I have *two* ears, a nose, and a mouth.

5. I *ate* all my vegetables.

6. We fixed the *sail* on the boat.

7. I *know* my ABCs.

8. Can I go fishing *too* ?

ate
eight

know
no

meat
meet

to
two
too

sale
sail

blew
blue

Word Study • **197**

Get Ready to Write

What Is a Research Report?

A **research report** tells about something real. It gives information about a topic. A good research report is about something you find interesting.

● **Read the research report. Then answer the questions.**

A tyrannosaurus is a well-known kind of dinosaur. The tyrannosaurus was enormous. It was 40 feet long and 20 feet tall. It had a huge head, sharp teeth, and a long tail. It could run up to 20 miles an hour. The tyrannosaurus is one of the most famous kinds of dinosaurs.

1. How big was the tyrannosaurus?

40 feet long and 20 feet tall

2. What did the tyrannosaurus look like?

It had a huge head, sharp teeth, and a long tail.

3. How fast could the tyrannosaurus run?

up to 20 miles an hour

198 • Chapter 6

Choosing a Topic

The **topic** is what your research report is about. Your topic should interest you. What do you want to know more about? If you are interested in your topic, your report will be more fun to write.

Your topic should not be too big. For example, U.S. Presidents is too big for a topic. You would have to write many pages about a topic that big. President Thomas Jefferson would be a better topic for a report.

Read the topics. Circle the topic in each group that would be a better research report topic. Be sure it's not too big.

1. (sharks)

   animals

2. the nine planets

   (Jupiter)

3. cowgirls

   (Annie Oakley)

4. (the Chicago White Sox)

   baseball

5. insects

   (ants)

Research Reports • **199**

Topic Sentences

The **beginning** of a research report has a **topic sentence**. The topic sentence tells your reader what your report is about.

A Draw a line to match each report to the correct topic sentence.

Research Reports

1. Some have long hair. Some have short hair. Some don't have any hair at all. There is even a kind of cat that does not have a tail.

2. They like the water. Alligators have rough scales that cover their bodies. They have long tails to help them swim.

3. They are not really spiders at all. They have a different body. They do not bite.

Topic Sentences

Many people think that daddy longlegs are spiders.

There are many kinds of cats.

Alligators are reptiles.

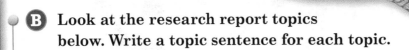

B Look at the research report topics below. Write a topic sentence for each topic.

1. elephants

_____

_____

2. frogs

_____

_____

Finding Facts

The **middle** of a research report tells more about the topic. It tells important **facts**. A fact is something that is true. Look for facts in encyclopedias, in other books, or on the Internet.

Here are some questions you might try to answer with facts.

What does it look like?   Where does it live?   How big is it?

What does it eat?   What does it sound like?

When you find a fact, don't just copy it. Rewrite the fact in your own words. That way, you will know the information better.

● **Find facts about each topic below. Remember to write them in your own words.**

Giraffes

FACT: Giraffes have long necks.

FACT: Giraffes live in Africa.

FACT: _____

Penguins

FACT: Penguins can't fly.

FACT: _____

FACT: _____

Organizing Facts

Before you write your research report, organize your facts. Use note cards to help you. Write each fact on a separate note card.

Sort your note cards with similar facts into piles. Your piles will help you keep your facts in order. It will be easier to write your report.

Draw a line to match each fact to the correct pile.

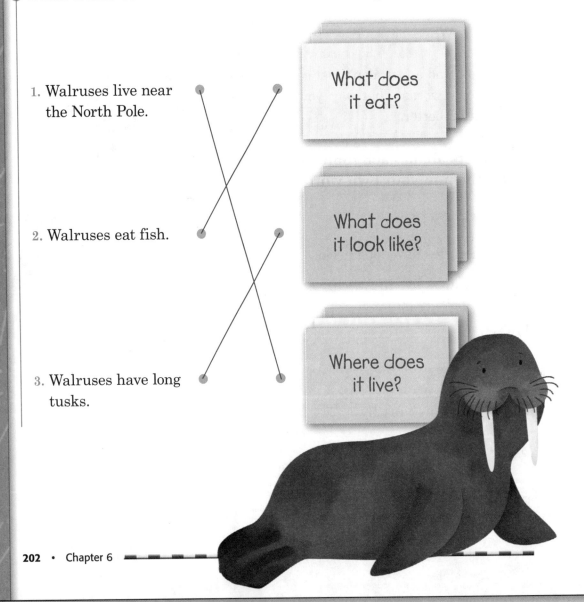

1. Walruses live near the North Pole.

2. Walruses eat fish.

3. Walruses have long tusks.

What does it eat?

What does it look like?

Where does it live?

202 • Chapter 6

Writing an Ending

The **ending** of a research report sums up the topic. It reminds your reader what you wrote about.

> Bats are unusual animals. They have wings and sharp claws. Bats use their ears instead of their eyes to see. They make a sound and listen for the echo. The echo tells them how close something is. Bats hang upside down when they eat and sleep. Bats are strange, but they are not scary.

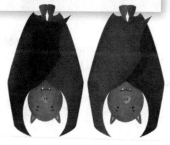

Imagine you wrote these research reports. Add an ending to each. Try to remind the reader what the report is about.

1. A koala is a mammal. It carries its babies in a pouch on its body. Koalas are usually gray and furry. They sleep up to 20 hours a day. They eat leaves from the trees where they live.

2. You have probably seen a skunk before. Its fur is black and white. It has a bushy tail. A skunk's color sends a warning to humans and other animals. If it gets bothered, it sprays a bad-smelling liquid.

Writer's Workshop

PREWRITING

Pick a Topic

Tara is writing a research report. First she has to pick a topic. Tara thinks of topic ideas that she wants to learn more about. She thinks of things that might be interesting to write about. Tara lists her ideas in her notebook. Then she circles the topic she will write about.

Grand Canyon

the first Thanksgiving

ladybugs

Ben Franklin

List topic ideas in your notebook. Think about what you'd like to know more about. Your topic can be

a famous person or event in history

an interesting thing or animal

an important place

Look at each of your ideas. Which one interests you the most? Circle the idea you like best.

PREWRITING

Plan Your Research Report

Tara goes to the library. She uses encyclopedias, other books, and the Internet. She looks for important facts about ladybugs.

Tara writes the facts she finds on note cards. She uses one note card for each fact. Tara writes the facts in her own words.

Tara puts her note cards into two piles. In one pile she puts all the note cards about what ladybugs eat. In another pile she puts all the note cards about how ladybugs look. The piles of note cards will help Tara write her draft.

Here are some of Tara's note cards.

Ladybugs eat aphids that can harm crops.

The spots on a ladybug fade as it gets old.

Find important facts about your topic at the library. Use encyclopedias, other books, and the Internet. Write each fact on a separate note card. Remember to write the facts in your own words. Then sort your note cards into piles.

Writer's Workshop

DRAFTING

Tara writes her draft. She uses her note cards to help her.
Here is Tara's draft.

*A ladybug is a helpful and pretty bug.
There are many ladybugs in my backyard.
Ladybugs eat aphids. Aphids are bugs that
can harm crops. That is why farmers like
ladybugs two. Ladybugs are red with black
spots. As a ladybug gets old, the spots fade.
The next time you see a ladybug, remember
that it is a useful bug.*

Write your draft in your notebook.
Use your note cards. Include facts
that you think are important
and interesting. Leave out
anything that isn't important.
Try to write as much as you can.
You can make changes to your
draft later.

EDITING

Tara edits her research report to make it even better. She uses an editing checklist.

A ladybug is a helpful and pretty bug.

There are many ladybugs in my backyard.

One of my facts isn't important!

Look at the mistake Tara finds. How does she fix it?

Edit your research report. Use the Editing Checklist. Make an **X** next to each question if you can answer yes. Make any changes that will improve your research report.

You might ask a classmate to read your research report. A classmate can check that your report makes sense and has important facts.

REVISING

Tara copies her draft. She includes all the changes she's marked. Tara knows that revising will make her report better than before.

Copy your draft. Fix any mistakes you marked. Make your research report the best it can be.

Writer's Workshop

PROOFREADING

Tara proofreads her research report for mistakes. She uses a proofreading checklist. She checks one question on the checklist at a time.

Proofreading Checklist

☐ Are all the words spelled correctly?

☐ Did I use capital letters?

☐ Did I use the right end marks?

☐ Can I replace any words with synonyms?

☐ Are antonyms used correctly?

☐ Are homophones used correctly?

can harm crops. That is why farmers like
                                          too
ladybugs ~~two~~. Ladybugs are red with black

Look at the mistake Tara finds. How does she fix it?

Proofread your research report. Use the Proofreading Checklist and check for one question at a time.

Mark your changes on your draft. Use the proofreading marks chart at the back of this book.

PUBLISHING

Tara is excited to publish her research report. She knows that it is her best work. She copies it neatly and adds a title. Tara is now ready to share her report with her teacher and classmates.

Copy your research report. Remember to write as neatly as you can. Write a title for your report at the top of your paper. You might include a drawing of the topic of your report.

How will you publish your research report? Use one of the following ideas or think of your own idea.

Make a class encyclopedia.

Read your report to someone special.

Display it on a class bulletin board.

Present your report as part of a play.

Ladybugs
A ladybug is a helpful and pretty bug. Ladybugs eat aphids. Aphids are bugs that can harm crops. That is why farmers like ladybugs too. Ladybugs are red with black spots. As a ladybug gets old, the spots fade. The next time you see a ladybug, remember that it is a useful bug.

Research Tools

In this chapter students will learn about

- ABC order
- dictionary skills
- encyclopedia skills
- fiction and nonfiction books
- the cover of a book
- the Internet

A Visual, Please

Parts of a Dictionary

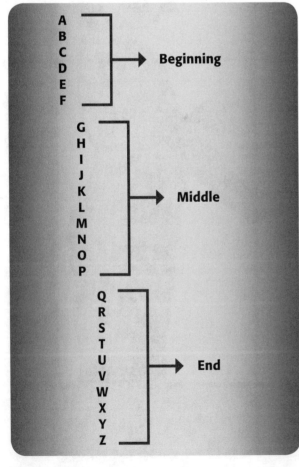

Tools of the Trade

Long Live the Library

Research tools provide students with an all-access pass to the world of knowledge and information. The library is a hub of research materials. Dictionaries, encyclopedias, fiction books, nonfiction books, and computers are all gathered under one roof for the purpose of discovering and sharing information. Teaching students how to tap into this information and familiarizing them with the library go hand in hand.

Library books are organized into three categories: fiction books; nonfiction books; and reference books, such as dictionaries and encyclopedias. In most libraries, fiction books are organized alphabetically by the author's last name, while nonfiction books are organized by subject.

Most libraries have either a card catalog or an electronic card catalog to help people search for books by title, author, or subject. Many libraries also have access to the Internet. Online search engines are a valuable resource, but with their advantages come pitfalls. Inappropriate and unreliable information is often included in search results. Encouraging students to use kid-friendly search engines not only is an effective way to avoid such information, it also promotes Internet safety.

Librarians are also an excellent resource. Librarians can help find the best sources for information and are there to answer any questions that may arise.

Common Errors

Otherwise Known as "First Comes First"

Some students, when searching for a word in a dictionary or an encyclopedia, forget to consider where the first letter of the word falls in the alphabet, and consequently where the word will fall in the book. These students waste time paging through the entire book instead of narrowing their search to the beginning, the middle, or the end of the dictionary.

To help students avoid this common error, display the visual on page 210a. Remind students to use this visual as a reference before looking up a word in a dictionary or an encyclopedia.

For Kids Who Are Ready

Or "Meet and Greet"

For students who are comfortable using a dictionary and an encyclopedia, introduce the thesaurus. The following is a sample entry from a thesaurus:

> **near** Within a short distance
> *Synonyms* **close, around**

Explain that a thesaurus lists synonyms. Remind students that synonyms are words that have almost the same meaning. Tell students that a thesaurus can help them find the exact word that they need and that many thesauruses are arranged like dictionaries. Keep a thesaurus in the room. Invite students to use it to find synonyms for words that they commonly repeat in their writing.

Ask a Mentor

Real Situations, Real Solutions

Dear Library Luminary,

My students are confused about when to use an encyclopedia instead of a dictionary. What should I tell them?

Help me clarify,
Cleo

Dear Cleo,

Students should use an encyclopedia instead of a dictionary when they are interested in learning more about a word than just its meaning—but only if the word is a noun. Encyclopedias contain general information about people, places, things, and events, and are usually used for research. Point out that an encyclopedia is a good place to look up proper nouns.

Now it should be clear,
Library Luminary

Dear Loyal Librarian,

In addition to using kid-friendly search engines, how can I help students be sure that a Web site is legitimate and that the information is reliable?

Web-site watchdog,
Mr. Rosati

Dear Mr. Rosati,

To decide whether a Web site is reliable, tell students to check the letters at the end of the address. Sites developed by organizations, which end in .org, or by the government, which end in .gov, are usually accurate. A site ending in .edu is often a reliable source if the pages were created by professors or a university. Encourage students to also check when a Web site was last updated.

Watchdogs are welcome,
Loyal Librarian

www.CartoonStock.com

"That's the best pop-up I've ever seen."

Research Tools

Teacher's Toolbox

Try the following ideas to help your students get the most out of this chapter:

- Ask the school librarian to give students a tour of the library and a presentation on how it is organized.

- Supply students with the following kid-friendly search engines: www.ajkids.com, www.kidsclick.org, www.yahooligans.com.

- Make a bulletin-board display of both fiction and nonfiction book covers.

Reasons to Research

Share with students the following situations in which the research tools learned in this chapter may be applied to writing projects throughout the year:

- using a nonfiction book about gardening to write a how-to article about planting a garden

- looking up an adjective in a dictionary to see if it is appropriate to use in a description

- finding in the library a fiction book to use for a book report

- finding in the library a map of the Grand Canyon to include with a personal narrative about a trip there

- using a kid-friendly search engine to find a Web site about ocelots to use for a research report

- using the Internet to look up the correct Zip Code when mailing a friendly letter

Chapter Adaptors

SPEAKING & LISTENING

Form the class into small groups and assign each group a brief encyclopedia article. Have students read the article and take notes on note cards. Then have each group give an oral summary of the article to the class. Be sure that each student in the group shares at least one fact. When each group is finished, invite the rest of the class to tell what they learned from the presentation.

FACT-FINDING MISSION

Invite students to go on a scavenger hunt for interesting facts. Provide small groups with encyclopedias or set aside time for students to use the library. Photocopy and distribute the following list of questions: *How many stars are there on the U.S. flag? Where is Yellowstone National Park? What are the names of the five Great Lakes? Which are the two largest planets?* Have students work together to find the answers to the questions. Award a prize to the first group to finish the list of questions correctly.

DICTIONARY DISCOVERERS

Allow students to browse more advanced dictionaries. Point out that all dictionaries are organized in the same way. Invite each student to find an interesting word that starts with the same first letter as his or her name. Have students write down their words. Help students use the dictionary to determine the meanings of their words. Then have students either draw pictures that represent their words or write sentences that use their words. Invite volunteers to share their work with the class.

RETEACHING

Provide students with fiction and nonfiction books that feature similar topics. *(Examples: whales, dinosaurs, airplanes)* Have students identify which books are fiction and which books are nonfiction. Ask students how they know. Remind students that fiction books tell about made-up people, places, things, or events and that nonfiction books contain facts about real people, places, things, or events.

RETEACHING

Write on the board in a horizontal line simple nouns with different first letters. *(Examples: tree, fish, bear, king)* Above the words, write horizontally the alphabet. Have students come to the board, circle the first letter of a word, and draw a line to the correct letter in the alphabet above. Then help students use the alphabet to put the words in ABC order.

ENGLISH-LANGUAGE LEARNERS

Invite English-language learners to create their own translation dictionaries. Have students choose five nouns and draw those nouns on separate sheets of paper. *(Examples: bicycle, dog, train, house, park)* For each drawing, have students write the noun in their primary language under the picture and in English above the picture. Then have students alphabetize their pages in English. You might have students who share a primary language work together to choose different nouns and build a bigger dictionary.

CHAPTER 7

Research Tools

Quotation Station

Someone who does not research has nothing to teach.

–proverb

Computer Area

Fiction Section

A-L

Librarian

Circulation Desk

Book Return

210 • Chapter 7

Nonfiction Section

Reference Area

Reading Area

Research Tools • 211

Name

ABC Order

Words are in **ABC order** when their first letters are in the order of the alphabet.

Aa Bb Cc Dd Ee Ff Gg Hh Ii Jj Kk Ll Mm

Nn Oo Pp Qq Rr Ss Tt Uu Vv Ww Xx Yy Zz

Circle the first letter of each word. Color the check mark if the words are in correct ABC order.

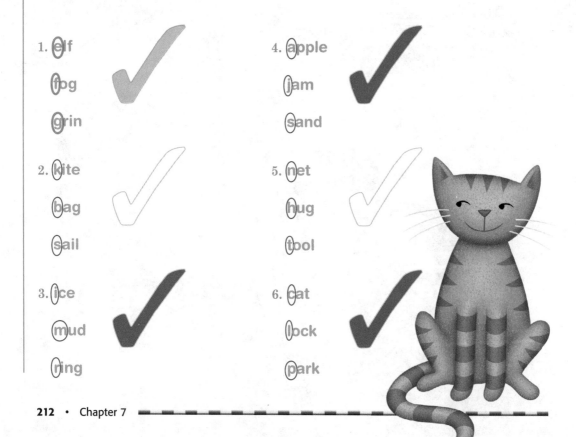

1. (e)lf
   (f)og
   (g)rin

2. (k)ite
   (b)ag
   (s)ail

3. (i)ce
   (m)ud
   (r)ing

4. (a)pple
   (j)am
   (s)and

5. (n)et
   (h)ug
   (t)ool

6. (c)at
   (l)ock
   (p)ark

212 • Chapter 7

Name

Practice with ABC Order

Circle the first letter of each word. Then write the words in ABC order.

1. (c)an   *ant*

   (d)og   *bat*

   (b)at   *can*

   (a)nt   *dog*

2. (f)lip   *egg*

   (e)gg   *flip*

   (h)at   *glass*

   (g)lass   *hat*

Name _____

Names in ABC Order

People's names can be put in ABC order.

Underline each person's last name. Circle the first letter in the last name. Write the last names in ABC order.

1. *Adams*

2. *Baxter*

3. *Cruz*

4. *Day*

5. *East*

6. *Farmer*

Meg D̲a̲y̲

Ann B̲a̲x̲t̲e̲r̲

Lana C̲r̲u̲z̲

Tom A̲d̲a̲m̲s̲

Dan E̲a̲s̲t̲

Sue F̲a̲r̲m̲e̲r̲

Name _____

Dictionary Skills

A **dictionary** is a book of words. It tells you how to spell a word. It also tells you what a word means. The words in a dictionary are in ABC order. **Guide words** help you find a word. Guide words tell the first and last words on a dictionary page. Look for guide words at the top of each page.

Look at this dictionary page. Then answer the questions.

guide words

garden   **gym**

entry

garden   a piece of ground used for growing vegetables, flowers, or fruits

gerbil   an animal that looks like a mouse

girl   a young female child

gym   a big room used for exercise and playing games

meaning

1. What are the two guide words?

garden   *gym*

2. What is the meaning of *gerbil*?

an animal that looks like a mouse

Name

Practice with Dictionary Skills

Write the letter you would look under to find each word in a dictionary.

1. doctor   *D*

2. eagle   *E*

3. milk   *M*

4. gorilla   *G*

5. button   *B*

6. clock   *C*

7. jacket   *J*

8. key   *K*

9. vest   *V*

10. wolf   *W*

11. rug   *R*

12. office   *O*

Name

More Practice with Dictionary Skills

Underline the word in each pair that comes first in a dictionary.

1.
star

<u>ball</u>

2.
<u>dragon</u>

heart

3.
<u>log</u>

man

4.
wheel

<u>umbrella</u>

5.
<u>nickel</u>

pants

6.
gate

<u>feet</u>

Name

Encyclopedia Skills

An **encyclopedia** is a group of books that has facts. The facts are about people, places, things, and events. Each book is called a **volume**. The topics in an encyclopedia are in ABC order.

Read this encyclopedia entry. Then answer the questions.

entry

volume

Snake

A snake is a reptile. It has scaly skin. A snake is cold-blooded. It warms itself in the sun. A snake does not have legs. It moves along the ground on its belly. A snake does not use its nose to smell. It flicks its tongue into the air to smell the world around it. Some snakes have poisonous venom.

They use it to kill their prey. A snake swallows its food whole. After eating a large meal, a snake may not eat again for days or even weeks.

1. Which volume number would you use to find facts about snakes?

19

2. What is one fact about snakes? **Answers will vary.**

Name

Fiction and Nonfiction

Fiction books tell about made-up people, places, things, or events. These books are on library shelves in ABC order by the author's last name. Fiction books are in a special part of the library.

Nonfiction books tell facts about real people, places, things, and events. These books are on library shelves in order by topic. Nonfiction books are in a different part of the library.

Decide which books are fiction and which are nonfiction. Put an **X** in the **Fiction** box for each fiction book title. Put an **X** in the **Nonfiction** box for each nonfiction book title.

	Fiction	Nonfiction
1. Ocean Animals		X
2. Henry the Happy Whale	X	
3. The Flying Boy	X	
4. Airplanes, Big and Small		X
5. Dances with Dinosaurs	X	

Name

The Cover of a Book

You can find out a lot about a book by reading the **cover**. The **title** tells the name of a book. The **author** is the person who wrote the book. The **illustrator** is the person who drew the pictures in the book.

● **Look at this book. Then answer the questions.**

cover

title

author

illustrator

1. What is the title of the book? <u>A Voyage into Space</u>

2. Who is the author? <u>Ronald Keller</u>

3. Who is the illustrator? <u>Tasha Berger</u>

Name _____

Using the Internet

Some people call the **Internet** the world's biggest library. You can use it to find facts about any topic you want to research.

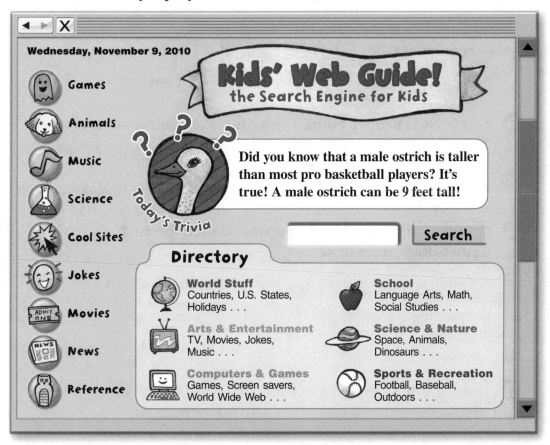

Make sure that the information you find on the Internet is true. Sometimes what you read on the Internet is made up. Use **search engines** made for kids. A kids' search engine helps you find Web sites that have true information.

Internet safety is very important. Don't give out information about yourself, such as your name or where you live. Make sure a grown-up is nearby when you are using the Internet. If you see something that makes you uncomfortable, tell a grown-up.

Research Tools • 221

Grammar Review

(A) Read each sentence. Add the correct end mark. Then write **t** for telling, **a** for asking, **c** for commanding, or **e** for exclaiming.

1. Stir the soup.   **c**   3. It is so cold today**!**   **e**

2. What is her name**?**   **a**   4. The ant is small.   **t**

(B) Circle each proper noun. Underline each common noun.

1. (Ally) went to the zoo.   3. (Jake) likes pizza.

2. We play soccer on (Mondays.)   4. My sister lives in (Chicago).

(C) Circle each noun that names one. Underline each noun that names more than one.

1. The (tiger) has stripes.   4. The (bike) has two tires.

2. The ships sailed on the (lake.)   5. My (teacher) grows flowers.

3. A (week) has seven days.   6. Our (school) has many classrooms.

(D) Draw a line to match each sensory word to the correct sense.

1. spicy	sight
2. blue	sound
3. smoky	smell
4. fuzzy	taste
5. crunching	touch

Name

E Underline the correct verb in each sentence.

1. Mom (<u>calls</u> call) us for dinner.
2. Sam and Betsy (sings <u>sing</u>) songs.
3. My sister (<u>has</u> have) new shoes.
4. Tate and Jacky (has <u>have</u>) a cat.
5. I (<u>talked</u> talk) to her yesterday.
6. Nat (see <u>saw</u>) a movie last night.
7. I (<u>am</u> is are) very tall.
8. Two frogs (am is <u>are</u>) in the pond.
9. The car (<u>was</u> were) dirty.

F Underline the correct pronoun in each sentence.

1. Ray and (<u>I</u> me) walked home.
2. Brett is my brother. (<u>He</u> She) is nine years old.
3. I lost the ball. I found (they <u>it</u>) in the backyard.
4. The dogs are thirsty. (We <u>They</u>) are drinking water.

G Draw a line to match the words in the first list to their contractions.

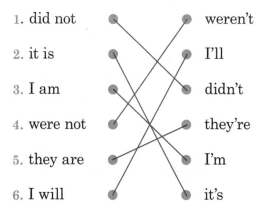

1. did not   weren't
2. it is   I'll
3. I am   didn't
4. were not   they're
5. they are   I'm
6. I will   it's

CHAPTER 1
Sentences and Personal Narratives

Introducing the Chapter   Pages 6–7

Students Should
- have a basic understanding of personal narratives
- have a basic understanding of sentences

Reading the Model
Read aloud the quotation. Ask students to name some things that they think about. Explain that everybody thinks by using words and pictures. Tell students that writers write their thoughts with words. Talk with students about why people write. Say: *Writing is a way people share information, ideas, and stories.* Discuss ideas and stories students like to share with others. (*Examples: stories of things that have happened to them, retelling a book or movie to a friend, showing someone how to do something*)

Direct students' attention to the picture. Then explain that the boys in the picture are meeting for the first time. Invite volunteers to tell their own stories about meeting someone new. Say: *When you tell a story about something that happened to you, the story is called a personal narrative.* Emphasize that a personal narrative is a true story about something that happened to the writer.

Read aloud the model personal narrative. Point out that this is a personal narrative because the story is true and because it happened to the writer. Explain that a personal narrative uses words like *I, me,* and *my* to show that it is a story about the writer.

Say: *Everyone shares stories. We all like to tell about funny and interesting things that happen to us. When we write stories, we write them by using sentences.* Write a sentence on the board and read it aloud. (*Example: Alfie saw a ladybug.*) Tell students that a sentence tells a complete idea. Point out that the sentence has two things: a capital letter and an end mark. Explain that the capital letter and the end mark show the beginning and ending of each sentence. Read aloud the model again, stopping after each sentence to point out the capital letter and end mark, and the fact that it tells a complete idea. Tell students that knowing how to write sentences is one of the most important skills for a writer.

Sentence Sense   Page 8

Students Should
- recognize sentences
- understand that the first word of every sentence begins with a capital letter
- understand that a sentence always ends with an end mark

Teaching the Lesson
Ask students to name three kinds of animals. (*Examples: horse, alligator, cat*) List their responses on the board. Point out that this is a list of things. Then ask students to name three actions. (*Examples: jump, eat, smile*) List their responses in a second column on the board. Point out that these words tell what someone or something does.

Guide students through the first paragraph. Point out that the words on the board name things and actions, but they are not complete sentences. Then go over the first two examples. Point out that *the pig* is not a complete sentence. Ask students whether the words name a thing or an action. *(a thing)* Explain that the second example is not a complete sentence because it only tells an action—*oinked*. Go over the rest of the teaching. Then use words from both lists on the board to write complete sentences. Read aloud the sentences. Explain that these word groups make sentences because they tell complete ideas; each names something and shows an action.

Remind students that a sentence begins with a capital letter. Point out the capital letter in the third example. Emphasize that the sentences on the board all begin with capital letters. Then remind students that a sentence ends with an end mark. Point out the end mark in the third example. Tell students that this end mark is called a period. Emphasize that the sentences on the board all end with end marks.

Go over the activity directions. When students have finished the activity, review their answers.

Extension

Have students practice saying complete sentences by finishing sentence starters. *(Examples: Dad's car, The slow turtle, The horse, Karen's eyes, For my birthday I)*

A little black dot that you can see,
Period is my name.
A telling sentence ends with me.
I play a telling game.

Making Sentences *and* Practice with Capital Letters   Pages 9–10

Students Should

• practice writing sentences

• understand the use of capital letters in sentences

Teaching the Lesson

Guide students through the teaching and the example on page 9. Review that a sentence must tell a complete idea. Invite volunteers to say sentences about themselves. Write students' sentences on the board without end marks or initial capital letters. Ask students to tell what goes at the beginning of a sentence. *(a capital letter)* Ask students what the capital letter in the example sentence is. *(A)* Demonstrate adding capital letters to the sentences on the board. Remind students that every sentence ends with an end mark. Ask students after which word the end mark is placed in the example sentence. *(pond)* Demonstrate how to add end marks to the sentences on the board.

Go over the activity directions on pages 9 and 10. When students have finished each activity, review their answers.

Extension

Explain that a capital letter at the beginning of a sentence shows that the sentence is starting. Tell students that the capital letter is like the starting line of a race and that the end mark is like the finishing line. Provide students with lined paper. Have them write on the first line *This is a short race.* Tell students to write the capital letter and end mark in a different color. Encourage students to draw cars, animals, runners, or other kinds of racers on the other lines. Allow students to decorate and display their race posters.

Practice with Sentences *and* Completing Sentences Pages 11–12

Students Should
- recognize complete sentences

Teaching the Lesson

Write on the board *Joe wants a, hops around., Maria plants flowers.* Ask students which word group is a sentence. Then ask volunteers to suggest ways to complete the incomplete sentences. Write their responses on the board. As you complete the first item, ask students how they should end the sentence. *(with an end mark)* As you complete the second item, ask students how they should begin the sentence. *(with a capital letter)*

Go over the activity directions on pages 11 and 12. When students have finished each activity, review their answers.

Extension

Have students draw a picture of their favorite animal. Ask students to write a sentence below their pictures telling what they like most about the animal. As students work, write the following questions on the board: *Does it tell a complete idea? Does it start with a capital letter? Does it have an end mark?*

Have students exchange drawings and sentences with a partner. Ask students to answer the three questions about the sentences they receive. Tell students that if they answer no to any question, they should fix their partners' sentences to make them correct.

Telling Sentences Page 13

Students Should
- recognize a telling sentence
- understand that a period is placed at the end of a telling sentence

Teaching the Lesson

Ask several students questions about their favorite colors, foods, and places. Help students to answer with complete sentences. *(Example: What is your favorite color? Yellow is my favorite color.)* Write on the board their responses without periods. Explain that the sentences on the board are telling sentences because students are telling things about themselves.

Go over the teaching and example with students. Point out that the example is a telling sentence that tells what *We* did. Ask students how telling sentences begin. *(with a capital letter)* Ask students what they put at the end of a sentence. *(an end mark)* Explain that telling sentences end with an end mark called a period. Point out the period in the example. Then have volunteers add periods to each sentence on the board. Remind students that an end mark shows that a sentence is ending.

Go over the activity directions. When students have finished the activity, review their answers.

Extension

Have the class recite the poem on page 13. Then call on a student to say a sentence and to say *period* when he or she reaches the end of the sentence. Repeat with additional volunteers.

Making Telling Sentences

Students Should

- understand that a telling sentence tells about something

Teaching the Lesson

Write *The old bear* on the board. Point out that this is not a complete sentence. Ask students what is missing. *(an action)* Point out that these words do not tell what the bear does. Invite volunteers to suggest words that could make this a complete sentence. *(Examples: slept, growled, ate dinner)* Write students' suggestions on the board as complete sentences without end marks. Point out that these are telling sentences. Ask students what end mark should be placed at the end of each telling sentence. *(a period)* Invite volunteers to add periods to the sentences on the board.

Go over the activity directions. When students have finished the activity, review their answers.

Read aloud the Writer's Corner. Allow time for students to write their sentences. Invite volunteers to share their sentences by reading the sentences aloud, beginning each sentence by saying the capital letter and ending each sentence by saying *period. (Example: "Capital M, my bike is red, period.")*

Extension

Have students copy one item from the activity, filling the blank with a word of their own. Have students share their sentences and check that each is a complete sentence.

Asking Sentences

Students Should

- recognize asking sentences
- understand that a question mark is placed at the end of an asking sentence

Teaching the Lesson

Choose an object in the room and have students guess what it is by asking you questions. Be sure that students form their questions as complete sentences. Write students' questions on the board. Ask students to tell what you are writing. *(questions)* Explain that questions are also sentences and are called asking sentences.

Go over the teaching and the example. Remind students that all sentences begin with a capital letter and end with an end mark. Explain that a question mark is the end mark for an asking sentence. Draw a box around the question marks on the board. Then write a series of asking sentences without question marks. *(Examples: May I play cards, Where are the jumping beans, Who is the pilot)* Have volunteers add question marks. Make certain that students write the marks correctly.

Go over the activity directions. When students have finished the activity, review their answers.

Extension

Have the class recite the poem on page 15. Then call on a student to say an asking sentence and to say *question mark* when he or she reaches the end of the sentence. Repeat with additional volunteers.

Making Asking Sentences *and* Find the Asking Sentences

Pages 16–17

Students Should

- recognize the use of question words and question marks in asking sentences

Teaching the Lesson

Guide students through the teaching on page 16. Explain that the words in the honey pot are often used to start questions, so they are called question words. Using all lowercase letters, copy on the board the list of question words. Have the class repeat after you as you read each word aloud. After you say each word, use the word to form a question directed at an individual student. Have students answer your questions. Then go through the list again, inviting volunteers to ask questions that start with the question words.

Write on the board _____ *are you?* Help students choose the question words that could be used in the blank to form an asking sentence. *(who, how, where)* Write *who* in lowercase letters in the blank. Ask students what needs to be done to the question word to make the sentence correct. *(The word needs to begin with a capital letter.)* Capitalize the first letter and read the sentence aloud. Then erase the question word and repeat this with *how* and *where*.

Go over the activity directions on pages 16 and 17. When students have finished each activity, review their answers.

Ask students to think of their favorite books. Tell students to pick one book and to draw a picture of something that happens in the book. Have students make their picture into a book cover by drawing a box around it and adding the title. Then read aloud the Writer's Corner on page 17 and allow students to write their asking sentences. Invite volunteers to share their pictures and to read aloud their asking sentences.

Extension

Have each student draw a large question mark on a sheet of paper. Then ask students to hold up their question marks whenever they hear an asking sentence in the poem you are going to read. Read the following poem to the class, pausing after each complete sentence:

"What Is Pink?"

What is pink? a rose is pink
By the fountain's brink.
What is red? a poppy's red
In its barley bed.
What is blue? the sky is blue
Where the clouds float thro'.
What is white? a swan is white
Sailing in the light.
What is yellow? pears are yellow,
Rich and ripe and mellow.
What is green? the grass is green,
With small flowers between.
What is violet? clouds are violet
In the summer twilight.
What is orange? why, an orange,
Just an orange!

—Christina Rossetti

I am a squiggle on your page
with a little dot below.
At the end of each asking sentence,
please place me just so.

Asking and Telling Sentences

Page 18

Students Should

- distinguish between asking and telling sentences

Teaching the Lesson

Review with students that asking sentences ask questions and that telling sentences tell about something. Point out that telling sentences are good sentences to use to answer questions. Write on the board three questions. *(Examples: When do you go to bed? What is your favorite sport? Who do you play with?)* Have volunteers answer the questions. Write students' answers on the board as telling sentences.

Go over the activity directions. When students have finished the activity, review their answers.

Extension

Have the class form two groups—an Asking Group and a Telling Group. Call on a member of the Asking Group to pick a member of the Telling Group and to ask that student a question. Have that student answer the question with a telling sentence. *(Example: What is your middle name? My middle name is Charles.)* Then have that student choose a member of the Asking Group to say a telling sentence to. The chosen student should reply with an asking sentence. *(Example: I went to the park last night. Where did you go after that?)* Have students continue until everyone has had a turn. If time allows, have students switch groups and play the game again.

Writing Telling Sentences

Page 19

Students Should

- understand how to write telling sentences

Teaching the Lesson

Ask a volunteer to explain what a telling sentence is. *(a sentence that tells about something)* Ask volunteers to say telling sentences about the pictures on the page. Write on the board students' sentences without capitalization or end marks. Remind students that a telling sentence begins with a capital letter and ends with a period. Invite volunteers to add capital letters and end marks to the sentences on the board.

Go over the activity directions. When students have finished the activity, review their answers.

Extension

Choose a sport that students are familiar with, such as baseball. Ask volunteers to name things that players do when they play that sport. *(Examples: run, throw, slide, catch)* Write students' answers on the board. Tell each student to pick one word from the list and to write a telling sentence using that word. Then have students draw and color pictures that illustrate their telling sentences. Invite volunteers to share their sentences and drawings. Consider displaying students' work on a bulletin board display titled *Tell Me About [name of sport]*.

Writing
Asking Sentences Page 20

Students Should

- understand how to write asking sentences

Teaching the Lesson

Bring to class one or more common objects that students are unlikely to be familiar with. (*Examples: a tire-pressure gauge, a lint brush, an eyelash curler, a staple remover, a thimble*) Have students ask questions about the object in order to guess what it is used for. As students guess, write several of their asking sentences on the board. Use the sentences to review that asking sentences begin with capital letters and end with question marks.

Go over the activity directions. When students have finished the activity, review their answers.

Extension

Have students find examples of telling and asking sentences in classroom reading materials. Invite volunteers to read aloud the sentences and to tell what kind of sentence each is and what end mark it has.

Commanding Sentences
and
Find the Commanding
Sentences Pages 21–22

Students Should

- recognize commanding sentences
- understand that a period is placed at the end of a commanding sentence

Teaching the Lesson

Write on the board a telling sentence, an asking sentence, and a commanding sentence. (*Examples: The apple smells good. What does it smell like? Take a bite.*) Use the first two examples to review that a telling sentence tells about something and that an asking sentence asks a question. Point to the third sentence and say that this sentence tells someone to do something. Explain that when you tell someone to do something, you are saying a commanding sentence. Go over the teaching and example on page 21. Explain that the example sentence tells someone to tie his or her shoe.

Write on the board commanding sentences appropriate to the game Simon Says. Do not write the end marks. (*Examples: Pat your head, Close your eyes, Raise your hand*) Remind students that telling sentences end with periods and asking sentences end with question marks. Explain that commanding sentences also end with periods. Read aloud each commanding sentence and have the class perform the action. Then have a volunteer add a period to the command on the board. Repeat with the remaining sentences.

Go over the activity directions on pages 21 and 22. When students have finished each activity, review their answers.

Read aloud the Writer's Corner on page 22 and allow time for students to write their commanding sentences. Invite volunteers to share their answers.

Extension

Have the class recite the poem on page 21. Then call on a student to say a commanding sentence and to say *period* when he or she reaches the end of the sentence. Repeat with additional volunteers.

Exclaiming Sentences
and
Find the Exclaiming
Sentences Pages 23–24

Students Should

- recognize exclaiming sentences
- understand that an exclamation point is placed at the end of an exclaiming sentence

Teaching the Lesson

Write *It is raining* on the board without an end mark. Have a volunteer say the sentence the way he or she might say it if someone asked what the weather was like. Explain that this is a telling sentence.

Guide students through the teaching and example on page 23. Then have a volunteer say the sentence on the board the way he or she might say it if excited that it is raining. Tell students that there is a way to show excitement or surprise in writing. Explain that these sentences are called exclaiming sentences. Tell students that exclaiming sentences end with an exclamation point. Write an exclamation point at the end of the sentence on the board and say the sentence aloud with excitement.

Ask volunteers to give examples of exclaiming sentences they might have said when excited or surprised. Write the suggested sentences on the board without end marks. Have the student who suggested each sentence say the sentence with excitement or surprise and have him or her add the exclamation point to the sentence.

Go over the activity directions on pages 23 and 24. When students have finished each activity, review their answers.

Read aloud the Writer's Corner on page 24 and allow students to write their exclaiming sentences. Invite volunteers to share their sentences. Ask students to name other things that might startle them. *(Examples: a car horn, a school bell, a dog's bark)* Have students pick something else that startles them and write an exclaiming sentence about it. Invite volunteers to share their sentences.

Extension

Have the class recite the poem on page 23. Then call on a student to say a telling sentence and to say *period* when he or she reaches the end of the sentence. Then have the student say the same sentence as an exclaiming sentence and say *exclamation point* at the end of the sentence. Repeat with additional volunteers.

Scrambled Sentences *and* Sentences to Complete Pages 25–26

Students Should

- distinguish among the four kinds of sentences
- understand which end marks are used with each of the four kinds of sentences

Teaching the Lesson

Begin by having the class recite the poem about telling sentences on page 13. Then write *Telling Sentence* as a column heading. Write an example of a telling sentence below the column heading. Have volunteers suggest their own examples of telling sentences. List their suggestions on the board without end marks. Repeat this procedure with the other three poems (on pages 15, 21, and 23) and kinds of sentences. When you have finished all four poems, have volunteers tell the definition of each kind of sentence. Ask students which end mark goes with each kind of sentence. Invite volunteers to add the correct end marks to the sentences on the board.

Go over the activity directions and example item on page 25. When students have finished the activity, review their answers. Help them check that each sentence begins with a capital letter and has the correct end mark. Go over the activity directions on page 26. When students have finished the activity, review their answers.

Extension

Display a picture of a farm, city, or zoo scene. Have students write one of each kind of sentence about the scene. Have volunteers stand beside the picture and read their sentences. Ask the class to identify each kind of sentence the volunteer reads.

More Sentences to Complete

Page 27

Students Should

- distinguish among the four kinds of sentences
- understand which end marks are used with each of the four kinds of sentences

Teaching the Lesson

Review with students the four kinds of sentences. Have students write a period, an exclamation mark, and a question mark on separate note cards. Say aloud examples of each kind of sentence and have students identify the kind of sentence you said by saying aloud its kind and by holding up the appropriate end mark.

Go over the activity directions. When students have finished the activity, review their answers.

Extension

Divide a bulletin board into four sections, each labeled with the name of a kind of sentence. Then prepare slips of paper, one for every student, each naming a type of sentence. Have students draw slips from a bag. Ask students to write that kind of sentence. Then have students attach their sentences to the correct section on the bulletin board.

Commanding Sentence is my name.
Giving directions is my aim.
I help you know the things to do
at home, at play, and in school too!

Show What You Know

Pages 28–29

Students Should

- recognize the four kinds of sentences
- know the correct end mark for each kind of sentence

Teaching the Lesson

Explain the directions for each activity. Assist students if necessary. When students have finished each activity, review their answers. Show What You Know may be used as a review or as a test.

My name is Exclamation Point.
Now if you are very wise,
you will put me at the end
of each sentence of surprise.

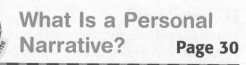

Get Ready to Write

What Is a Personal Narrative?　　Page 30

Students Should

- understand the purpose of a personal narrative
- identify the parts of a personal narrative

Teaching the Lesson

Ask a volunteer to read aloud the title. Say: *The word* personal *means "about a person." The word* narrative *means "story." So a personal narrative is a story about a person.* Ask students if they remember the personal narrative that they read at the beginning of the chapter. Review what happened in that story. Then go through the first two paragraphs of the teaching. Tell students that no matter how long or how short a story is, it always has a beginning, a middle, and an ending. Explain that when they write their own personal narratives, they should always include a beginning, a middle, and an ending.

Direct students' attention to the definition of *beginning* and read it aloud. Tell students that every story has a beginning. Then read aloud the example beginning sentence. Help students understand what this story is about and how the beginning gives readers a hint of the topic.

Point out the definition of *middle* and read it aloud. Tell students that the middle is where writers tell their stories. Explain that the middle is usually the longest part of the story. Read aloud the middle of the example narrative. Use the example to help students understand that the middle is the most important part of the story. Talk to students about how the beginning and the middle tie together, and how the middle tells more about what is told in the beginning.

Go over the definition of *ending*. Tell students that the ending tells how a story turns out and lets readers know that the story is over. Explain that sometimes endings tell what the story meant or why it was important. Read aloud the ending

example. Use the example to emphasize how the ending ties up the story. Guide students to understand how the beginning, middle, and ending are connected to form a complete story.

Read aloud the activity directions. Have students complete the activity as a class. Ask students to explain their answers.

Extension

Using reading materials in your classroom, have students identify the beginning, middle, and ending in several different stories. Talk with students about how in each story the beginning, middle, and ending tie together and connect to one another. Cite specific examples in each story that illustrate this concept.

Plan a Story　　Page 31

Students Should

- understand how to plan a story
- use drawings as a graphic organizer

Teaching the Lesson

Review with students that a beginning tells what the story is about, a middle tells what happened in the story, and an ending finishes the story. Ask students to talk about the funniest, scariest, or most interesting thing that has happened to them during the last week. After a student has shared a story, help the class to identify which part of each story is the beginning, middle, and ending. Remind students that any time they tell a story about themselves, they are telling a personal narrative.

Go over the activity directions. Tell students that when they write personal narratives, they should first plan what they want to write about. Explain that drawing pictures of the important parts of their story will help them keep the events in order. Tell students that sometimes they will have to draw more than one picture for the middle of their stories. Tell students that they should draw as many pictures as they need for all the parts of their narratives.

Allow time for students to complete the activity. As students work, circulate among them to offer help and support. When students have finished, invite volunteers to share and explain their drawings and sentences.

Extension

Have students choose a new personal narrative topic and draw pictures for their beginnings, middles, and endings. Encourage students to write sentences that go with each picture. Repeat this activity to offer additional practice using pictures to help plan a story.

I, Me, and *My*   Page 32

Students Should

- understand that personal narratives use the words *I, me,* and *my*

Teaching the Lesson

Review with students how the beginning, middle, and ending function in a personal narrative. Invite students to share their drawings from page 31 to illustrate the importance of each part and to demonstrate how drawings helped them plan their stories.

Go over the teaching. Point out that students use the words *I, me,* and *my* when they talk about themselves. Tell students that when they write, the words *I, me,* and *my* show that the story is about them.

Allow time for students to color the words. Then guide them to complete the activity. Emphasize that the words in this story help us know that the story is about the writer.

Extension

Have students practice writing sentences about themselves, using *I, me,* and *my.*

Finish a Story   Page 33

Students Should

- understand how to combine the beginning, middle, and ending to form a personal narrative

Teaching the Lesson

Review with students the elements and characteristics of personal narratives. *(A personal narrative has a beginning, a middle, and an ending. Writers can draw pictures to help plan their story. Personal narratives use the words* I, me, *and* my.*)*

Go over this page. Point out the word bank. Then allow time for students to complete the activity. Consider having students draw pictures of their beginnings, middles, and endings before they begin to write. As students work, circulate through the room to offer help and support. When students have finished, invite volunteers to share their personal narratives with the class.

Extension

Have students draw additional pictures about their stories. Encourage students to think of at least two other things they might include in the middle of their personal narratives. Have students write sentences for each picture. Then guide students to understand how they might add these details to their stories.

Writer's Workshop

Prewriting— Pick a Topic   Page 34

Students Should

- understand how to brainstorm topics
- identify appropriate topics for their personal narratives

Review with students what personal narratives are. *(true stories about the writer)* Talk to students about the elements and characteristics of personal narratives. *(beginning, middle, ending; using* I, me, *and* my*)*

Invite a volunteer to read aloud the title. Say: *During prewriting we think about a topic for our personal narratives. When we do prewriting, we think of a lot of topics. That way we can pick the best one.*

Go over the first paragraph. Say: *A topic is what a personal narrative is about. A topic might be* I went to the circus, my walk to school this morning, *or* what I did last summer. *These might all be good personal narrative topics.* Emphasize that before they write, students will first have to pick topics.

Read aloud the second paragraph. Explain that Luis is a first-grade student who is writing a personal narrative. Tell students that they will follow Luis as he writes his own personal narrative. Have students read aloud Luis's topics. Explain that Luis wrote down many different topics for his personal narrative so that he could choose the best one. Help students understand that each item on the list is a possible topic for Luis's personal narrative because the topic is something that happened to him. Tell students that Luis circled the topic he wanted to write about.

Read aloud the third paragraph and the topic prompts. For each prompt, invite volunteers to name possible topics. For each suggestion, guide students to understand that the topic is a true story about something that happened to that student.

Model how to brainstorm and choose your own personal narrative topic. Use the topic prompts on the page to guide your own brainstorming list. As you work, explain to students why you prefer some topics to others. Choose one topic and circle it.

Go over the last paragraph. Then allow time for students to write their topic ideas in their notebooks. Encourage students to pick the topic that seems most interesting. Circulate among students to provide encouragement and to be sure that they are listing appropriate topics. Help students to understand which topics are appropriate for personal narratives.

Prewriting—Plan Your Story   Page 35

Students Should

- use drawings to plan and organize their personal narratives

Review with students what a topic is. *(what a personal narrative is about)* Invite volunteers to share the topics they have chosen to write about. Talk to them about why their topics are appropriate for personal narratives. *(The topics are things that happened to them.)*

Invite a volunteer to read aloud the title. Say: *First we listed possible topics. Then we chose a topic. The next thing we have to do is organize our ideas.* Explain that when students organize, they make sure that the beginning comes first, the middle comes next, and the ending comes last. Tell students that when they do this part of prewriting, they have to figure out what they want to say in their personal narratives.

Guide students through the first paragraph. Tell students that when they write personal narratives, a good way to start is by drawing pictures. Explain that Luis has drawn pictures that show the parts of his personal narrative. Remind students that pictures help them make sure that their stories have all the important parts.

Remind students of the topic that you chose for your personal narrative. Model drawing pictures that represent the beginning, middle, and ending of your personal narrative. Explain how you can use the pictures to help plan your story. Say: *Drawing pictures can help me to remember what happened. Drawing pictures also helps me figure out what parts of the story are important. When I am done, I can put numbers on the pictures to show in what order the parts of my story happened.* Save pictures for the drafting stage of the writing process.

Go over the rest of the page. Then allow time for students to complete their pictures. Encourage students to draw several pictures for the middle of their stories. As students work, move through the class to offer help and support. Guide students to put their pictures in the order they will use when they begin to write. Help students to identify which pictures are important to their stories and which show things that do not belong.

Drafting

Students Should

- use their prewriting pictures to write first drafts
- write first drafts of their personal narratives, using complete sentences

Ask volunteers to share the pictures they drew and to explain what part of their story each picture represents. As volunteers share, prompt them to say complete sentences about their stories. Explain that these sentences might go in their personal narratives.

Invite a volunteer to read aloud the title. Say: *During prewriting we drew pictures about our ideas. During drafting we will write sentences about our topics.* Remind students that we use the words *I, me,* and *my* when we write personal narratives.

Read aloud the first paragraph. Then direct students' attention to Luis's draft. Ask students to identify in the draft words Luis used to talk about himself. *(I, me)* Tell students that Luis turned his pictures into sentences. Point out that later he will have time to make his story better.

Using the pictures that you drew during prewriting, model how to write a draft. As you work, point out sentences that are part of the beginning, middle, and ending of your narrative. Explain to students how the sentences are connected to your prewriting pictures. Include in your model draft at least one mistake from the Editing Checklist on page 37 and one mistake from the Proofreading Checklist on page 38. Save your draft to use during the Editing stage.

Go over the rest of the page. Then allow time for students to complete their drafts. Circulate through the class to provide students with encouragement and support. Explain that there are steps to complete before finishing a personal narrative. Tell students that later they will have time to look closely at correcting their mistakes.

Editing

Page 37

Students Should
- edit their personal narratives

Invite a volunteer to read aloud the title. Say: *During editing you make sure that your writing makes sense. When you edit, you look for places where someone else might get confused, and you fix the problems.*

Guide students through the first paragraph. Explain that a checklist can help writers remember the important things to check as they edit. Read aloud the Editing Checklist. As you read each item on the checklist, pause to clarify students' understanding of the question and to explain how students might check for that item in their drafts.

Go over the next paragraph and the thought bubble. Ask students which item on the checklist helped Luis find the mistake in his draft. *(Do I have an ending?)* Ask students how Luis fixed his draft. *(He added the sentence Now Matt is my best friend.)* Talk with students about why the sentence makes the draft stronger. *(It tells how the story turned out.)*

Direct students' attention to your personal narrative. Help students use the checklist questions to find the mistake in your draft. Guide students to help you fix the mistake. Say: *We all make mistakes when we write. That is why we edit. Now that we have found this mistake, I can correct it and make my story better.*

Tell students that a friend can often catch mistakes that the writer missed. Emphasize the importance of appropriate behavior and language for peer-editing sessions. Say: *When we edit other people's writing, we use helpful words. We always start by saying what we liked about the story. Tell the writer if you thought the story was funny or interesting. If you see a mistake, say "I think you could make your story better if you made this change." Never use hurtful words like* bad, boring, *or* I didn't like it.

Choose a volunteer to model peer-editing behavior, using your personal narrative as a model. Use appropriate language to reinforce how students should interact during peer-editing conferences.

Go over the rest of this section. Then allow time for students to edit their drafts. Circulate among students to be sure that they are giving consideration to each item on the checklist. Ask students to give reasons for making or not making changes in their work. Then allow time for partners to edit each other's drafts. Observe students as they edit and hold their peer-editing conferences. Check that students are using appropriate peer-editing behavior and language. When they have finished, say: *When a friend edits your work, check it over. Your friend might suggest a change that you do not agree with. It is a good idea to check your editor's changes, using the checklist. You can also ask a teacher, a parent, or another friend for help. You want your writing to be correct, but it is your story. You should decide what to change.*

Revising

Page 37

Students Should
- use editing changes to revise their drafts

Ask a volunteer to read aloud the title of this section. Say: *When we revise our writing, we change it to make it better. Some changes are our own ideas. Some changes are from suggestions that a friend or a teacher has made.*

Go over the first paragraph. Point out the partial student model. Guide students to notice the use of proofreading marks to add a sentence. Point out the thought bubble above Luis's head. Explain that Luis knew that he forgot to write an ending, so he added a sentence. Say: *When we edit, we mark what we want to change. Later we rewrite the changes correctly. Marks like this help us show where we want to change things. This mark means to add something to the story.*

Guide students through the Proofreading Marks chart on the inside back cover of the book. Help students understand the function of each proofreading mark, using the examples in the chart and additional examples of your own.

Point out the mistake in your draft that the class found during editing. Demonstrate how to mark the correction. Talk about how making this change helps to make the story clearer. Then rewrite your draft on the board, incorporating into the new copy your marked change. Remember to include your mistake from the Proofreading Checklist on page 38. Tell students that a new copy of the draft can help us see other mistakes. Explain that the revised story is not the best it can be yet, but now it will be easier to spot mistakes.

Read aloud the last paragraph. Then allow time for students to revise their drafts. As they work, circulate among students to be sure that they are making their editing changes correctly.

Proofreading   Page 38

Students Should

- understand the function of proofreading marks
- proofread their revised drafts

Invite a volunteer to read aloud the title. Say: *During proofreading we make sure that all the words are spelled the right way and that the sentences are correct. Proofreading is important because misspelled words and mistakes in sentences can bother the reader. Readers might not pay attention to the story because they are looking at misspelled words or other mistakes.*

Go over the first paragraph and the Proofreading Checklist. For each checklist item, help students understand what the question means and how to check for it in their drafts.

Read aloud the next paragraph and direct students' attention to the partial student model. Ask students what mistake Luis finds in his story and which item in the checklist helped him find the mistake. *(an incomplete sentence; Are the sentences complete?)* Help students explain why the sentence is incomplete. *(It does not tell an action.)* Ask students how Luis fixed the mistake. *(He added an action— said his name was Matt.)* Point out the proofreading mark Luis used to add to his draft. Say: *Proofreading marks are marks we use to show what changes we want to make to a draft.* Go over the Proofreading Marks chart and review the function of each proofreading mark.

Point out your model revised draft. Help students use the Proofreading Checklist to find the mistake in your personal narrative. Remind students that everyone makes mistakes when they write, and that by proofreading, they can make their stories better. Demonstrate how to use proofreading marks to correct your error.

Go over the rest of the page. Then allow time for students to proofread their drafts. Tell students to check for only one kind of mistake at a time. Circulate through the class to offer students assistance and support. Tell students that they can use reference materials, such as a picture dictionary, to check and correct mistakes.

If time allows, have partners trade drafts and proofread each other's work. Be sure that students work with different partners from those they had during editing. Remind students that a friend might catch mistakes that the writer missed. If you choose this option, circulate among students to be sure that they are using appropriate peer-conferencing language. When students have finished, remind them to double-check their partner's work.

Publishing

Page 6e provides a full-sized, reproducible copy of the student's Personal Narrative scoring rubric. Students can use the rubric when assessing their own personal narratives.

Page 6f provides a full-sized, reproducible copy of the Teacher's Scoring Rubric for personal narratives. The rubric can be used when assessing students' understanding of the genre.

Students Should

- understand what publishing means
- produce final copies of their personal narratives

Have a volunteer read aloud the title. Say: *Publishing happens when a writer decides to share his or her work with an audience.* Explain that an audience is the people who read their writing. Tell students that their audience might be you or it might be their parents, their brothers or sisters, or their friends. Explain that their audience is anyone with whom students share the final copy of their writing. Tell students that publishing might mean handing in the personal narrative to a teacher, giving it to their parents, or sharing it with the class. Explain that publishing is an exciting time for writers because after all that hard work, it is nice to share their work with an audience.

Go over the first paragraph. Allow students to answer the question. *(Luis will publish his story by reading it to his mom.)* Talk with students about ways they could publish their work. Then model for students how to produce a final copy. You might write your final copy on the board, or you might use one of the publishing ideas listed in the student book. As you work, explain that first you wrote this personal narrative, then you edited it, revised it, and proofread it. Tell students that now you are ready to share your story with an audience.

Go over the rest of the page. Talk with students about how they will publish their own personal narratives. Then allow time for students to make their final copies. Remind students to write slowly and carefully, and to check each sentence to be sure they do not make any new mistakes. Allow time for students to create artwork or other items to accompany their published pieces.

When students have finished, distribute copies of the student's Personal Narrative scoring rubric. Help students understand what each item means and how to apply it to their own writing. Then allow time for students to self-evaluate their work.

Have students begin keeping a portfolio of their finished work. Distribute folders or have students use their own. Ask students to decorate their folders in any way they choose. Tell students that a portfolio will help them see what they are learning and how far they have come since the beginning of the year.

CHAPTER 2

Nouns and Friendly Letters

Introducing the Chapter
Pages 40–41

Students Should
- have a basic understanding of friendly letters
- have a basic understanding of nouns

Reading the Model

Talk with students about the personal narratives they wrote. Invite volunteers to retell their stories. Then read aloud the quotation. Say: *When you write a story, you can share it with many different people, even if they live far away.* Ask students how they might share their stories with someone far away. *(letters, e-mails, phone)* Tell students that when they write messages to people they know, they are writing friendly letters. Invite volunteers to name people they know who live far away. Prompt students to suggest messages they might send to those people. Guide students to understand that there are many kinds of messages we can share with others, such as saying thank you or asking a favor.

Read aloud the friendly letter model. Ask students to tell what is happening in the picture. *(a birthday party)* Say: *Ana is having a birthday party with her friends. But to tell her friends about the party, she had to write a friendly letter.* Ask questions to guide students to identify the kinds of information in the letter. *(Examples: On what date was this letter written? To whom is the letter written? Who wrote the letter?)* Say: *Letters can be about many different things, but all friendly letters have the same parts.* Point out the date, greeting, body, and closing as parts that appear in all

friendly letters. Ask students to imagine that their next birthday party can be anywhere they want. Guide students to say what they might write in a friendly letter that invites people to the party.

Write on the board *ice cream*. Ask students to name other things they might find at a birthday party. *(Examples: balloons, clowns, cake)* Write students' suggestions on the board. Point out that these words all name people, places, and things. Explain that words that name people, places, and things are called nouns. Point out that nouns are important words. Then read aloud the friendly letter model again, pausing and not reading aloud the nouns in the letter. Say: *Without nouns we couldn't talk or write about the things around us.*

May 10, 2008

Dear Mike,
My birthday is on Friday.
I am having a party at Big
Pond Park. We will play games.
We will have ice cream too.
Can you come?

Your friend,
Ana

Students Should

- recognize nouns

Teaching the Lesson

Display pictures showing people, places, and things. Have students name what is shown in each picture. Write students' responses on the board, underlining the nouns. Explain that these words are nouns. Tell students that nouns are words that name people, places, or things.

Guide students through the teaching, using the words on the board to emphasize each noun category. Go over the examples and pictures. Write on the board *Person, Place,* and *Thing* as column headings. Then help students think of more nouns that fit each category and write them on the board.

Guide students through the activity directions. When students have finished the activity, review their answers.

Extension

Have students line up in the front of the room. Designate three different areas of the room as the person zone, place zone, and thing zone. Say a noun and have the student at the head of the line identify it as person, place, or thing and move to the appropriate zone. When all students have found the zones that match their nouns, have each zone group take turns reciting the poem on page 42. As students recite the poem, have them hold up their hands when they name their zone. *(Example: Students in the place zone would raise their hands when they say* place *in the first line of the poem.)*

Students Should

- recognize proper nouns
- understand that a proper noun begins with a capital letter

Teaching the Lesson

Review that nouns name people, places, and things. Then say the nouns *boy, park,* and *toy* and have students identify each noun as naming a person, place, or thing. Then say the proper name of a student, a local park, and a popular toy that students would likely know. Write on the board these proper nouns. Explain that these words are called proper nouns because they name a special person, place, or thing. Tell students that because these nouns are special, they are written a special way, by beginning with a capital letter.

Go over the teaching and examples. Point out the capital letter that begins each proper noun. Explain that some proper nouns are made up of two words. Emphasize that when a proper noun is two words, each word is capitalized. To reinforce this concept, explain that students capitalize the first letters of their own names when they write them because their names are proper nouns. Write a few students' names on the board. Circle the names and write outside the circle *students.* Tell students that because the names inside the circle are special names, they are proper nouns. Draw another circle on the board and label it *city.* Help students think of proper nouns that name cities. Write their responses inside the circle.

Go over the activity directions. When students have finished the activity, review their answers.

Extension

Have the class recite the poem. Then say sentences that use proper nouns. Have volunteers identify the proper nouns and tell what letter or letters should be capitalized.

Proper Nouns Name Special People
Page 44

Students Should

- identify proper nouns that name people
- use capital letters to write proper nouns

Teaching the Lesson

Review that a proper noun can name a special person, place, or thing. Write on the board your name without capitalization and point out that your name is a proper noun. Ask students to identify which letters should be capitalized. Then write on the board a few students' names without capitalization. Have students add the correct capital letters.

Go over the teaching and examples. Have students suggest proper nouns for people at their school, in their community, or at home.

Go over the activity directions. When students have finished the activity, review their answers.

Extension

Write on the board the following sentences, including the errors: *My sister is anne. my dad is Mr. Gomez. Have you seen earl? here comes Dolly.* Read aloud the sentences, pausing after each one to help students determine which letter needs to be capitalized and why. Then for each sentence, have a volunteer add the capital letter.

Proper Nouns Name Special Places
Page 45

Students Should

- recognize proper nouns that name places
- use capital letters to write proper nouns

Teaching the Lesson

Review that a proper noun names a special person, place, or thing and that all proper nouns begin with capital letters. Have volunteers say their names, indicating which letters should begin with capital letters. (*Example: Capital M, Maria, capital L, Lopez*)

Go over the teaching. Then draw on the board a simplified street map of a part of your community with which students are familiar. Help students to name stores, parks, and landmarks that would appear on the map. Indicate the location of these places on the map and label each one with its name. Point out that these are special places on the map and that they are proper nouns.

Go over the activity directions and help students complete the activity. When students have finished the activity, review their answers.

Extension

Help students think of a name for a made-up character and write the name on the board. Invite a volunteer to give a telling sentence about the character that says where he or she visits in the map you drew on the board. Encourage the volunteer to tell something the character does there. (*Example: Milo McNoodle went to Jones Park. He played on a slide.*) Have the rest of the class identify the proper nouns. Invite other volunteers to tell where the character went next and what he or she did.

A noun names a person, a place, or a thing—
a friend, the park, or a bell that rings,
a boy, a building, a bat, or a ball.
Nouns are words that name them all.

Proper Nouns Name Special Things Page 46

Students Should

- recognize that proper nouns name things
- use capital letters to write proper nouns

Teaching the Lesson

Review proper nouns that name people and places. Write several examples on the board and circle the capital letters.

Go over the teaching. Have students think of the names of candy bars, cars, and games. Write their responses on the board. Write beside their responses the broader common noun that describes each proper noun. Use the lists to emphasize that a proper noun names a special thing.

Go over the activity directions. When students have finished the activity, review their answers.

Read aloud the Writer's Corner. Invite volunteers to name special things they own. Then have students write their sentences. Ask students to draw pictures of their special things. Invite volunteers to share their sentences and pictures.

Extension

Provide each student with photocopies of a sheet of paper with the following written at the top: _____ *drove to* _____ *in a* _____.

Ask students to draw an imaginary car from the future and to think of a name for the car. When students have finished, have them write the name of the car in the last blank. Then help the class come up with a character name and have students write it in the first blank. Have students draw the character inside the car.

Display a map that shows major cities and have students choose a city to write into the middle blank. Ask students to imagine that city and to draw it in the background behind the car. Invite students to share their work.

Common Nouns Page 47

Students Should

- recognize common nouns

Teaching the Lesson

Write on the board the proper nouns *Judy, Lincoln Zoo,* and *Chocolate Crunch.* Help students explain why these are proper nouns and have them identify which names a person, a place, and a thing. Review that all nouns name people, places, and things. Then help students name a common noun for each of the proper nouns on the board. *(Examples: girl, zoo, candy)* Write each common noun under the appropriate proper noun. Tell students that these nouns are called common nouns.

Guide students through the teaching and examples. Write on the board other proper nouns with which students are familiar. Help them to name common nouns that go with each proper noun.

Go over the activity directions. When students have finished the activity, review their answers.

Extension

Have available a set of picture cards that illustrate common nouns. Place the picture cards face-down. Have a volunteer come to the front of the room, pick a card, and identify the noun.

Common Nouns Name People

Page 48

Students Should

- recognize common nouns that refer to people

Teaching the Lesson

Review that common nouns name people, places, or things. Then go over the teaching. Play a riddle game to help students name common nouns that refer to people. *(Example: I am a person who grows food. Who am I? You are a farmer.)* Write on the board students' responses. Invite volunteers to tell other nouns that name people. Add correct responses to the list on the board.

Go over the activity directions. For each item help students determine what the picture represents before they write their response. When students have finished the activity, review their answers.

Read aloud the Writer's Corner. Allow time for students to write their sentences. As students work, check that they are using common nouns, not proper nouns. When students have finished, invite volunteers to read aloud their sentences. Challenge students to name the common noun in each volunteer's sentence.

Extension

Assign small groups one of the common nouns from the activity on page 48. Have one member of each group say a telling sentence about that group's noun. *(Example: The firefighter rides on a truck.)* Then have the next group do the same with their assigned common noun. Continue with each group.

Common Nouns Name Places

Page 49

Students Should

- recognize common nouns that refer to places

Teaching the Lesson

Review that common nouns name people, places, or things. Then go over the teaching. Ask students to name places. Guide them to use common nouns. Draw on the board a simple map of streets. Explain that students are going to help you build an imaginary town. Ask students to name places found in most towns. Draw and label their suggestions on the map on the board. *(Examples: store, park, school, police station)* Help students add natural features to the map. *(Examples: lake, forest, beach)*

Go over the activity directions. Read aloud the story without naming the nouns represented by the pictures. Then reread the story, stopping at each picture to allow students to write their answers. When students have finished, review their answers.

Extension

Provide magazines and have students cut out pictures of places, glue them on poster board, and write the common noun name of the place below the picture. Have students present their pictures to the class, telling the proper noun and common noun that name the place. *(Example: The proper noun is* Caldwell Park. *The common noun is* park.*)*

Common Nouns Name Things
Page 50

Students Should
- recognize common nouns that refer to things

Teaching the Lesson
Review that common nouns name people, places, or things. Go over the teaching. Play a riddle game to help students name common nouns that refer to things. (*Example: I am a thing you sleep in. What am I? You are a bed.*) Then play the riddle game with objects in the room. Have students point to the correct object as they give their telling sentences.

Go over the activity directions. Read aloud the story without saying the nouns. Then reread the story, stopping at each beginning letter to allow students to write their answers. When students have finished, review their answers.

Read aloud the Writer's Corner. Allow time for students to write their sentences. Invite volunteers to read aloud their sentences and have the rest of the class identify the common noun or nouns used.

Extension
Ask students to think of an activity they know how to do. Then have students draw and label pictures of items involved in that activity. (*Example: to set the table: dishes, spoons, knives, forks*) Have students present their pictures to the class or display them on a bulletin board.

The Days of the Week
Page 51

Students Should
- recognize the names and the order of the days of the week
- understand that the names of the days of the week are proper nouns

Teaching the Lesson
Display a calendar. Point to today's date and ask students what day of the week it is. Ask students additional questions to elicit the names of the other days of the week. (*Examples: What day is tomorrow? What day was yesterday?*) Write their responses on the board. After all seven days have been written on the board, read them aloud one by one and have the class repeat after you. As you read, point to each day and emphasize the *day* part of its name. Then help students use the calendar to review the order of the days of the week.

Review the difference between common nouns and proper nouns. Write the word *day* on the board. Explain that *day* is a common noun because it doesn't name a special day. Tell students that the names of the days of the week are proper nouns because they name special days. Ask students to tell how we write proper nouns. (*with capital letters*)

Go over the teaching and activity directions. When students have finished the activity, review their answers.

Extension
Provide each student with one note card with a day of the week written on it. Write on the board one-word descriptions of weather conditions. (*Examples: hot, rainy, snowy, sunny, windy*) Ask students to imagine what the weather will be like on that day and to write their weather word on the card. Allow students to draw simple pictures of the weather. Then beginning with Sunday, invite a volunteer from each day of the week to deliver an oral weather report.

The Months of the Year
Pages 52–53

Students Should
- recognize the names of the months of the year
- understand that the names of the months of the year are proper nouns

Teaching the Lesson
Ask volunteers to tell their birthdays. Write the dates on the board. Circle the months and read them aloud. Explain that each of the circled words is a month. Write on the board *month* and underline it. Ask students if they can name other months. Prompt students by suggesting holidays and school-related days. Write their responses on the board. Pass out photocopies of small calendars. Ask students to tell the order of the months as you write them on the board.

Go over the teaching on page 52. Review that the days of the week are proper nouns. Explain that the months of the year are also proper nouns. Then go over the activity directions on pages 52 and 53. When students have finished each activity, review their answers.

Extension
Have the class recite the poem on page 53. Then distribute note cards with the names of the months on them. Call out a month. Have a student with that month's card stand and say the month's name, the capital letter, and one special thing about that month. *(Example: The month is July. The capital letter is J. July is a special month because we can go swimming.)* Then ask the class how many days are in that month. Allow students to use a calendar or the poem if they need help. Repeat with the other months.

Days and Months Review
Page 54

Students Should
- distinguish among months of the year
- distinguish among days of the week
- write months and days as proper nouns

Teaching the Lesson
Use a calendar to review the days of the week and the months of the year. List on the board the days of the week in one column and the months of the year in another column. Assign a day of the week to each of seven students. Then play the part of a parade leader and lead a days-of-the-week parade. Say: *Who will join my weeklong parade?* Have students take turns responding "I will join! I am Sunday, the first day of the week!" and continue until all seven days are in the parade. Then stop the parade. Say: *This parade is not long enough. We need another week.* Assign seven more days to students and repeat. Conduct a similar parade with the months of the year.

Go over the activity directions. When students have finished the activity, review their answers.

Extension
Have students write on note cards their names and birthdays. Then collect and shuffle the cards. Pass out the cards and have students make a birthday card for the person whose note card they receive. Ask students to write the date on the front cover of the card and to decorate around the date. Encourage students to draw pictures of things they associate with that month. As students work, circulate among them and use a calendar to find out on which day that birthday next falls. Have students write down the day. When students have finished decorating their cards, have them write inside *It's a special,* finishing the phrase with the day of the week they wrote down. Encourage students to add any other friendly messages they wish to share on the inside of the card. Distribute envelopes and help students write the name of the receiver on the envelope and seal it. Pass out the birthday cards over the school year.

Proper Nouns and Common Nouns Review *and* More Proper Nouns and Common Nouns Review Pages 55–56

Students Should
- distinguish between common and proper nouns

Teaching the Lesson

Write on the board examples of common and proper nouns. Have volunteers underline each common noun and circle each proper noun. If students have difficulty, remind them that proper nouns begin with capital letters.

Guide students through the activity directions on pages 55 and 56. When students have finished each activity, review their answers.

Extension

Read aloud a story. Stop when you read various nouns. Have students tell whether they are common nouns or proper nouns.

Compound Words *and* Practice with Compound Words Pages 57–58

Students Should
- recognize compound words

Teaching the Lesson

Write on the board two lists of words: *sea, tree, rain* and *coat, shell, top*. Invite volunteers to read aloud the words. Explain that some words can be put together to make a new word. Ask students to raise their hands when they hear you say a word they know. Then pair words from the first list with words from the second list, one at a time. When students correctly identify a compound word, invite a volunteer to tell what it means.

Go over the teaching and example on page 57. Guide students to understand that *sail* is a word, that *boat* is a word, and that *sailboat* is a word that names a certain kind of boat that has a sail. Point out that the two words are written as one word when they are put together.

Go over the activity directions on pages 57 and 58. When students have finished each activity, review their answers.

Read aloud the Writer's Corner on page 58. Invite volunteers to name words they use to talk about winter. (*Examples: snow, cold, snowball, snowflake*) Write on the board students' responses. Help students distinguish between the words on the board that are or are not compound words. Then allow time for students to write their sentences. Invite volunteers to share their work.

Extension

Have the class recite the poem on page 58. Then say several words, some that are compound words and some that are not. For each word, invite a volunteer to tell whether it is a compound word. If it is a compound word, have the student identify the two words that make it up. Then have the student tell what the compound word means. Guide the student to use the meanings of the two words that make up the compound word to determine the compound word's meaning. Use the compound words on pages 57 and 58 and some compound words not studied in the book.

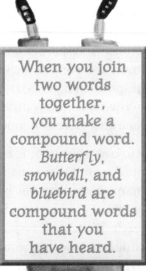

When you join two words together, you make a compound word. *Butterfly, snowball,* and *bluebird* are compound words that you have heard.

One and More Than One
and
Practice with One and More Than One
and
More Practice with One and More Than One   Pages 59–61

Students Should

- understand that some nouns can name one and more than one

- recognize that most nouns name more than one by adding *-s*

Teaching the Lesson

Hold up objects and ask students to say telling sentences that tell what you have. *(Example: You have a pencil.)* After the first few items, begin alternating between holding up one item and holding up more than one of the same item. Guide students to understand one and more than one. For the final two items, hold up one item and write students' responses on the board. Then hold up more than one of the same item and write students' responses on the board. Point out that we say and write some nouns differently when we talk about one and more than one.

Go over the teaching on page 59. Guide students to understand that most nouns can be changed to name more than one by adding *-s*. Then hold up pictures or objects and ask students to identify each. Write their responses on the board. Ask students how they would name the object if there were more than one. Write their response on the board. Repeat with other pictures and objects. Underline the *s* added to the words. Help students form sentences with the words on the board, with both singular forms and plural forms.

Go over the activity directions on pages 59–61. When students have finished each activity, review their answers.

Extension

Read aloud children's poems. Have students raise one hand when they hear a noun that names one, and two hands when they hear a noun that names more than one.

Show What You Know   Pages 62–63

Students Should

- distinguish between common and proper nouns

- identify compound words

- identify nouns that name more than one

Teaching the Lesson

Explain the directions for each activity. Assist students if necessary. When students have finished each activity, review their answers. Show What You Know may be used as a review or a test.

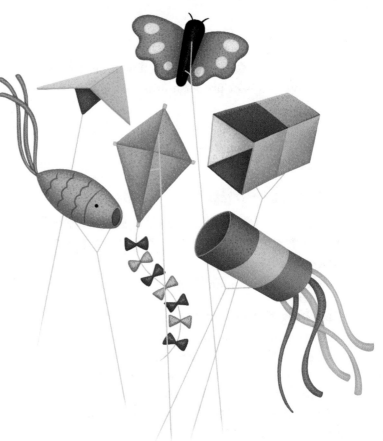

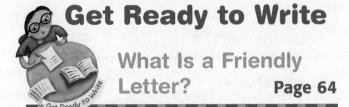

Get Ready to Write

What Is a Friendly Letter?   Page 64

Students Should

- understand what friendly letters are
- understand the reasons to write a friendly letter

Teaching the Lesson

Ask a volunteer to read aloud the title. Talk about times students have written or received letters, cards, or e-mails. Explain that these are all forms of friendly letters. Say: *Friendly letters are letters that we send to people we know. Friendly letters can share a story or message, say thank you, or ask a favor.* Review the friendly letter students read on page 41. Ask a volunteer why Ana wrote her letter to Mike. *(to invite Mike to her birthday party)*

Go over the teaching and the first example letter. Explain that one reason to write a friendly letter is to share a story or message. Ask: *What is this friendly letter telling Aunt Marlo?* (the writer went to swimming lessons and learned to float) Point out that the writer wanted to share a story. Help students understand that the letter might change if the reader were a different person.

Go over the teaching and the second example letter. Ask: *What is this friendly letter telling Uncle Tim?* (The writer is thanking Uncle Tim for the football.) Point out that the writer wanted to thank a special person for a gift. Explain that the writer would only write this letter to the person who gave the gift.

Go over the teaching and the third example letter. Ask: *What is this friendly letter asking Mrs. Jensen?* (if the writer can play with Mrs. Jensen's puppy) Point out that the writer has a favor to ask this person. Help students understand that the writer would not have written this letter to a different person.

Go over the activity directions. Guide students to complete the activity as a class. Invite volunteers to explain how each sentence fits the listed reasons to write.

Extension

Have students choose a reason to write a friendly letter and someone to write the friendly letter to. Have students draw a picture of what their letter will be about. When students have finished, invite them to explain their reason for writing.

Parts of a Friendly Letter   Page 65

Students Should

- recognize the parts of a friendly letter

Teaching the Lesson

Remind students that friendly letters are letters that we send to people we know. Review the reasons friendly letters are written. *(to share a story, to say thank you, or to ask a favor)* Ask students to look back at the model letter on page 41. Direct students' attention to the date, the greeting, the body, the closing, and the writer's name. Tell students these are called parts of a friendly letter. Explain that students will use these parts in the letters they write.

Ask a volunteer to read aloud the title. Go over the first sentence of the teaching. Then guide students through the example letter and the callouts. Read aloud each callout and emphasize where each part of the friendly letter is in the example. Explain that no matter how long or short a friendly letter is, it should always have these parts.

Go over the activity directions. Guide students to complete the activity as a class.

Extension

Write on the board a model of a friendly letter with blank callouts. Invite volunteers to fill in the names of the parts of a friendly letter, using as a guide the model on page 65. Repeat this activity as necessary for additional practice.

Complete a Friendly Letter

Page 66

Students Should

- understand how to complete a friendly letter

Teaching the Lesson

Review the parts of a friendly letter. Help students understand that a friendly letter must tell when it was sent, to whom it was written, what the writer wanted to say, and who sent it.

Ask a volunteer to read aloud the title. Go over the activity directions. Help students read the words in the word bank and the body paragraph of the letter. Then have students complete the activity. Circulate among students and guide those who are having trouble to understand the appropriate place for each part of the letter.

Extension

Write on separate note cards the parts of a letter. Make enough sets of cards to distribute to small groups of students. Have groups work together to place the cards in the correct order on a large sheet of paper. Monitor students as they work to be sure that each part is in the correct place.

Finish a Friendly Letter

Page 67

Students Should

- understand how to write a friendly letter

Teaching the Lesson

Review the parts of a friendly letter. Help students understand the order and placement of the parts of a friendly letter.

Have a volunteer read aloud the title. Then go over the activity directions and review the reasons for writing a friendly letter. Ask students to name people to whom they might write their letters of thanks. Have students complete the activity. When students have finished, encourage them to share their work with the class.

Extension

Ask students to imagine they are writing to a first grader in another country to tell him or her about what the class is doing today. Help students compose a friendly letter on the board. Prompt students to provide the information needed for the date, greeting, closing, and signature. Guide students to write the body of the letter. If time allows, repeat the activity with different recipients and topics.

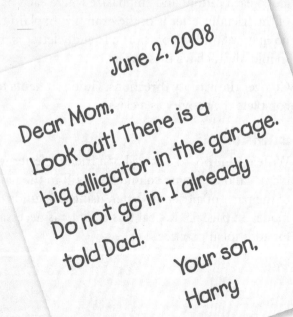

June 2, 2008

Dear Mom,
Look out! There is a big alligator in the garage. Do not go in. I already told Dad.

Your son,
Harry

Writer's Workshop

Prewriting— Pick a Topic
Page 68

Students Should
- brainstorm topics
- identify appropriate topics for their friendly letters

Review the reasons to write a friendly letter. Then ask students from whom they have received letters and why the letters were written. Remind students that friendly letters can be written to many people. Talk about the people to whom they might write a friendly letter. *(a friend, a classmate, a teacher, a family member)*

Ask a volunteer to read aloud the title. Say: *Remember that during prewriting we think about the person to whom we will write and what we will write about. The topic is what the letter is about. When we do prewriting, we think of a lot of topics. That way we can pick the best one.*

Go over the first two paragraphs and the people to whom students might write. Ask volunteers to provide names for each person listed. Write students' responses on the board. Say: *These are the names of people you know. They can be people who get a friendly letter from you.*

Go over the next paragraph and the messages that students might write in their friendly letters. Invite those students who named specific people to tell what their letters to those people would be about. Write their responses next to the appropriate name. Explain that students have just brainstormed topics and people to whom they might write a friendly letter.

Point out Ana's list of friendly letter ideas. Explain that each idea is information she wants to share with someone she knows. Point out that Ana

decided that inviting Mike to her birthday party was an important message she needed to share right away.

On the board, model for students how to brainstorm a list of receivers and topics for a friendly letter. Use the topic prompts on the page to guide your brainstorming list. As you work, explain why you think each topic might make a good friendly letter and to whom you might write. Then choose one topic by circling it. Talk about how the topic relates to the friendly letter that you will write and why it is appropriate for the reader that you chose.

Go over the rest of the page. Then allow time for students to brainstorm ideas in their notebooks. Circulate among students to provide encouragement and to be sure that they are listing appropriate topics. Help them to understand which topics are appropriate for friendly letters and why those topics are appropriate. Encourage students to pick the topic that seems most interesting to them.

Prewriting— Plan Your Letter
Page 69

Students Should
- plan their friendly letters

Invite volunteers to share their topic ideas. Ask students to explain why the topic they chose is appropriate for the person to whom they are writing.

Invite a volunteer to read the title. Say: *First we chose someone who will get our friendly letter. The next step is to plan our letters.* Tell students that planning a friendly letter means thinking about what will go in each part of the letter. Tell students that when they do this part of prewriting, they decide what they want to write.

Go over the first paragraph. Use Ana's chart to review what information belongs in each part of a friendly letter. Explain that by using a chart Ana will be sure to include all the parts of her friendly letter.

Write on the board a copy of the chart. Model for students filling in parts of the chart for the friendly letter topic you chose on page 68. Explain how using a chart helps you to plan your friendly letter. Say: *Filling in this chart helps me remember to include all the parts of my friendly letter. It also helps me remember the right order of all the parts of the letter. Writing ideas in the* What I want to say *space helps me remember what I want to say in the letter.* Save your chart for the drafting stage of the writing process.

Go over the second paragraph and allow time for students to complete their charts. Circulate among students to provide encouragement and support.

Students Should
- use their prewriting charts to write their first drafts

Ask volunteers to share their prewriting charts with the class. Talk with students about each part of a friendly letter. Invite students to explain what they want to say in their letters and to whom they will write. As volunteers share, prompt them to say complete sentences. Explain that these sentences might go in their friendly letters.

Ask a volunteer to read aloud the title. Say: *Remember that during drafting we write our letters. First we planned our letters in prewriting. Now we will write down what we want to say. When we write our drafts, we include all of the parts of a friendly letter.*

Read aloud the first paragraph. Then direct students' attention to Ana's draft. Tell students that Ana used her chart to help write her friendly letter. Remind students that Ana may have made mistakes in her first draft, but that she will look for those mistakes later.

Go over the two paragraphs following Ana's draft. Tell students that they might have more ideas for their letters after they have finished prewriting. Allow time for students to add to their charts any other ideas that they have. Monitor students as they work to be sure that the additional details stay on the topic and do not add unnecessary information.

On the board, model for students how to use your prewriting chart to write a draft of your own friendly letter. As you write, have students identify which part of the letter you are writing. Include in your model draft at least one mistake from the Editing Checklist on page 71 and one mistake from the Proofreading Checklist on page 72. Save your draft to use during the editing stage.

Go over the rest of the teaching and the word bank. Explain that the word bank can help students think of the right words to use in their friendly letters. Allow time for students to complete their drafts. Circulate through the class to provide students with encouragement and support. Tell students that they might make mistakes but that they can look for them later.

Students Should

- edit their friendly letters

Invite a volunteer to read aloud the title. Say: *Remember that when we edit, we make sure that our writing makes sense. We look for places where the person reading the letter might get confused.*

Read aloud the first paragraph and each item on the Editing Checklist. As you read, guide students to understand what each question means.

Go over the next paragraph and the thought bubble. Ask students which item on the checklist helped Ana find the mistake in her draft. *(Do I have a closing?)* Talk with students about why a closing is important in a friendly letter. *(It says goodbye in a friendly way.)*

Direct students' attention to the draft of your friendly letter. Guide students to use the Editing Checklist to help you find your mistake. Invite volunteers to suggest ways to fix the mistake and improve the draft. Remind students that everyone makes mistakes and that is why we edit. Say: *It's a good thing we found this mistake. Now I can fix it and make my letter better.*

Go over the third paragraph. Allow time for students to edit their drafts. Circulate among them to be sure that they are giving consideration to each item on the checklist. Ask students to give reasons for making or not making changes to their work.

Read aloud the last paragraph of this section. If time allows have students read one another's drafts. Remind students that a friend can often catch mistakes that the writer missed. If necessary, review appropriate language and behavior for peer-editing sessions. Remind students to check over any editing comments they receive from a friend. Say: *Remember that a friend might suggest a change that you do not agree with. Always check your friend's changes, using the checklist. If you aren't sure about a change, ask a teacher, a parent, or another friend for help.*

Students Should

- use editing changes to revise their drafts

Ask a volunteer to read aloud the title. Say: *Remember that when we revise our writing, we change it to make it better. We use ideas of our own from editing to make our drafts better. We use ideas that friends or a teacher have.*

Go over the first paragraph of this section and direct students' attention to the partial student model. Remind students that Ana forgot to include her closing. Invite a volunteer to explain how she fixed her draft. *(She added* Your friend, *as a closing.)* Point out the proofreading mark that Ana used to mark the change in her draft.

Point out the mistake in your draft found during editing. Demonstrate how to mark your correction. Talk about how making this change improves the draft. Then rewrite your draft on the board, incorporating into the new copy your marked change. Remember to include your mistake from the Proofreading Checklist on page 72. Remind students that a new copy of the draft can help writers see other mistakes that might be in the letter.

Read aloud the last paragraph. Then allow time for students to revise their drafts. As they work, circulate among students to be sure that they are writing their editing changes correctly.

I don't have a closing!

Proofreading

Page 72

Students Should
- proofread their revised drafts

Ask a volunteer to read aloud the title. Say: *Remember that when we proofread, we make sure that all the words are spelled the right way, that the sentences are correct, and that we have used the right capital letters, end marks, and words.*

Guide students through the first paragraph and the Proofreading Checklist. As you read, talk about what each question means and how students can check the question in their drafts. If necessary, review with students the Proofreading Marks chart on the inside back cover of their book.

Read aloud the next paragraph. Invite a volunteer to identify Ana's mistake. (Friday *should start with a capital letter.*) Point out the proofreading mark that Ana used to correct the mistake. If time allows, write on the board additional examples of proofreading errors, and invite volunteers to correct the sentences with the appropriate proofreading marks.

Guide students to proofread your revised draft by using the Proofreading Checklist. Help students use the questions to find the mistake in your letter. Remind students that people make mistakes when they write, and that by proofreading, you have made your draft better. Demonstrate how to use proofreading marks to correct the error.

Go over the rest of the page. Then allow time for students to proofread their drafts. Tell students to check for only one kind of mistake at a time. Circulate through the class to offer students assistance and support. Guide students to understand how to use references such as a picture dictionary, a word wall, and their book to check and correct mistakes.

If time allows, have partners trade drafts and proofread each other's work. Remind students that a friend might catch mistakes that they have missed. If you choose this option, circulate among students to be sure that they are using appropriate peer-conferencing language. When students have finished, remind them to double-check their partner's suggestions.

Publishing

Page 40e provides a full-sized, reproducible copy of the student's Friendly Letter scoring rubric. Students can use the rubric when assessing their own friendly letters.

Page 40f provides a full-sized, reproducible copy of the Teacher's Scoring Rubric for friendly letters. The rubric can be used when assessing students' understanding of the genre.

Students Should

- produce final copies of their friendly letters

Ask a volunteer to read aloud the title. Remind students that publishing happens when a writer decides to share his or her work with an audience. Explain that an audience is the people who read their writing. Tell students that the audience for a friendly letter is the person to whom the letter is being written. Tell students that publishing a friendly letter means mailing it to the person it is addressed to. Say: *Publishing is an exciting time for writers. After all that hard work, it's nice to share your letter with someone you like.*

Go over the first paragraph. Model for students how to produce a clean copy of your friendly letter. You might write your final copy on the board, or you might use one of the publishing ideas listed in the student book. As you work, say: *First I wrote my friendly letter. Then I edited it, revised it, and proofread it. Now I am ready to share this letter with the person it is addressed to.* Share with students other ways you might publish a friendly letter, such as bringing it home, putting it on the class bulletin board, or personally delivering it to the person to whom it is written.

Read aloud the second paragraph. Then allow time for students to make final copies of their letters. Tell students to write slowly and carefully. Remind them to check each sentence to make sure they do not make any new mistakes.

When students have finished, read aloud the rest of the page. Talk with students about how they would like to publish their letters. Allow time for students to work on additions to their letters, such as a drawing to accompany the letter. If you plan to have students send the letters through the mail, model on the board how to properly address an envelope. Allow time for students to complete their envelopes. Make sure students understand that their letters should be mailed to family members or friends, not to people that they do not know well. Emphasize that students should let a parent or teacher read their letter before they send it.

When students have finished, distribute copies of the student's Friendly Letter scoring rubric. Read aloud each item from the rubric. Guide students to understand what each item means and how to apply it to their own writing. Then allow time for students to self-evaluate their letters.

Remind students to add their finished letters to their portfolios. Explain that their portfolios will help them see what they are learning and how their writing has improved throughout the year.

CHAPTER 3

Verbs and How-to Articles

Introducing the Chapter
Pages 74–75

Students Should
- have a basic understanding of how-to articles
- have a basic understanding of verbs

Reading the Model
Read aloud the quotation. Then review with students the writing they have done. Say: *You have already had practice writing personal narratives and friendly letters. The more you practice writing, the better you will get.*

Direct students' attention to the picture. Invite volunteers to tell what the child lying in the snow is doing. *(making a snow angel)* Invite volunteers to tell things they like to do. *(Examples: ride a skateboard, play checkers, make popsicle-stick castles)* Ask volunteers to tell how to do the activity. Say: *When you know how to make or to do something, you can teach others. One way to teach others is to write a how-to article. How-to articles tell how to make or to do something.*

Read aloud the title of the model how-to article. Explain that this boy liked making snow angels, so he wrote a how-to article to teach others how to make snow angels. Then read aloud the model how-to article. Point out that the steps in the how-to article are numbered. Explain that this makes it easy to tell in what order to do the steps. Say: *It is important to tell how to do something in order. If the steps are out of order, the reader may get confused.*

Ask volunteers to tell other things they could teach people to make or to do. As students suggest ideas, write on the board verbs taken from their answers. *(Examples: make, play, build)* Tell students that these are words that tell what something or someone does. Explain that the steps of a how-to article usually tell people to do things. Explain that verbs are important words that help to make sentences complete. Point out the verbs in the steps of the model how-to article. Say: *Without these words, readers wouldn't know what to do to make a snow angel.*

Action Verbs
Page 76

Students Should
- recognize verbs that show action

Teaching the Lesson
Review what telling sentences are. Then pantomime for the class several actions and have students guess what the action is. *(Examples: blink, tap, whistle, point)* Write on the board telling sentences that describe what you did. Point out that these telling sentences tell something you do. Ask volunteers to underline the words in the sentences on the board that show action. Explain that words that show action are called verbs.

Go over the teaching and example. Have students identify the word in the example that shows action. Then write on the board *The dog* three times. Ask students to tell what kind of word *dog* is. *(a noun)* Point out that these words are not sentences because they do not tell complete ideas. Help students think of action words that might tell something a dog does. Write their responses on the board. *(Examples: eats, jumps, runs, fetches)* Point out that these words form complete sentences.

Go over the activity directions. When students have finished the activity, review their answers.

Extension

Have students recite the poem on page 76. Then assign each student one of the following words: *run, jump, play, sing.* Have students form four groups according to the verbs they were assigned. Have each group recite the poem, pantomiming their assigned verb when they read it in the poem. Repeat for all four groups.

Verbs Ending in *s*
and
Practice with Verbs
Ending in *s*   Pages 77–78

Students Should

- recognize that some verbs add -*s* when used with a noun that names one person or one thing

Teaching the Lesson

Review singular nouns and plural nouns. Write on the board *boy* and *girl.* Ask volunteers whether the words tell one or more than one. Then review action verbs and have students suggest action verbs that might be used with *boy* and *girl.* Write on the board their responses as complete sentences. *(Example: The boy plays. The girl sings.)* Have volunteers underline the action verb in each sentence.

Go over the teaching and example on page 77. Ask students to tell whether *frog* tells one or more than one. Point out that the verb *hop* adds -*s* because *frog* tells only one. Circle the *s* in each verb on the board. Draw an arrow from the circle to the noun in each sentence. Point out that the verbs for those sentences end in *s* because the nouns name only one.

Go over the activity directions on pages 77 and 78. When students have finished each activity, review their answers.

Read aloud the Writer's Corner on page 78. When students have finished writing their sentences, invite volunteers to share their work. Show students a book about spiders or insects. Read sentences

aloud and have students identify the action verbs in the sentences.

Extension

Have students draw pictures of a superhero with *s* on the superhero's chest. Then write on the board sentences with singular subjects and regular present tense verbs. Write some with the verbs correctly ending in *s* and others written incorrectly without *s*. Read each sentence aloud and have students decide if the verb is written correctly. Have a volunteer indicate that a sentence is written incorrectly by flying his or her superhero to the board and adding *s* to the verb.

Verbs Not Ending in *s*
and
Practice with Verbs
Not Ending in *s*   Pages 79–80

Students Should

- recognize that some verbs do not add -*s* when used with a noun that names more than one person or thing

Teaching the Lesson

Write on the board the following: *The dog runs. The cat climbs.* Have volunteers underline the nouns in the sentences. Review that some nouns tell one and some nouns tell more than one. Invite volunteers to circle the action verbs in the sentences. Point out that each verb adds -*s* because it tells what more than one person or thing does.

Go over the teaching and example on page 79. Have students identify the noun and whether it names one or more than one. Write on the board the example sentence and *The girl plays* below it. Have students read aloud both sentences. Point out how *s* is used in each sentence. Invite volunteers to tell how to make the words *dog* and *cat* into words that tell more than one. Then have students use the words to make telling sentences with the same verbs as the previous examples. *(The dogs run. The cats climb.)*

Go over the activity directions on pages 79 and 80. When students have finished each activity, review their answers.

Extension

Write on the board verbs such as *ring, read,* and *chirp* and nouns such as *phone, people,* and *birds.* Play a game with students in which you say one of the nouns and the class then says the verb that goes with it. Read aloud each of the three nouns and have the class answer with the corresponding verb. Then mix up the order of the nouns and say them aloud, some singular and some plural. Be sure that students are responding with the correct form of the verb.

Action Verbs Review
and
More Action Verbs Review   Pages 81–82

Students Should

- distinguish between singular and plural verb forms

Teaching the Lesson

Write on the board the verbs *sings, laughs, bounces, shouts,* and *hears.* Invite volunteers to give a telling sentence for each word. Write on the board students' sentences. Then write *sing, laugh, bounce, shout,* and *hear.* Have students give telling sentences that use these verbs correctly. Write on the board students' responses. Have volunteers circle the action verb in each sentence and underline the noun or nouns it tells about. Ask other volunteers whether the noun or nouns tell one or more than one.

Go over the activity directions on pages 81 and 82. When students have finished each activity, review their answers.

Extension

Have the class form an even number of small groups. Ask the groups to work together to write short stories about a talking duck named Egbert who is lost in a big city. As students work, circulate among them to be sure they are using action verbs correctly in their stories. When students have finished, have groups exchange their stories. Invite groups to find and circle the action verbs in the story they receive. Have students check that action verbs were used correctly.

Has and *Have*
and
Practice with
Has and *Have*   Pages 83–84

Students Should

- understand when to use *has* and *have*

Teaching the Lesson

Review action verbs students have learned. Write on the board examples of regular action verbs. (*Examples: run, jump, leap, hop, sing*) Review that verbs used with nouns that name one add *-s* and that verbs used with a noun or nouns that name more than one do not add *-s*. Explain that many verbs follow this rule but that some verbs are special. Write on the board the following sentences: *The robot _____ metal arms. The robots _____ metal arms.* Then write on the board *has* and *have.* Guide students to choose which sentence takes *has* and which takes *have.* Explain that *has* and *have* are special verbs.

Go over the teaching and examples on page 83. Use the sentences on the board to emphasize that *has* is used with nouns that name one and that *have* is used with a noun or nouns that name more than one. Write on the board additional example sentences. (*Examples: The elephant has wrinkled skin. The elephants have wrinkled skin.)* Have students read aloud each sentence, emphasizing the word *has* or *have*. For each sentence, circle *has* or *have* and draw an arrow to the noun. Above the appropriate noun write *one* or *more than one*.

Go over the activity directions on pages 83 and 84. When students have finished each activity, review their answers.

Read aloud the Writer's Corner on page 84. Allow time for students to write their sentences. Invite volunteers to share their sentences with the class.

Extension

Have volunteers use *has* or *have,* and a noun phrase, to complete the following sentence starters:

The bear	This classroom
Some bears	Some classrooms
That book	The tree
Those books	Other trees

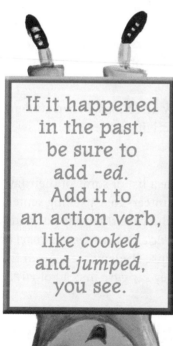

If it happened
in the past,
be sure to
add -*ed.*
Add it to
an action verb,
like *cooked*
and *jumped,*
you see.

Verbs Ending in *ed* and Practice with Verbs Ending in *ed*   Pages 85–86

Students Should

- recognize that many verbs can show what happened in the past by adding -*ed*

Teaching the Lesson

Review that verbs show action. Write on the board *The stars twinkle.* Have a volunteer underline the verb. Then write on the board *The stars twinkled last night.* Have a volunteer underline the verb. Ask the class what is different about the two verbs. Point out that the second sentence tells what happened in the past. Tell students that the past is anything that happened before right now. Explain that writers can add -*ed* to many verbs to tell what happened in the past.

Go over the teaching and example on page 85. Point out that *this morning* means before now, so this sentence is telling about the past. Circle *ed* in the sentence on the board. Then write *The stars twinkled last week.* Circle *ed* in the sentence and point out that last week and last night are both in the past.

Go over the activity directions on pages 85 and 86. When students have finished each activity, review their answers.

Read aloud the Writer's Corner on page 86. Encourage students to use the words on pages 85 and 86 to write their sentences. Then have volunteers read aloud their sentences.

Extension

Help students decide on a name for a fictional zookeeper. Write the name on the board. Then help students make up a story about what the zookeeper did this morning, one sentence at a time. Have students make each sentence with the past tense form of one of the words in the word bank on page

86. *(Examples: Odie Farnsworth brushed the zebras. Odie Farnsworth talked to the bears.)* Write each sentence on the board. When the story is complete, have volunteers underline the verbs in the story. Then have students recite the poem on page 85. Have them recite the poem a few more times, substituting the verbs in the last line of the poem with the verbs on the board as you point to them.

Eat and *Ate* Page 87

Students Should

- use *ate* as the past tense form of *eat*

Teaching the Lesson

Review that many verbs can tell what happened in the past by adding *-ed*. List on the board several examples of regular present tense verbs. Ask volunteers to use the verbs to make sentences in the past tense. Point out that all of these verbs form the past tense by adding *-ed*. Then explain that some verbs do not add *-ed*. Tell students that some verbs change to a different spelling when they tell about the past. Write on the board *The cows eat hay*. Have students identify the verb. Explain that *eat* is a verb that changes spelling in the past tense.

Go over the teaching. Then write on the board *The cows _____ hay this morning*. Have a volunteer fill in the blank. Say other sentences with *eat* and have students say the sentence with the past tense form of the verb. *(Example: The frogs eat flies. The frogs ate flies yesterday.)*

Go over the activity directions. When students have finished the activity, review their answers.

Extension

Show students a wand or some other prop and ask them to imagine that you are the Food Fairy. Circulate among students and choose a student at random, touching his or her desk with the wand and saying a commanding sentence that asks that student to eat a type of food. *(Example: Robert, eat a peach.)* Have the student pantomime eating the food you named. When the student has finished, have the class recite a telling sentence with a verb

in the past tense that tells what the student ate. *(Example: Robert ate a peach.)* Repeat with other students and types of food.

Give and *Gave* Page 88

Students Should

- use *gave* as the past tense form of *give*

Teaching the Lesson

Review that many verbs tell about something that happened in the past by adding *-ed*. Remind students that some verbs are spelled differently to tell what happened in the past. Point out that *eat* is one of those verbs. Tell students that *give* is another verb that changes spelling to tell about something that happened in the past.

Go over the teaching. Then call a student to the front of the room and say *I give stickers to my students*. Give the student a sticker. When he or she sits down, have the class recite a telling sentence with *gave*. *(Example: Mrs. Lono gave Tony a sticker.)* Repeat by giving other objects. *(Examples: apples, gold stars, pencils)*

Go over the activity directions. When students have finished the activity, review their answers.

Extension

Have students make a list of some of their favorite gifts. Then ask volunteers to say telling sentences about the person who gave them the gift and what it was. *(Example: Uncle Pak gave me a model car.)* Reinforce that because students were given their gifts in the past, they say *gave* instead of *give*.

See and *Saw* Page 89

Students Should

- use *saw* as the past tense form of *see*

Teaching the Lesson

Review the past and present tense forms of *eat* and *give*. Then explain that *see* is another verb that changes spelling to tell about something that happened in the past.

Go over the teaching. Write on the board *I see chalk*. Have students read aloud the sentence. Then write *I saw chalk*. Have students read aloud the second sentence. Explain that *saw* tells what happened in the past.

Go over the activity directions. When students have finished the activity, review their answers.

Extension

Have students draw a picture of something in the room. Then have them write a sentence telling what they see. *(Example: I see a book.)* Then ask students to remember a trip they took. Have students draw a picture of something they saw on the trip. Then have students write a sentence telling what they saw on the trip. *(Example: I saw a zebra.)*

Write and *Wrote*   Page 90

Students Should

- use *wrote* as the past tense form of *write*

Teaching the Lesson

Review the past and present tense forms of *eat, give,* and *see*. Then explain that *write* is another verb that changes spelling to show something that happened in the past.

Go over the teaching. Then write on the board the following sentences: *The poets write poems. The authors write books. The singers write songs.* Have students give complete sentences in the past tense, using the examples on the board. *(The poets wrote poems. The authors wrote books. The singers wrote songs.)* Guide students to understand which sentences tell about something that happened in the past.

Go over the activity directions. When students have finished the activity, review their answers.

Extension

Assign each of four groups one of the irregular verbs they learned. *(ate, gave, saw, wrote)* Have each

group write their appropriate sentence at the top of a large sheet of poster board: *Everybody eats food. Everybody gives gifts. Everybody sees pretty things. Everybody writes stories.* Then have each student write on his or her group's poster a first-person sentence that uses their assigned verb. *(Examples: I ate tuna. I gave my friend a necklace. I saw the mayor. I wrote a letter.)* Then have groups decorate their posters with appropriate pictures from magazines. Allow groups to present their posters to the class.

Being Verbs   Page 91

Students Should

- understand that being verbs do not show action

Teaching the Lesson

Go over the first two sentences of the teaching. Invite volunteers to pantomime each of the example action verbs. Point out that these verbs are called action verbs because they show action. Then go over the rest of the teaching and read aloud the words in the word bank. Emphasize that these verbs cannot be acted out because they do not show action. Tell students that being verbs tell what something or someone is, not what something or someone does. Hold up a common object, such as a ruler. Have students give telling sentences that use the being verb *is* to tell about the ruler. *(Examples: The ruler is straight. The ruler is yellow.)* Repeat with other objects.

Go over the activity directions. When students have finished the activity, review their answers.

Extension

Have the class recite the poem on page 91. Then write on the board telling sentences, some with action verbs and some with the being verbs *am, is, are, was,* and *were.* Read aloud each sentence and have a volunteer underline the verb. Ask if any students can pantomime the underlined words. When students discover that a verb is a being verb and cannot be pantomimed, have them recite the poem again.

Am, Is, and Are
and
Practice with
Am, Is, and Are   Pages 92–93

Students Should

- recognize that *am, is,* and *are* are being verbs
- understand when to use the verbs *am, is,* and *are*

Teaching the Lesson

Review that being verbs do not show action. Write on the board *am, is,* and *are.* Explain that these are being verbs and that they do not show action.

Go over the teaching on page 92. Then write on the board the following sentences: *I am tall. The cat is black. The camels are thirsty.* Read aloud each sentence. Circle the verb and underline the noun. Give students sentence starters to help them form sentences using each of these being verbs. *(Examples: The mountains _____. The table _____. I _____.)*

Go over the activity directions on pages 92 and 93. When students have finished each activity, review their answers.

Extension

Assign small groups different occupations. *(Examples: writer, bus driver, artist, firefighter, teacher)* Call on students and ask: *What are you? What is he or she? What are they?* Have students give telling sentences that use *am, is,* or *are* to answer your questions.

Was and Were
and
Practice with
Was and Were   Pages 94–95

Students Should

- recognize that *was* and *were* are being verbs that tell about the past
- understand when to use the verbs *was* and *were*

Teaching the Lesson

Review the being verbs students have learned. Write on the board sentences with *am, is,* and *are.* Then explain that like action verbs, being verbs can also tell about the past.

Go over the teaching on page 94. Then pick up an eraser and put it down again. Write on the board *The eraser was in my hand.* Underline the word *eraser.* Explain that because the word *eraser* names one thing, the verb *was* is used. Pick up two erasers and put them down again. Write on the board *The erasers were in my hand.* Underline the word *erasers* and circle the *s.* Explain that because the word *erasers* names more than one, the verb *were* is used.

> Am, is, are, was, and were—
> these are being words.
> When you do not show action,
> use a being verb.

Help students turn the sentences on the board that use *am, is,* and *are* into sentences that tell about the past. Help students understand how the meaning of each sentence changes.

Go over the activity directions on pages 94 and 95. When students have finished each activity, review their answers.

Read aloud the Writer's Corner on page 95. When students have finished, invite volunteers to read aloud their sentences. Help students determine whether each sentence tells about now or the past.

Extension

Ask students to imagine that they saw two unusual people or things on the way to school. Have students express their ideas in sentences with the verbs *was* and *were*. (*Examples: A monster was on the school bus. Leaping lizards were on the playground.*)

Show What You Know
Pages 96–97

Students Should

- use action verbs and being verbs with singular and plural subjects

- add *-ed* to show past tense

- use the past tense of the irregular verbs *eat, give, see,* and *write*

- use past and present forms of being verbs

Teaching the Lesson

Explain the directions for each activity. Assist students if necessary. When students have finished each activity, review their answers. Show What You Know may be used as a review or a test.

Get Ready to Write

What Is a How-to Article? Page 98

Students Should

- understand the purpose of a how-to article

Teaching the Lesson

Talk about times students have followed art project instructions, read the directions for a game, or helped someone make cookies from a recipe. Ask students to describe what they made or did. Talk about what might have happened if students had not followed the instructions or directions. (*The project would have been harder. They might not have finished the project.*) Then have a volunteer read aloud the title. Say: *The instructions or directions we have been talking about are all how-to articles. How-to articles teach how to make something or how to do something.*

Have students turn back to the how-to article on page 75. Ask students what this how-to article teaches. (*how to make a snow angel*) Explain that the writer of this how-to article knew how to make a snow angel. He wrote his how-to article to teach others how to make a snow angel.

Go over the first paragraph. Guide students to understand that when they write their own how-to articles, they should teach something that they know how to make or to do. Invite volunteers to name things they know how to make or to do. Encourage students to write their answers as possible topics for their how-to articles.

Go over the activity directions and topic ideas. Have students complete this activity independently. When students have finished, invite them to share their answers with the class. Go over each item and guide students to understand why the item is or is not a good topic for a how-to article.

Extension

Have students share things they know how to make or to do. *(Examples: turning cartwheels, washing dishes, riding a sled)* Have students draw pictures of themselves doing that activity. When students have finished, invite volunteers to share their drawings and to explain what they are doing.

Order in a How-to Article
Page 99

Students Should
- understand order in a how-to article

Teaching the Lesson

Invite students to explain what a how-to article is. Then review appropriate topics for a how-to article. Remind students that how-to articles can be about anything that they know how to make or to do.

Invite a volunteer to read aloud the title. Go over the first paragraph. Explain that before writers write how-to articles, they think about the order in which the steps should be done. Say: *A writer might do the activity and write down the steps as he or she does them. That way no steps are left out.*

Demonstrate sharpening a pencil. After you complete each step, write it on the board. When you have finished, read aloud all the steps. Talk about what might happen if the steps were in a different order. To reinforce the importance of order, invite a volunteer to try sharpening a pencil, using the steps out of order. Guide students to understand that doing things in order helps people to make or to do things correctly.

Go over the activity directions. Complete the first item as a class. Then have students complete the rest of the page independently. Circulate through the class to be sure students are placing items in the correct order. When students have finished, invite volunteers to share their answers with the class.

Extension

Assign each student one of the activities on this page. Tell students to draw separate pictures for each step of their activity. Then have students mix the pictures up and trade sets of pictures with a partner. Ask students to put in the correct order the pictures they receive.

Steps in a How-to Article
Page 100

Students Should
- understand the steps of a how-to article

Teaching the Lesson

Review that order in a how-to article is telling which steps come first, second, third, and so on. Ask students to explain why knowing this is important. *(If the reader doesn't know the order of the steps, he or she cannot complete the activity or project.)* Invite volunteers to share simple steps for writing on the board. *(Example: Walk to the board. Pick up the chalk. Write on the board.)* Talk about what might happen if the steps were presented out of order.

Have a volunteer read aloud the title. Then go over the activity directions. Guide students to complete the first set as a class. Have students complete the second set independently. Encourage students to explain why the steps belong in the order they have chosen.

Extension

Ask students to think of three things they did to get ready for school today. Have students draw what they did on three sheets of paper. Invite volunteers to tell what each picture shows, but tell them to show the pictures out of order. Invite other volunteers to tell in what order the pictures should be. If time allows, give each student a turn.

Plan a How-to Article   Page 101

Students Should
- plan a how-to article

Teaching the Lesson
Review the importance of writing the steps of a how-to article in the correct order. Tell students that if the steps are not in the right order, the reader may not be able to make or to do the thing they are trying to teach.

Ask a volunteer to read aloud the title. Then go over the activity directions. Remind students that drawing pictures can be a useful way to plan their writing. Help the class brainstorm topics for how-to articles and write appropriate responses on the board. As students name topics, talk about why each topic is or is not appropriate for a how-to article. When you have written several topic ideas, encourage students to choose a topic from the board. Have students write their topic on the first line of the activity. Explain that this is the title of their how-to article. Tell students that how-to articles usually name the topic in the title.

Allow time for students to draw a picture for each step of their chosen topic. As students work, circulate among them to make sure that their pictures are about the steps that are needed to complete the activity. When students have finished, invite volunteers to share their pictures. Encourage students to say for each drawing a sentence that they might write in their how-to article.

Extension
Suggest as a topic a simple activity, such as making a peanut butter and jelly sandwich. Invite students to tell the steps needed to complete the activity. Write students' suggested steps on the board without correcting any errors. When the class thinks that the how-to article is complete, have a volunteer follow the steps as written on the board and pantomime the activity. If steps are missing, inaccurate, or incomplete, talk with the class about changes they could make to improve the steps on the board. Repeat with other simple activities.

Writer's Workshop

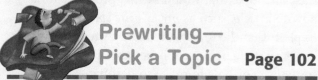

Prewriting— Pick a Topic   Page 102

Students Should
- brainstorm topics for their how-to article
- identify appropriate how-to article topics

Ask students to name things they know how to make or to do. *(Examples: make a paper-bag puppet, braid hair, take care of a pet)* Talk about times students have taught someone else to make or to do something. Remind students that a how-to article tells how to make or to do something. Review the importance of steps being in the right order. *(so that readers can complete the how-to article without getting lost or confused)*

Invite a volunteer to read aloud the title. Remind students what they did during prewriting when they wrote their personal narratives and friendly letters. *(wrote lists of topics, chose the best topic, used drawings or charts to organize ideas)* Say: *Prewriting is a time to think about what your how-to article might be about. It is a time to think about what you want to teach readers to do or to make.*

Go over the first two paragraphs and direct students' attention to the notebook graphic. Tell students that Kyle wasn't sure what he wanted to write about, so he made a list of several things he knows how to do. Go over each item on the list and ask students whether it is appropriate for a how-to article. Point out that Kyle wrote down many topic ideas so that he could choose the best one. Explain that Kyle decided to write about how to make a snow angel because he thought it was fun and because he thought other people might find it fun too.

Model on the board brainstorming a list of topics for a how-to article. Emphasize that each topic is something that you know how to do. Explain that you know enough about each topic to teach it to others. For each idea explain why that topic might be good for a how-to article. Include on your list at least one topic that would be inappropriate for a how-to article, such as *my favorite sports team.* Explain that the topic would not be good for a how-to article because it is not about how to do something or how to make something. Then choose one topic by circling it. Explain why you chose that topic over the others.

Go over the rest of the page. Write on the board the following questions: *What do you know how to make? What do you know how to do?* Encourage students to think about these questions as they brainstorm topics.

Allow time for students to draw or write their topic ideas in their notebooks. Encourage students to pick the topic that seems most interesting to them. As they work, circulate among students to provide encouragement and to be sure that they are choosing appropriate topics.

Prewriting—Plan Your How-to Article   Page 103

Students Should
- use drawings to plan their how-to articles

Ask a volunteer to read aloud the title. Review ways in which students planned or organized their personal narratives and friendly letters. Say: *We have each picked a topic for a how-to article. But we are not finished with prewriting. Now that we have picked topics, we need to plan what we want to write in our how-to articles.* Tell students that planning a how-to article includes thinking about the order of the steps.

Go through the first paragraph. Direct students' attention to Kyle's What You Need list. Explain that a What You Need list is a list of all the things a person needs to do or to make something. Tell students that Kyle wrote these things down so that he would not forget them when he wrote his first draft.

Direct students' attention to Kyle's drawings. Review the importance of writing clear, ordered steps. Go over each drawing and talk about why each step is necessary. Explain that Kyle has drawn pictures of his steps to help him remember to include everything.

Model on the board writing a What You Need list for the topic that you chose for your own how-to article. Explain why you are including each item on the list. Invite students to help you identify any other things a person might need to complete the activity. Then draw on the board pictures of each step. Help students understand how the pictures can help you plan your article. Say: *Writing a What You Need list and making sure that my steps are in order helps me to write a better first draft. I can make sure that the most important things are included. Later I can look at ways to make my how-to article better.*

Go over the last paragraph. Then allow time for students to make a What You Need list and to draw the steps. Circulate through the class to be sure students are including the necessary items on their What You Need lists and that they are clearly drawing each step. Tell students that writing is a process and that they are planning the ideas they will write about in the next stage of the process.

Drafting   Page 104

Students Should
- use their prewriting notes to write their first drafts

Invite a volunteer to read aloud the title. Talk about students' experiences drafting their personal narratives and friendly letters. Emphasize how students used their prewriting notes when writing their first drafts. Say: *Drafting is the first opportunity to write down your ideas as sentences.*

Read aloud the first paragraph. Direct students' attention to Kyle's draft. Explain how Kyle's draft was written using the list and the drawings he made during prewriting. *(Example: The sentence* You need warm clothes and a snowy patch of ground *came from the What You Need list.)*

Model how to use your What You Need list and drawings to write your own how-to article. Write on the board the title of your how-to article and a short sentence that tells what is needed. Then write the steps of your how-to article. As you work, explain how the steps you are writing come from the drawings you made. Remember to include in your draft at least one mistake from the Editing Checklist on page 105 and one mistake from the Proofreading Checklist on page 106. Save your draft for use during the Editing stage.

Go over the rest of the page. Allow time for students to complete their drafts. As they work, circulate among students to provide encouragement and support. Remind students that in the Drafting stage they should get all of their ideas on paper. Emphasize that students will be able to make their drafts better later.

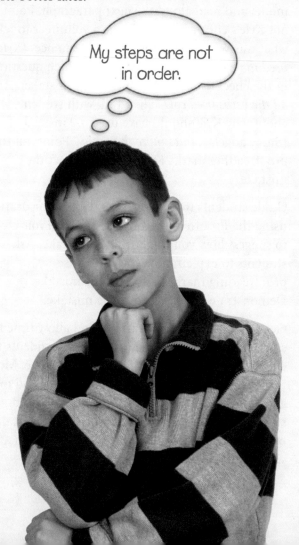

My steps are not in order.

Students Should

- edit their how-to articles

Ask a volunteer to read aloud the title. Talk about how editing students' personal narratives and friendly letters made their writing better. Then say: *When you edit a how-to article, you look for places where readers might get confused and you fix the problems.* Tell students that when they edit a how-to article, they should pay special attention to whether they included the things that are needed to complete the activity. Tell students that they should also make sure that the steps are complete and in the correct order.

Go over the first paragraph and each item on the checklist. As you read, explain what each question means and how students should check for it when they edit their drafts. Emphasize the importance of checking for one question at a time to make sure that they do not miss anything.

Guide students through the next paragraph and the thought bubble. Ask students which item on the checklist helped Kyle find the mistake in his draft. *(Are the steps in order?)* Ask students how Kyle fixed his draft. *(He switched the first and third lines.)*

Direct students' attention to your how-to article. Guide students to use the Editor's Checklist to edit your draft. When students find your mistake, invite volunteers to suggest ways that you might fix the draft. Remind students that mistakes are part of the writing process and that every writer makes them. Emphasize that we edit to catch these mistakes.

Go over the next paragraph. Remind students that reading aloud their drafts is a good way to catch mistakes. Then allow time for students to edit their drafts. As students work, move through the class to be sure students are answering each question on the checklist. Guide students who are having trouble to make appropriate changes to their work.

If students read each other's drafts, remind them of the proper language and behavior for peer-editing sessions. Tell students that when a friend edits their work, they should check over what their friend finds in the draft. Say: *Remember to check your friend's changes, using the checklist. If you aren't sure about a change, ask a teacher, a parent, or another friend for help.*

Revising   Page 105

Students Should

- use editing changes to revise their drafts

Invite a volunteer to read aloud the title. Remind students that revising means to change a draft to make it better. Point out that some of our ideas for how to revise our draft are our own while others might come from a friend, a teacher, or a parent.

Guide students through the first paragraph. Point out the mistake in your draft that the class found during Editing. Demonstrate how to mark the correction. Guide students to understand how correcting this mistake makes the draft better. Then rewrite the draft on the board, incorporating into the new copy your marked change. Remember to include your mistake from the Proofreading Checklist on page 106.

Read aloud the last paragraph. Allow time for students to revise their drafts. As they work, check students' progress to be sure they are correctly writing their editing changes. Emphasize the importance of not putting any new mistakes into the revised draft.

Proofreading   Page 106

Students Should

- proofread their revised drafts

Invite a volunteer to read aloud the title. Say: *We do proofreading to check spelling, punctuation, capitalization, and grammar. We make sure each sentence begins with a capital letter and ends with the right end mark. We look at things such as whether the verbs in each sentence are used correctly.* Emphasize that mistakes in spelling, punctuation, capitalization, and grammar might distract or confuse the readers.

Go over the first paragraph and the Proofreading Checklist. For each item on the checklist, talk about what the question means. Guide students to understand how to check for each item in their drafts.

Direct students' attention to the partial student model and read aloud the next paragraph. Point out Kyle's correction and invite a volunteer to tell what was wrong with the original sentence. *(Kyle used the wrong verb.)* Ask students which question in the checklist helped him find the mistake. *(Are all the verbs used correctly?)* Talk with students about why Kyle should have used *are* instead of *is*. *(Snow angels names more than one.)* Point out the proofreading marks Kyle used to correct the mistake.

Guide students to find the mistake in your draft, using the Proofreading Checklist. Invite volunteers to suggest how you might fix the mistake. Ask students to explain how you might use proofreading marks to correct the mistake. Demonstrate how to correct the mistake.

Go over the rest of the teaching and allow time for students to proofread their drafts. Tell students to check for only one kind of mistake at a time. Move through the class to check students' work and to assist those who are having difficulty. Remind students that they may check and correct mistakes by using references such as a picture dictionary, a word wall, and this book.

If time allows, have partners trade drafts and proofread each other's work. Remind students that a friend might catch mistakes that they have missed. Be sure that students use appropriate peer-conferencing behavior and language. Remind them to double-check their friend's suggestions, using the checklist. Encourage students to ask a parent, teacher, or other friend for help if they are unsure whether a marked change is correct.

Publishing   Page 107

Page 74e provides a full-sized, reproducible copy of the student's How-to Article scoring rubric. Students can use the rubric when assessing their own how-to articles.

Page 74f provides a full-sized, reproducible copy of the Teacher's Scoring Rubric for how-to articles. The rubric can be used when assessing students' understanding of the genre.

Students Should

- produce final copies of their how-to articles

Ask a volunteer to read aloud the title. Say: *Remember that publishing happens when writers share their work with an audience. We publish our work when we display it on a bulletin board, put it in a book, or give it to our parents.* Talk with students about how they published their personal narratives and friendly letters. Invite students to share how their audience reacted to their published work. Tell students that the audience for a how-to article is anyone who wants to make or to do what the article teaches.

Go over the first paragraph. Point out Kyle's published draft. Explain that Kyle was probably excited to share his work with an audience. Ask students whether they might try making a snow angel.

Model how to produce a final copy of your how-to article. You might write your final copy on the board, or you might use one of the publishing ideas listed in the book. As you work, say: *First I made notes about my topic. Then I wrote a draft. I edited, revised, and proofread the draft. Now I am ready to share my how-to article with my audience. My audience is anyone who wants to learn to do or to make what my article teaches.* Discuss ways that you might publish your how-to article.

Guide students through the second paragraph. Then allow time for students to make a final copy of their how-to articles. As they work, move through the class to provide encouragement and support. Tell students to write slowly and carefully. Emphasize the importance of making sure they do not make any new mistakes. When students have finished, allow time for them to draw pictures to accompany their how-to articles.

Go over the rest of the page. Talk with students about how they would like to publish their how-to articles. If students are publishing their work as suggested on the page, allow them time to work on any additional components of their published work.

When students have finished, distribute copies of the student's How-to Article scoring rubric. Guide students to understand what each item means and how to apply it to their own writing. Then allow time for students to self-evaluate their work.

Have students add to their portfolios their finished how-to articles. Remind students that their portfolios will help them see what they are learning and how their writing has improved throughout the year.

CHAPTER 4

Pronouns, Adjectives, and Descriptions

Introducing the Chapter

Pages 108–109

Students Should
- have a basic understanding of descriptions
- have a basic understanding of pronouns
- have a basic understanding of adjectives

Reading the Model

Read aloud the quotation. Explain that many activities are best learned through practice. Talk with students about other activities that are best learned through practice. *(Examples: ice-skating, hitting a baseball, riding a bike)* Say: *For many of these activities, other people can help you learn. But you really learn how to do these things by practicing. When you make mistakes, you get better. You learn not to make the same mistakes again.* Explain that practicing writing is the best way to learn to write better. Tell students that when they edit and proofread, they will catch mistakes. Explain that learning from those mistakes will make them better writers. Point out that you will be their writing coach and help them as they practice.

Direct students' attention to the picture. Invite volunteers to tell what they see. Point out that the children are playing in the snow. Then point out the model description. Say: *This is a description. The writer enjoys playing in the snow. She wrote a description to tell others what it is like to play in the snow.* Point out that as students talked about the picture, they were describing the scene.

Invite volunteers to tell about their favorite toys, people, and places. If necessary, ask questions to prompt students to provide more details. *(Examples:*

What color is your teddy bear? What does it sound like at the amusement park?) Say: *A description is a way to share people, places, things, and events with others. A description helps people imagine what something or someone is like.*

Ask students to close their eyes. Tell them to listen as you read and to try to imagine what you are describing. Then read aloud the model description. Have students open their eyes. Invite volunteers to tell what they imagined as you read the description. Point out that people have five senses. List them on the board. *(sight, sound, smell, taste, touch)* Point to each of the five senses and have students find a sentence in the description that tells about that sense. Say: *A good description makes a clear picture by telling about the five senses.*

Point out the word *We* in the last sentence of the model. Help students determine who *we* tells about. *(Sophie and the writer)* Read aloud the last sentence, substituting *Sophie and I* for *We*. Explain that *We* takes the place of *Sophie and I*. Point out *Pronouns* in the chapter title and explain that words that take the place of nouns are called pronouns.

Point out the words *long* and *cold* in the model. For each word invite a volunteer to name what that word is telling about. *(long tunnels, cold snowflakes)* Tell students that some words tell about nouns. Point out *Adjectives* in the chapter title and explain that words that tell about nouns are called adjectives. Say: *Pronouns keep us from repeating the same nouns over and over. They make our writing easier to read. Adjectives help our readers imagine what we are describing. They make our descriptions clearer and more interesting.*

Pronouns

Students Should

- recognize pronouns

Teaching the Lesson

Write on the board sentence pairs that have the same subject. (Examples: Ed crossed the street. Ed bought an apple. Trisha flew on an airplane. Trisha landed in Chicago. The soccer players won the game. The soccer players got a trophy.) Review with students that nouns are words that name people, places, and things. Invite students to identify the nouns in the sample sentences. (Ed, street, apple, Trisha, airplane, Chicago, soccer players, game, trophy) Explain that pronouns are words that can take the place of nouns. Underline the subject of each second sentence. Explain that a pronoun can replace these words. Replace the underlined subjects with appropriate pronouns. (Examples: He bought an apple. She landed in Chicago. They got a trophy) Tell students that using pronouns means we do not have to use the same nouns over and over.

Go over the teaching. Then invite volunteers to read aloud the pronouns on the balloons. For each pronoun, invite a volunteer to use the word in a sentence.

Go over the activity directions. When students have finished the activity, review their answers.

Extension

Show students pictures of people and things. For each picture, help students make up sentences using the pronouns on page 110. Write on the board students' sentences. Invite volunteers to underline the pronouns. Then have the class recite the poem. While students recite the poem, point to the pronouns underlined on the board as students say them.

The Pronoun *It*

Students Should

- understand how to use the pronoun *it*

Teaching the Lesson

Review that pronouns are words that take the place of nouns. Invite volunteers to read aloud the pronouns on page 110. Write on the board *Elliot ate the pizza.* Ask students what pronoun they could use to replace *the pizza.* Guide students to answer *it.* Write on the board *Who ate the pizza?* Invite a volunteer to answer the question using *it.* Write on the board the correct response.

Go over the teaching and examples. Explain that a thing cannot be called *he* or *she.* Emphasize this point by naming things. (Examples: a toaster, a sandwich, an alarm clock) Then write on the board more sentences. (Examples: Allen took my ball. Cheryl cleaned the table.) Ask questions about the sentences and guide students to answer the questions by using *it* in sentences. (Examples: Who took my ball? Allen took it. Who cleaned the table? Cheryl cleaned it.)

Introduce the robot R.E. to students. Explain that R.E. is a thing. Go over the activity directions. When students have finished the activity, read aloud the story.

Read aloud the Writer's Corner. Have students write their sentences. Invite volunteers to share their work.

Extension

Have students give two sentences about objects in the room, using *it* in the second sentence about the same object. (Examples: This is my desk. I keep it very neat. Here is your pencil. I found it on the floor.)

The Pronouns
He and *She*   Page 112

Students Should

- distinguish between the pronouns *he* and *she*

Teaching the Lesson

Review that pronouns are words that take the place of nouns. Remind students that nouns that name things can be replaced with the pronoun *it*. Then stand near one of the girls in the class. Introduce the student, and say a sentence about her, using the pronoun *she*. (*Example: This is Gina. She plays the piano.*) Explain that the pronoun *she* takes the place of the noun *Gina*. Tell students that any noun that names a girl or a woman can be replaced with the pronoun *she*. Stand next to a boy in the class and repeat this procedure. (*Example: This is Mike. He plays soccer.*)

Go over the teaching and examples. Then call on students to introduce a student near him or her and to say a sentence about that student, using *he* or *she*.

Go over the activity directions. When students have finished the activity, review their answers.

Extension

Help the class choose names for a female and a male science fiction character. (*Examples: Captain Delia Starburst, Space Cadet Miles Nova*) Write on the board as column headings the names students choose. Select a character and invite a volunteer to describe something about the character with a complete sentence that uses *he* or *she*. (*Examples: She wears a silver jacket. He has purple hair.*) Write students' sentences in the appropriate columns. When the characters are developed with several sentences, have each student choose one character to draw. Have students write above their pictures the name of the character and under their pictures a sentence that uses *he* or *she* to describe the character.

The Pronoun *I*   Page 113

Students Should

- recognize the pronoun *I*
- understand that the pronoun *I* is used before the action verb in a sentence
- recognize that *I* is used last when the writer is referring to himself or herself and others

Teaching the Lesson

Review pronouns that students have studied. (*it, he, she*) Write on the board sentences that use names of students in the class. (*Examples: Kathy ate an orange. Jorge rode a horse.*) Review how to use *he* and *she* with these sentences. Point out that these pronouns are used when writing about other people or things. Remind students that when they wrote personal narratives they used the words *I* and *me*. Explain that *I* is a pronoun used when a writer is talking about himself or herself.

Go over the teaching and example. Point out that in the example the writer is writing about himself and another person. Emphasize that when students are writing about themselves and another person, they should use the pronoun *I* last. Explain that it is polite to let others go first, even in writing. Then call on the students whose names appear on the board to say the sentences, using *I* where their names appear. (*Examples: I ate an orange. I rode a horse.*) Invite volunteers to circle the action verb in each sentence. Point out that in each sentence *I* appears before the action verb. Ask volunteers to tell something about themselves in a sentence that uses *I*. Repeat each sentence, emphasizing the placement of *I* before the action verb.

Go over the activity directions. When students have finished the activity, go over each item and have them identify the action verb. Point out items in which *I* is part of a compound subject. Explain that *I* always comes last because it is polite to let others go first.

Extension

Create a large *I* cut from poster board. Hand the *I* to a student and form a sentence that says that you and the student share an occupation. Then say a sentence using *I* that tells what you both do in your occupation. *(Example: We are artists. Katy and I paint pictures.)* Have that student hand the *I* to another student and form two sentences, using the same format but a different occupation. Suggest occupations for students if they are having trouble. *(Examples: astronauts, rodeo clowns, gardeners)*

I, me, she, he, it, we, and *they*—
these pronouns might
come your way.
They stand for nouns;
they take their place,
like *he* for Jim or *it* for vase.

The Pronoun *Me*   Page 114

Students Should

- recognize the pronoun *me*
- understand that the pronoun *me* is used after the action verb in a sentence
- recognize that *me* is used last when the writer is referring to himself or herself and others

Teaching the Lesson

Write on the board *Jim and I play baseball.* Review that the pronoun *I* is used when the writer is talking about himself or herself. Remind students that *I* is written last when the sentence is about the writer and someone else. Circle the action verb and point out that *I* is used before the action verb. Explain that there is another pronoun that writers use when talking about themselves.

Go over the teaching and example. Explain that both *me* and *I* refer to the writer. Emphasize that *I* is used before the action verb, and *me* is used after the action verb. Write on the board *Eric played baseball with Jim and me.* Explain that *me* is written last when the writer is referring to himself or herself and others. Write on the board additional sentences that use *me.* *(Examples: Miss Jones gave me a new book. My brother took Pat and me to the circus.)* Invite volunteers to circle *me* in each sentence and to identify the action verb.

Go over the activity directions. When students have finished the activity, go over each item and have them identify the action verb. Point out items 7 and 8. Explain that *me* always comes last because it is polite to let others go first.

Extension

Have two volunteers stand at the front of the room. Give a pencil to each student. Have each student say a sentence using *me* that expresses the action that was performed. *(Example: Mrs. Collins gave Ken and me pencils.)* Then have another volunteer stand at the front of the room. Give a book to the student. Have that student give a sentence using *me.* *(Example: Mrs. Collins gave me a book.)* Repeat this procedure with different objects and students.

The Pronouns *I* and *Me* and Practice with *I* and *Me*

Pages 115–116

Students Should

- distinguish between the uses of *I* and *me*

Teaching the Lesson

Review that the pronouns *I* and *me* are used when the writer is talking about himself or herself. Write sentences on the board that use *I* and sentences that use *me*. (*Examples: I swim at the park. Jamie laughs with me.*) Ask students to explain when to use *I* and when to use *me*. (*I is used before the action verb, and* me *is used after the action verb.*)

Distribute note cards, each with a sentence that uses either *I* or *me*. Then have one student stand at the front of the room, holding a sign that reads *action verb*. Invite a student to read aloud the sentence on his or her note card. Have the class identify the action verb in the sentence. Then have the student who read aloud stand to the right of the student holding the sign if the sentence uses *I* or to the left of the student holding the sign if the sentence uses *me*. Repeat this procedure until all sentences have been read.

Go over the activity directions on pages 115 and 116. When students have finished each activity, review their answers.

Read aloud the Writer's Corner on page 116. Talk about hobbies or sports students could write about. Then have students write their sentences. When students have finished, have partners check that they have used *I* or *me* correctly.

Extension

Write on separate sentence strips the following sentences: *I know you. You know me.* Cut the sentence strips into individual words. Repeat with other action verbs. (*Examples: I see you. You see me. I like you. You like me. I hear you. You hear me.*) Give partners these sentence puzzles to unscramble. If students have difficulty, tell them to pick out the action verb first and to put *me* after the action verb or *I* before the action verb. Invite students to read their sentences aloud.

The Pronouns *We* and *They*

Page 117

Students Should

- distinguish between the pronouns *we* and *they*

Teaching the Lesson

Briefly review pronouns that students have studied. (*it, he, she, I, me*) Point out that these pronouns take the place of nouns that name one person or thing. Write on the board the following sentences: *Ally plays checkers. Grant plays checkers.* Review with students that *he* and *she* could take the place of *Grant* and *Ally* because each proper noun names one person. Then write on the board *Ally and Grant play checkers.* Underline *Ally and Grant* and ask students which pronoun could take the place of the underlined words. Replace *Ally and Grant* with *They.* Then write on the board *Ally and I ran home.* Replace *Ally and I* with *We.* Explain that when writing about other people, students should use the pronoun *they.* Point out that when writing about themselves and other people, students should use the pronoun *we.*

Go over the teaching and examples. Lead students in contrasting their class with an army of knights. (*Examples: We study English. They fight dragons. We ride the bus. They ride horses. We wear school uniforms. They wear armor.*)

Go over the activity directions. When students have finished the activity, review their answers.

Extension

Have partners talk about one food they both like. Then call on one pair to share the food they both like by saying *We like* _____. Call on another pair to say what the first pair liked as the sentence *They like* _____ followed by the sentence *We like* _____. Continue with other students. Emphasize that *we* and *they* tell about more than one person or thing.

Pronouns Review   Page 118

Students Should

- identify and use pronouns correctly

Teaching the Lesson

Review pronouns that students have studied by playing a guessing game. Say: *I am thinking of a pronoun that can be used in place of* _____. Fill in the blank with a variety of nouns. *(Examples: I am thinking of a pronoun that can be used in place of* boy. *I am thinking of a pronoun that can be used in place of* children. *I am thinking of a pronoun that can be used in place of* book. *I am thinking of a pronoun that can be used in place of* Anna and I.*)*

An adjective's a special word that tells about a noun. Some adjectives to describe a shoe are *big, smelly,* and *brown.*

Go over the activity directions. When students have finished the activity, review their answers.

Extension

Have students read their work written for previous Writer's Workshops and other writing assignments. Ask students to find pronouns they have already used in their writing. Invite volunteers to share the sentences that they find. Guide students to tell what nouns the pronouns are replacing.

Adjectives   Page 119

Students Should

- recognize adjectives

Teaching the Lesson

Show students a picture of an animal. Guide students to suggest words that describe the animal. *(Examples: big, furry, spotted, wrinkled)* Tape the picture to the board and write underneath it the words that students suggest. To the right of the list write the name of the animal. Point out that the name of the animal is a noun. Explain that the words in the list tell about the noun. Read aloud one adjective from the list and the noun. *(Example: big bear)* Repeat with other adjectives listed. Explain that words that tell about nouns are called adjectives. If time allows, repeat with another picture.

Review that a noun can name a person, a place, or a thing. Then go over the teaching and the example. Point out that the adjective *long* tells about the noun *tail.*

Go over the activity directions. When students have finished the activity, review their answers.

Extension

Assign adjectives to small groups of students. *(Examples: happy, soft, small, big)* Have groups cut out pictures from magazines that go with their assigned adjectives. Help students make posters with their adjectives written in the middle and their pictures glued around it. Invite groups to share their posters. Then have them recite the poem on page 119.

Students Should

- recognize adjectives that tell about color

Teaching the Lesson

Review that adjectives are words that tell about nouns. List on the board names of various objects around the room. Then invite students to tell what color each object is. Write on the board to the left of each noun the colors students suggest. Explain that adjectives can tell many things about nouns. Tell students that one thing adjectives can tell about is color.

Go over the teaching and example. Ask students to draw their own umbrellas and to color them. Then invite volunteers to show their umbrellas and tell what color they chose. (Example: I have a yellow umbrella.)

Go over the activity directions. Help students locate in the picture the relevant nouns. When students have finished the activity, review their answers.

Extension

Choose a place or scene that has many colors that students could draw on the board. (Example: a home, a zoo, the inside of a library, a park) Use colored chalk to draw one item from the scene. Use a complete sentence with a color word to tell students what you are drawing. (Examples: I'm drawing a red house. I'm drawing a yellow lion at the zoo.) Invite students to add to the scene by saying a sentence that uses a color word to tell what they want to add. (Examples: I want to add green grass. I want to add a red bird.) Allow students who use color words correctly to use that color of chalk to add to the drawing. Use questions to guide students when necessary to add other appropriate objects to the picture. (Examples: What else do you find outside a house? What else do you find at the zoo?)

Students Should

- recognize adjectives that tell how many

Teaching the Lesson

Use different colors of chalk to draw on the board a moon and stars. Include between one and six stars of each color. (Example: three green stars, two red stars, five blue stars) Ask students to use complete sentences to tell how many stars they see of each color. (Example: I see three green stars. I see two red stars.) Review that color words are adjectives. Remind students that color words tell what color something is. Explain that number words are also adjectives.

Go over the teaching and example. Emphasize that in the example five is an adjective that tells how many birds. Invite a volunteer to name the other noun in the sentence. (trees) Point out that five does not tell about the trees.

Go over the activity directions. When students have finished the activity, review their answers.

Extension

Explain to students that a group of fish traveling in the ocean is called a school of fish. Tell students that they are going to make schools of fish. Then have students roll a die and choose a crayon. Explain that students should draw that number of fish of that color on a sheet of paper. Allow students time to draw and color their fish. Then have students write on the other side of the paper My school has [number] [color] fish. Invite students to share their pictures. Ask volunteers to identify the adjectives that describe that school of fish. Create an ocean-themed bulletin board display and allow students to decorate it with their schools of fish.

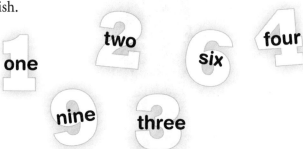

Size Words and Shape Words   Page 122

Students Should
- recognize adjectives that tell about sizes and shapes

Teaching the Lesson
Review that adjectives are words that tell about nouns. Remind students that color words and number words are adjectives. Point out that adjectives can tell many different things about nouns. Write on the board *round* and *square* as column headings. Ask students to name nouns that fit under each heading. Write students' suggestions on the board. Point out that *round* and *square* are adjectives that tell about nouns. Help students form sentences using the adjective and one of the nouns listed in its column. *(Examples: I threw a round ball. I saw a square book.)* Repeat for the adjective pairs *tall-short* and *large-small*.

Go over the teaching and examples. Emphasize that *little* tells about the kitten. Invite volunteers to tell other things that are little. Have students use their suggestions in sentences.

Go over the activity directions. When students have finished the activity, review their answers.

Read aloud the Writer's Corner. Have students draw a picture of a library. Then have students write their sentences. Invite volunteers to share their work.

Extension
Distribute sticky notes. Invite students to write an adjective from the activity on page 122 on the sticky note. Ask students to find an object in the room that their adjective describes and to attach their sticky note to the object they find. Have students remain standing beside their objects. Invite volunteers to share their answers by describing the object in a sentence that uses their adjective. *(Example: This is a tall chalkboard. Here is a little pencil.)* Talk with the class about whether they agree with each sentence.

Feeling Words   Page 123

Students Should
- recognize adjectives that tell about feelings

Teaching the Lesson
Pantomime adjectives from the word bank on page 123 and have the class guess what you are feeling. When students guess the feeling, write on the board *I feel* and the feeling you pantomimed. Then explain that adjectives can tell how someone feels. Write on the board *when* after each of the sentences. Invite volunteers to complete these sentence starters. *(Example: I feel sorry when I break something.)*

Go over the teaching and example. Invite volunteers to tell things that make them feel excited. Talk with students about other feelings they may have that could be described with feeling words.

Go over the activity directions. When students have finished the activity, review their answers.

Extension
Read aloud an age-appropriate story. Pause occasionally during the story to ask how a character might be feeling. Have students answer with complete sentences. *(Example: Skipper is excited. He got a new spaceship.)*

Sensory Words *and* Practice with Sensory Words

Pages 124–125

Students Should
- recognize adjectives that describe sensory experiences

Teaching the Lesson

Review that adjectives are words that tell about nouns. Write on the board sentences that use adjectives that students have studied. Ask volunteers to underline the adjective in each sentence and to circle the noun it describes.

Explain that people have five senses. Invite volunteers to name the five senses. Write on the board as column headings students' responses. Point to the senses one at a time and invite volunteers to tell something that could be described for each sense. When volunteers suggest nouns, ask them to describe how that noun looks, sounds, smells, tastes, or feels. (*Example: If a student suggests a lemon for taste, ask the student to tell how a lemon tastes.*)

Go over the teaching on page 124. Then point out each of the illustrations on the page and ask students to tell which sense each illustration represents. Write on the board above the column headings *popcorn*. Invite volunteers to suggest words that describe popcorn for each of the five senses. If necessary, guide students' answers by asking questions. (*Examples: What does popcorn sound like when you make it? What does popcorn sound like when you eat it?*) List students' responses on the board. Point out that these words are sensory words. Explain that sensory words are adjectives because they tell about nouns.

Go over the activity directions on pages 124 and 125. When students have finished each activity, review their answers.

Read aloud the Writer's Corner on page 125. Have students draw pictures of a food they like. Then ask students to write their sentences underneath their pictures. Invite volunteers to read aloud their sentences. For each sentence, ask volunteers to tell which sense is being described.

Extension

Help students come up with a gesture to represent each of the five senses. (*Examples: squeezing their noses for smell, rubbing their stomachs for taste, touching a finger to their desktops for touch*) Then have students recite the poem on page 124, performing their gestures when they read each of the five senses. Say aloud a sensory word, such as those listed on pages 124 and 125, paired with a noun it might describe. (*Example: crunchy gravel, sour grapes, orange sunset*) Have students identify the adjective and which sense it describes by performing the gestures they used during the poem.

Sound, smell, taste, touch, and sight—sensory words make descriptions clear and bright.

Adjectives Ending in er and est
Page 126

Students Should
- understand that adjectives can compare by adding the letters *er* or the letters *est*

Teaching the Lesson
Bring to class three pieces of yarn of different lengths, three pencils sharpened to different lengths, and three toys of different heights. Review that adjectives tell about nouns. Write on the board *long, short,* and *tall.* Invite volunteers to use each adjective in a sentence.

Dangle the shortest of the three pieces of yarn from your fingers and tell students that this is long yarn. Then hold up the next longest piece of yarn. Shaking the first piece of yarn, say: *This is long yarn.* Shaking the second piece of yarn, say: *This yarn is what?* (longer) Write on the board the following sentences: *This is long yarn. This is longer yarn.* Underline *long* and *longer* and invite volunteers to tell what is different about the words.

Explain that adjectives can tell how two things are different. Tell students that *long* and *longer* compare the two pieces of yarn. Point out that adjectives that compare two things add the letters *er.* Hold up all three pieces of yarn. Shaking the appropriate pieces of yarn, say: *This is long yarn. This is longer yarn. But this yarn is what?* (the longest) Write on the board *This is the longest yarn.* Underline *longest.* Invite volunteers to tell what is different about the word. Explain that when adjectives compare more than two things, they add the letters *est.*

Go over the teaching and examples. Repeat the activity above with the pencils and the adjective *short* and with the toys and the adjective *tall.* After you write the sentences on the board, have volunteers underline the endings.

Go over the activity directions. Invite volunteers to share their answers.

Extension
Draw on the board eight basketballs. In each basketball write a word to which *-er* and *-est* can be added without changing the spelling of the base word. Divide the class into two teams and assign each team a different ending. Have a volunteer from one team select a basketball, pronounce the word, and add the assigned ending. Ask another volunteer from that team to use the word correctly in a sentence. Give a team one point for saying the word with its ending correctly and another point for correctly using the word in a sentence. Then let the other team have a turn. If time allows, add new words to the board and repeat.

Practice with Adjectives *and* More Practice with Adjectives *and* Adjectives Review
Pages 127–129

Students Should
- identify and use adjectives

Teaching the Lesson
Display a poster that shows a scene with people and things. Play an I Spy game with students in which they choose an object or a person in the picture and use adjectives to give hints as to what they chose. (*Examples: I spy something red. I spy something stinky.*) Encourage students to use words to describe senses other than just sight. Write students' adjectives on the board and allow the rest of the class to guess. When the class guesses the object or person, lead them in saying sentences that use the adjectives on the board to describe that person or thing. (*Examples: I spy a red dump truck. I spy a stinky garbage can.*)

Go over the activity directions on pages 127–129. When students have finished each activity, review their answers.

Extension

Photocopy a short, age-appropriate story and distribute copies to students. Read aloud the story. Then have small groups go on an adjective scavenger hunt. Tell students to circle each adjective they find and to underline the noun that it tells about. When they have finished, invite students to share their adjectives. Talk with students about what each adjective tells about its noun. *(Examples: color, number, shape, size, feeling, how things compare)*

Show What You Know   Pages 130–131

Students Should
- identify pronouns and adjectives

Teaching the Lesson

Explain the directions for each activity. Assist students if necessary. When students have finished each activity, review their answers. Show What You Know may be used as a review or a test.

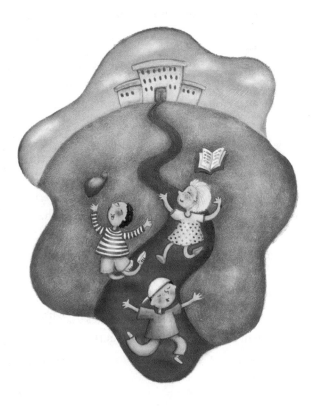

Get Ready to Write

What Is a Description?   Page 132

Students Should
- understand the purpose of a description
- understand how to use sensory words

Teaching the Lesson

Invite a volunteer to read aloud the title. Talk with students about times they have told a friend or family member about something that happened at school, about a person that they know, or about a place that they visited. Tell students that when they tell others about something or someone, they are giving descriptions. Say: *Descriptions help us imagine things that we read or that we hear about. Descriptions paint pictures in readers' minds about things, people, places, and events.* Explain that descriptions can appear in every kind of writing.

Go over the first two paragraphs. Then have students turn back to the description on page 109. Prompt discussion with the following questions: *What is being described?* (playing in the snow) *Is what is being described a person, a place, a thing, or an event?* (an event) *What words help you know that the description is about playing in the snow?* (snow, long tunnels, cold snowflakes, see my breath, snow crunches, South Pole) Explain that good descriptions tell how something looks, sounds, smells, feels, and tastes. Read aloud the first sentence of the model on page 109. Explain that this beginning tells readers what the topic of the description is. Say: *It's important to tell readers right away what you are describing. When you tell what you are going to describe in the beginning, readers can enjoy what you say about your topic without having to guess what it is.*

Go over the pictures and the example sensory words. Ask volunteers to name things that we might see, hear, smell, taste, and touch. *(Examples: desk, school bell)* For each example, invite additional volunteers to name sensory words that relate to the example. *(Examples: desk—hard, shiny, brown, cold; school bell—loud, noisy)*

Explain that sensory words are important because readers like to imagine the things they read about. Tell students that sensory words help readers to know how things that they read about look, sound, taste, smell, or feel. Say: *When we write descriptions, we want readers to see, hear, taste, smell, and feel what we are describing. Sensory words help readers imagine those things.*

Go over the activity directions. Have students complete the activity as a class. Invite volunteers to say other sensory words that might describe each item.

Extension

Choose five objects from around the room. Set the objects in a place that can easily be seen by students. Create on the board a chart with each item in a horizontal column and the five senses in vertical columns. Have students use sensory words to describe the objects. Write their responses in the chart. Encourage students to use as many sensory words as possible.

Use Sensory Words to Describe   Page 133

Students Should
- understand how to use sensory words in a description

Teaching the Lesson

Remind students that a description tells about a person, a place, a thing, or an event. Review the five senses and ask students to name words that relate to the five senses. Talk with students about why words that appeal to the five senses are important in a description. *(They help readers imagine what is being described.)*

Have a student read aloud the title. Then go over the first paragraph. Tell students that to make a description more real for the reader, they need to

help the reader imagine what is being described. Explain that sensory words should help readers experience what is being described. Invite volunteers to say short descriptions of what they had for dinner last night. Guide students to use sensory words in their descriptions.

Go over the activity directions. When students have finished the activity, invite them to share their answers with the class.

Extension

Play a sensory words version of I Spy with students. Begin by choosing an object in the room and describing it, using sensory words. Invite students to guess what the object is. Allow the student who correctly guesses your object to choose another object in the room and describe it, using sensory words. Continue with other students. Monitor students' use of sensory words and encourage them to describe more than just the appearance of each object.

Complete a Description   Page 134

Students Should
- understand how sensory words function in a description

Teaching the Lesson

Review that sensory words tell how things look, sound, smell, taste, or feel. Invite volunteers to describe their favorite foods. Prompt students to use sensory words by asking questions that appeal to the five senses. *(Examples: What does it look like? How does it smell? How does it taste?)* Talk about how sensory words help us imagine what things look, smell, taste, feel, and sound like.

Go over the activity directions. Guide students to complete the first item as a class. Then have students complete the rest of the page independently. When students have finished, invite them to share their answers.

Extension

Have students draw pictures of a family pet or an animal that they like. Then have students list on the picture sensory words that describe the animal. Guide students who are having trouble by asking questions such as: *Does it have fur? Is the fur soft or prickly?* Challenge students to write at the bottom of the picture sentences that describe their animal, using sensory words from their lists.

Finish a Description   Page 135

Students Should
- practice writing a description

Teaching the Lesson

Ask students what a description might be about. *(a person, a place, a thing, or an event)* Talk with students about some things they have described in this chapter. *(food, animals, people, a day at school)* Say: *We say descriptions all the time. When we talk to people, we are often describing someone or something. It's the same when we write. Descriptions are used in almost every kind of writing.*

Review what sensory words are. Talk about how sensory words tell readers how things taste, sound, smell, look, and feel. Remind students that the beginning of a description tells the topic.

Go over the activity directions. Then read aloud the beginning sentence of the first item. Ask students what the topic of this description will be. *(a rainy day)* Then read aloud the words in the word bank. Help students complete the first item as a class by having them suggest sentences that could go in a description of a rainy day.

Go through the words in the next word bank and the beginning sentence. Then have students complete this item independently. When they have finished, invite volunteers to share their work with the class.

Extension

Draw on the board a blank two-column five-senses chart similar to the one on page 137. Invite volunteers to name things that can be described by using all five senses. List their suggestions next to the chart. Then choose one topic and write it in the top row of the chart. Invite volunteers to write in the chart sensory words that describe the topic. When the chart is complete, explain that a five-senses chart is a good way to think of and to organize sensory words for a description.

Writer's Workshop

Prewriting— Pick a Topic   Page 136

Students Should

- brainstorm description topics
- identify appropriate topics for their descriptions

Review what a description is. *(writing that tells about a person, a place, a thing, or an event)* Talk with students about why sensory words are important in descriptions. Remind students that the beginning of a description tells what will be described.

Invite a volunteer to read aloud the title. Talk with students about their prewriting experiences when they wrote personal narratives, friendly letters, and how-to articles. Remind students that prewriting is a time to think of what they want to write about. Say: *Descriptions can be about almost anything. There are a lot of topics we can choose. Prewriting can help us think about and choose the best topic for a description.*

Go over the first paragraph and guide students to read Nora's list of topics. Explain that to think of a topic for a description, Nora thought about people, places, things, and events that she knew something about. Tell students that she wrote on her list things that she might describe by using sensory words. Point out that each item on the list is something that Nora knows well. Talk about why each item might be a good topic for a description. Invite volunteers to say sensory words that Nora might use for each topic.

Model on the board brainstorming a list of topics for your own description. For each idea, talk with students about why the topic might be good for a description. Explain that the best descriptions are the ones that can be described using the most senses. Then choose one topic and circle it.

Go over the next paragraph and the topic prompts. Remind students that the topics that they list should appeal to as many senses as possible. Then allow time for students to list possible topics. As students work, circulate to provide encouragement and to be sure that they are listing appropriate topics. Help students understand why each topic they list might make a good description.

Go over the last paragraph. Emphasize to students that they should think about which topic they can describe by using the most senses. Then have students choose and circle the topic they like best.

Prewriting—Plan Your Description   Page 137

Students Should

- use a chart to plan their descriptions

Invite a volunteer to read aloud the title. Review with students how they planned the drafts of their personal narratives, friendly letters, and how-to articles. *(drawing pictures, making charts)* Say: *When we do prewriting, we first pick a topic. Then we plan our drafts. Planning our drafts helps us make sure that we don't forget anything when we begin to write. When we plan a description, we can use a five-senses chart.*

Go over the first paragraph. Emphasize that after students have chosen their topics, they should think about the sensory words they will use in their descriptions. Direct students' attention to Nora's five-senses chart. Invite students to close their eyes as you read aloud the sensory words on the chart. Talk with students about how the sensory words helped them to picture playing in the snow. Point out that Nora tried to appeal to as many of the five senses as she could.

Model on the board creating a five-senses chart for the topic you chose for your own description. Say: *A five-senses chart helps me to think about what I will write in my draft. Thinking about the sensory words I will want to use helps me to write a better description.* As you fill in each section of the chart, talk with students about why you chose particular words and how those words relate to each sense.

Go over the next paragraph. Then allow time for students to fill in their five-senses charts. Circulate through the class to provide students with assistance and support. Guide students who are having trouble by asking questions such as the following: *What color or shape is it? Is it fuzzy, furry, rough, or smooth? Does it look like something else?* Ask questions that pertain to each of the five senses. Have students write the answers to your questions on a sheet of paper. Then help them identify in their answers sensory words to write in their five-senses charts.

Drafting
Page 138

Students Should
- use prewriting notes to write their first drafts

Ask a volunteer to read aloud the title. Talk with students about their experiences writing drafts for their personal narratives, friendly letters, and how-to articles. Then invite students to share their five-senses charts with the class. Guide each student to say sentences using the sensory words in his or her chart. Tell students that these sentences might be used in the drafts of their descriptions. Remind students that drafting is the first opportunity to put their thoughts and ideas into sentences.

Go over the first paragraph. Then guide students through Nora's draft. Emphasize that the items from Nora's five-senses chart can be found in her draft. Help students identify words and phrases in the draft that are from Nora's five-senses chart. *(Examples: long tunnels, snowflakes, snow crunching)*

Go over the next paragraph. Allow time for students to add additional sensory words to their five-senses charts. Be sure that the sensory words students add to their charts are appropriate to their descriptions. Tell students that the more sensory words they use in their descriptions, the better the reader will be able to imagine the topic.

Model for students how you will use the words in your five-senses chart to write your draft. Emphasize how your beginning tells what your description is about. Try to include in your draft at least one sentence for each of the five senses. As you work, explain how your description relates to your five-senses chart. Include in your draft one mistake from the Editing Checklist on page 139 and one mistake from the Proofreading Checklist on page 140. Save your draft to use during the Editing stage.

Go over the last paragraph. Then allow time for students to complete their drafts. Circulate through the class to assist students who are having difficulty writing their drafts. Remind students that drafting is a time to capture ideas. Encourage them to turn their thoughts into sentences. Remind students that they will have time to look for mistakes when they edit and proofread their drafts.

I forgot to tell my topic!

Editing Page 139

Students Should
- edit their descriptions

Ask a volunteer to read aloud the title. Talk with students about their experiences editing their personal narratives, friendly letters, and how-to articles. Say: *When we edit a description, we look for places that might confuse the reader. We also look for places that make it hard for the reader to imagine what is being described. We fix those places so that the description is clearer.*

Go over the first paragraph. Explain that Nora uses an Editing Checklist to make sure she checks for all the important parts of a description. Remind students that using an Editing Checklist helps them make their drafts better. Then go over each item on the checklist. Help students understand what each question means and how they might check for it in their drafts.

Direct students' attention to the partial student draft. Then go over the next paragraph and the thought bubble. Ask students which item on the checklist helped Nora find the mistake in her draft. *(Do I have a beginning that tells the topic?)* Ask students how Nora fixed her draft. *(She added I love to play in the snow.)* Explain that adding this sentence will help readers know what Nora is describing.

Direct students' attention to the draft that you wrote on the board. Guide students to use the Editing Checklist to identify the editing mistake that you included in your draft. Say: *When we write, it is important to have good editors. You are good editors because you helped me find this mistake. Now I can correct the mistake and make my draft better.* Remind students that everyone makes mistakes and that we edit to find those mistakes and make our drafts better.

Go over the last paragraph of this section. Then say: *Sometimes when we read aloud, we hear things that we don't see when we read to ourselves. Try reading your draft aloud to see if you can hear any mistakes.*

Allow time for students to edit their drafts. Circulate among students to be sure that they are giving consideration to each item on the checklist. Check students' justifications for making or not making changes to their work. If students edit each other's work, remind them of the proper language and behavior for peer-editing sessions. Tell students that when a friend edits their work, they should check over the mistakes that the friend marks. Emphasize that if they disagree with a mistake marked by their friend, they should ask a teacher, a parent, or another friend for help.

Revising Page 139

Students Should
- use editing changes to revise their drafts

Ask a volunteer to read aloud the title of this section. Ask students to explain what they did when they revised their personal narratives, friendly letters, and how-to articles. *(wrote new copies of the draft, including changes from editing)*

Guide students through the first paragraph. Point out the mistake in your draft that the class found during editing. Demonstrate how to mark the correction using proofreading marks. Explain that correcting this mistake helps to make your draft better. Then rewrite your draft on the board, incorporating into the new copy your marked change. Remember to include your mistake from the Proofreading Checklist on page 140. Explain that a new copy of the draft can help us see any other mistakes that might be in the description.

Go over the last paragraph. Then allow time for students to revise their drafts. As they work, circulate through the class to be sure that students are correctly writing their editing changes.

Proofreading

Students Should

- proofread their revised drafts

Invite a volunteer to read aloud the title. Say: *Proofreading is the time when we make sure that words are spelled correctly. We also make sure that capital letters and end marks are correct. We proofread because these kinds of mistakes can make it hard for readers to understand the description.* Talk with students about their experiences proofreading their personal narratives, friendly letters, and how-to articles. Ask students to explain why their drafts were better after proofreading.

Go over the first paragraph and the Proofreading Checklist. As you go over the checklist, help students understand what each question means. Encourage students to use what they learned in this chapter about pronouns and adjectives as they check that item in their drafts. Remind students to use references such as a picture dictionary or a word wall as they check and correct mistakes.

Read aloud the next paragraph and direct students' attention to the partial student model. Ask students what Nora noticed about her draft. *(She used the wrong pronoun. She should have used* I *instead of* me *in the sentence.)* Point out the proofreading marks Nora used to correct her draft.

Direct students' attention to your revised draft. Help students use the Proofreading Checklist to find the mistake in your description. Remind students that everyone makes mistakes when they write and that by proofreading they can make their descriptions better. Demonstrate how to use proofreading marks to correct your mistake.

Go over the rest of the page. Tell students that reading their drafts more than once can help them catch mistakes. Then allow time for students to proofread their drafts. Tell students to check for only one kind of mistake at a time. Circulate through the class to offer students assistance and support.

If time allows, invite partners to trade drafts and proofread each other's work. Remind students that a friend might catch mistakes that they have missed. If you choose this option, circulate among students to be sure that they are using appropriate peer-conferencing language. When students have finished, remind them to double-check their friend's suggestions.

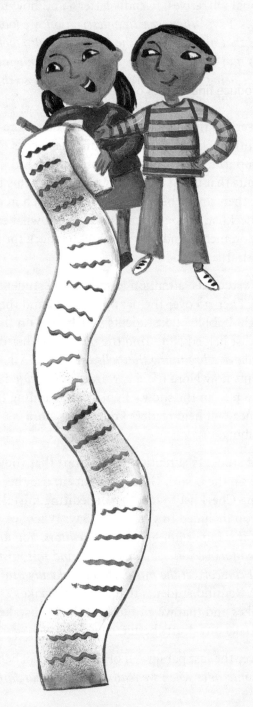

Publishing   Page 141

Page 108e provides a full-sized, reproducible copy of the student's Description scoring rubric. Students can use the rubric when assessing their own descriptions.

Page 108f provides a full-sized, reproducible copy of the Teacher's Scoring Rubric for descriptions. The rubric can be used when assessing students' understanding of the genre.

Students Should
- produce final copies of their descriptions

Ask a volunteer to read aloud the title. Remind students that publishing happens when a description is shared with an audience. Say: *Anyone who is interested in your topic can be the audience for your description.* Explain that their audience might be friends, family members, or people at school.

Go over the first paragraph. Direct students' attention to the picture of Nora publishing her description. Explain that Nora carefully copied her description and made sure that no new mistakes were added before she published it.

Model how to produce a clean copy. Then select a way to publish your piece. You might display your final copy on the board, or you might use one of the publishing ideas listed in the student book. Explain why you have chosen a particular publishing method.

Mail it to someone special.

Frame it.

Put it on a bulletin board.

Hang it up.

Read it to the class.

Make a book of People, Places, Things, and Events.

Go over the next paragraph. Allow time for students to make a final copy of their descriptions. Tell students to write slowly and carefully and to check each sentence to make sure they do not make any new mistakes.

When students have finished, read aloud the last paragraph and invite students to read the publishing suggestions. Guide students to choose a method of publishing. Allow time for students to create any additional items they need to publish their work, such as binding the descriptions in a book or reading them to the class.

When students have finished, distribute copies of the student's Description scoring rubric. Guide students to understand what each item means and how to apply it to their own writing. Then allow time for students to self-evaluate their descriptions.

Have students add their finished descriptions to their portfolios. Remind students that their portfolios will help them see what they have learned and how their writing has improved throughout the year.

CHAPTER 5

Contractions and Book Reports

Introducing the Chapter
Pages 142–143

Students Should
- have a basic understanding of book reports
- have a basic understanding of contractions

Reading the Model

Read aloud the quotation. Then have students recite the quotation along with you. Ask students to tell what the quotation is about. *(reading)* Explain that this quotation is from *I Can Read with My Eyes Shut!* by Dr. Seuss. Point out that the quotation is saying that reading is learning and that learning helps them do things and go places.

Invite volunteers to name their favorite books. For each response, ask questions to prompt that student to tell more about the book. *(Examples: Did you like the book? What was it about? Who was in the book? Where did the story take place?)* Then ask students if they told others about the books. Say: *We tell others about books we like. That way our friends and family can enjoy the same books we do.*

Point out the model book report on page 143. Read aloud the title and the name of the writer of the book report. Explain that Dermot Gibson wrote this book report about a book called *Get Well, Good Knight.* Read aloud the model book report. Explain that all book reports tell the title of the book and who wrote the book. Explain that book reports also tell who the book is about.

Ask students the following questions and help them locate the answers in the model: *Who wrote the book* Get Well, Good Knight? (Shelley Moore Thomas) *Who is the book about?* (a Good Knight and three little dragons) Explain that book reports

also tell what happens in the book. Reread the portion of the model that summarizes the plot of *Get Well, Good Knight.* Ask students if they would be interested in reading the book.

Remind students that people often write book reports because they liked a book. Explain that book reports usually tell what someone felt about the book. Ask students to tell how Dermot Gibson felt about *Get Well, Good Knight. (He liked the book.)* Point out that Dermot also explained why he liked the book.

Read aloud and point out in the model the sentence *The dragons don't like the soup at all!* Write on the board the contraction *don't.* Explain that this word is a short way of writing *do not.* Tell students that *don't* is a contraction. Write on the board *do not.* Say: *A contraction is a short way to write two words. Contractions help us write sentences that sound more like the way people talk. Contractions can make it seem as if you are talking to the reader.*

Contractions *and* More Contractions
Pages 144–145

Students Should
- recognize contractions

Teaching the Lesson

Write *I do not like to play* on the board. Invite volunteers to tell something they do not like to play, using the sentence starter. *(Example: I do not like to play soccer.)* Write on the board students' responses. Then write *I don't like to play.* Read aloud the new sentence starter and complete it by using items students have already listed. Underline *do not* and *don't*. Point out that *do not* and *don't* have the same meaning. Explain that *don't* is a short way of writing the two words *do not*. Tell students that *don't* is a contraction.

Go over the teaching on page 144. Point out the apostrophe in *don't* on the board. Have students compare *don't* and *do not* and tell what letter is missing. Explain that the apostrophe replaces the letter *o* in *not*. Have students practice spelling *don't* in the air, including the apostrophe. Tell students that there are many contractions.

Go over the activity directions on pages 144 and 145. When students have finished each activity, review their answers.

Extension

Invite volunteers to use in sentences the contractions from the activities on pages 144 and 145.

A contraction is a way
to write two words as one.
Replace a letter or letters
with an apostrophe,
and it's already done.

The Contraction *Don't* and
The Contraction *Didn't*   Pages 146–147

Students Should

- understand how to form the contractions *don't* and *didn't*

Teaching the Lesson

Review that *don't* is a contraction that is short for *do not*. Write on the board *do not*. Have students help you form *do not* into a contraction by asking them which letter you should erase and what you should use to replace it. Then invite volunteers to use *don't* in sentences.

Go over the teaching on page 146 and have students trace over the words in activity **A**. Then go over the directions for activity **B**. When students have finished the activity, review their answers.

Write on the board *didn't* and *did not*. Explain that *didn't* is the contraction of *did not*. Demonstrate how to use *didn't* in a sentence by providing an example sentence using *did not* and saying the sentence again with *didn't*.

Have students trace over the words in activity **A** on page 147. Then go over the directions for activity **B**. When students have finished the activity, review their answers.

Extension

Have the class recite the poem on page 146. Then have students write on one side of a sheet of paper *don't* and on the other side *didn't*. Select several students to stand at the front of the room holding their signs. Say a sentence that uses either *do not* or *did not* and have students hold up their signs to show the contraction that would fit in that sentence. Call on one student to repeat the sentence, substituting the contraction for *do not* or *did not*. Select another group to play the game.

The Contraction *Doesn't* and The Contraction *Couldn't*

Pages 148–149

Students Should

- understand how to form the contractions *doesn't* and *couldn't*

Teaching the Lesson

Invite volunteers to spell the contractions *don't* and *didn't*. Write on the board their responses. Point out that in the contractions *don't* and *didn't*, the letter *o* is dropped and is replaced by an apostrophe. Then write *does not* and *could not*. Explain that *does not* and *could not* can also be written as contractions. Invite volunteers to predict how *does not* and *could not* might be formed into contractions. Write on the board the contractions *doesn't* and *couldn't*.

Say funny sentences using *does not* that tell what people or things do not do. (*Examples: A kite does not eat spaghetti. A lion does not read books.*) Have students repeat the sentences, substituting *doesn't* for *does not*. Repeat with the contraction *couldn't*. (*Examples: A banana could not reach the moon. A volcano could not learn to count.*)

Go over the activity directions on pages 148 and 149. When students have finished each activity, review their answers.

Read aloud the Writer's Corner on page 149. Talk with students about some things they can do now that they could not do last year. Have students write their sentences. Invite volunteers to share their work.

Extension

Have students write funny sentences of their own, using *doesn't*. (*Examples: A balloon doesn't chew. A raindrop doesn't talk.*) Then have students draw a picture that shows what the sentence says does not happen. (*Examples: a balloon chewing, a raindrop talking*)

The Contraction *Isn't* and The Contraction *Aren't*

Pages 150–151

Students Should

- understand how to form the contractions *isn't* and *aren't*

Teaching the Lesson

Write *The ocean is not* on the board. Invite volunteers to complete the sentence starter. (*Examples: The ocean is not orange. The ocean is not dry.*) Write on the board students' responses. Then write *The ocean isn't*. Read aloud the new sentence starter and complete it by using items listed on the board. Underline *is not* and *isn't*. Point out that *is not* and *isn't* have the same meaning. Explain that *isn't* is another contraction formed with *not*.

Write on the board *The bear is not awake*. Have a volunteer erase *is not* and write in the contraction *isn't*. Then write *The bears are not awake*. Point out that by adding *-s* to *bear*, you have changed the noun so that it names more than one. Remind students that the verb *are* is used with nouns that name more than one. Underline *are not* and explain that there is a contraction for these two words. Write on the board *The bears aren't awake*. Point out that the *o* in *not* is dropped and is replaced with an apostrophe. Invite volunteers to say sentences that use *isn't* and *aren't*.

Go over the activity directions on pages 150 and 151. When students have finished each activity, review their answers.

Read aloud the Writer's Corner on page 150. Talk about what life on the moon might be like. Then have students write their sentences. Invite volunteers to share their work.

Extension

Have students write on one side of a sheet of paper *isn't* and on the other side *aren't*. Select several students to stand at the front of the room holding their signs. Say a sentence that uses either *is not* or *are not* and have students hold up their signs to show the contraction that would fit in that sentence. Call on one student from the group to repeat the sentence, substituting the contraction for *is not* or *are not*. Have students sit down. Select another group to play the game.

The Contraction *Hasn't* and The Contraction *Haven't*　Pages 152–153

Students Should

* understand how to form the contractions *hasn't* and *haven't*

Teaching the Lesson

Write on the board *The airplane has not left*. Underline *has not* and explain that it can be written as a contraction. Review how to form contractions with *not*. Then ask a volunteer to predict how *has not* might be formed into a contraction. Erase *has not* and write *hasn't*. Then write on the board *The airplanes have not left*. Point out that by adding *-s* to *airplane*, you have changed the noun so that it names more than one. Remind students that the verb *have* is used with nouns that name more than one. Underline *have not* and explain that it can be formed into a contraction. Erase *have not* from the sentence and write *hasn't*. Point out that the *o* in *not* is dropped and is replaced with an apostrophe. Have students practice spelling the contractions in the air. Say sentences that use *has not* and *have not* and have students say the sentences back with the contractions.

Go over the activity directions on pages 152 and 153. When students have finished each activity, review their answers.

Extension

Have students create contraction mobiles. Ask students to write a contraction on a strip of cardboard. Then have students write on separate strips the two words that make up the contraction. Help students attach string to hang the two words from the contraction. Display the contraction mobiles around the room.

The Contraction *Can't*　Page 154

Students Should

* understand how to form the contraction *can't*

Teaching the Lesson

Talk with students about things that they cannot do yet but will be able to do some day. (*Examples: driving a car, touching the top of a refrigerator, going to high school*) Write on the board *I can't do these things yet*. Underline *can't* and explain that it is another contraction with *not*. Tell students that *can't* is a special contraction because it shortens one word instead of two words. Write on the board *cannot* and demonstrate for students how to change *cannot* to *can't*. Have students practice using *cannot* in sentences by renaming some of the things they cannot do yet. (*Example: I cannot drive a car.*) Have another student repeat the sentence, substituting *can't* for *cannot*.

Go over the activity directions. When students have finished each activity, review their answers.

Read aloud the Writer's Corner. Have students write their sentences at the top of a sheet of paper. Then have students draw a picture of their animal doing the thing they said it could not do. (*Example: a picture of a lion dancing*)

Extension

Ask students questions and have them answer the questions with complete sentences that use *can* or *can't*. (*Examples: Can a monkey play baseball? A monkey can't play baseball. Can an airplane fly through the air? An airplane can fly through the air.*)

The Contraction *Wasn't* and The Contraction *Weren't*   Pages 155–156

Students Should
- understand how to form the contractions *wasn't* and *weren't*

Teaching the Lesson
Review contractions with *not* that students have studied. Remind students that contractions with *not* are formed by dropping the *o* in *not* and replacing it with an apostrophe. Then write on the board *The plant was not watered*. Underline *was not* and explain that these two words can be written as a contraction. Have students predict how the contraction will be spelled. Write on the board *The plant wasn't watered*. Underline *wasn't*.

Write on the board *The plants were not watered*. Remind students that the verb *were* is used with nouns that name more than one. Underline *were not* and tell students that there is a contraction for these two words. Write on the board *The plants weren't watered*. Invite volunteers to say sentences that use *wasn't* and *weren't*.

Go over the activity directions on pages 155 and 156. When students have finished each activity, review their answers.

Extension
Read aloud a story or poem that uses contractions formed with *not*. Have students raise their hands when they hear a contraction with *not*. Then invite a volunteer to repeat the contraction and tell what two words make up that contraction.

Contractions Review   Page 157

Students Should
- understand how to form contractions with *not*

Teaching the Lesson
Work with students to list on the board the steps for making contractions with *not*. (*Drop the letter* o, *and replace it with an apostrophe.*) Use flash cards to help students review contractions formed with *not*. Invite volunteers to say sentences that use the contractions.

Go over the activity directions. When students have finished the activity, review their answers.

Extension
Have available cards that each show one letter of the alphabet. Have five students come to the front of the room. Hand each student one letter needed to spell *do not*. Have students hold their cards and arrange themselves in a line to spell the two words. Be sure that students leave a space between the two words. Hand another card with an apostrophe to a seated student. Have the rest of the class tell the students with alphabet cards how to arrange themselves to spell out the contraction *don't*, including having one student sit down and having the student with the apostrophe replace him or her. Be sure students close the space between the two words. Repeat with other contractions and groups of students.

The Contraction *I'm* and The Contraction *I'll*   Pages 158–159

Students Should
- understand how to form the contractions *I'm* and *I'll*

Teaching the Lesson
Review that a contraction is a short way to write two words. Write on the board examples of contractions

with *not* that students have studied. Point out that these contractions are all made with *not* and another word. Tell students that there are other contractions besides those that are made with *not*.

Write on the board *I am*. Invite volunteers to tell about themselves, using the sentence starter. Write on the board *I'm*. Tell students that *I'm* is the contraction for *I am*. Ask the same volunteers to repeat their sentences, substituting *I'm* for *I am*. Invite volunteers to explain what changes are made to make *I am* into the contraction *I'm*.

Go over the teaching on page 158 and have students trace over the words in activity **A**. Then go over the directions for activity **B**. When students have finished the activity, review their answers.

Explain that another contraction can be made from *I* and *will*. Write on the board *I will call you later*. Invite a volunteer to read aloud the sentence. Underline *I will* and write underneath the first sentence *I'll call you later*. Invite volunteers to tell what letters have been dropped. Remind students that an apostrophe replaces the dropped letters.

Go over the teaching on page 159 and have students trace over the words in activity **A**. Then go over the directions for activity **B**. When students have finished the activity, review their answers.

Read aloud the Writer's Corner on page 159. Talk with students about things they typically do on weekends. Then have students write their sentences. Invite volunteers to pantomime their sentences. Have the rest of the class guess what the activity might be. Ask the pantomiming student to read aloud his or her sentence to reveal the answer.

Extension

Invite a volunteer to be interviewed in front of the class. Have the student respond as himself or herself, as a celebrity, or as a fictional character. Ask the volunteer questions to be answered with sentences beginning with *I'm*. Then ask questions about future plans to be answered with sentences beginning with *I'll*. Repeat with other volunteers. Point out that *I'm* and *I'll* are contractions often used in speech.

The Contraction *It's* and The Contractions *He's* and *She's*   Pages 160–161

Students Should

- understand how to form the contractions *it's*, *he's*, and *she's*

Teaching the Lesson

Hold up common objects and ask students what each one is. Have students answer with complete sentences, using *it is*. (Examples: *It is a book. It is a pencil.*) Write on the board students' responses. Underline *It is* and tell students that these words can be written as a contraction. Write *it's* and point out how the contraction is formed. Continue holding up common objects and asking students to name them, using the contraction *it's*. (Examples: *It's a flower. It's a lunch bag.*)

Go over the teaching on page 160. Remind students that *it* is a pronoun used to talk about things. Then ask volunteers to tell what pronouns are used for a boy and a girl. *(he, she)* Write on the board the following sentences: *He is a nice boy. She is a nice girl.* Underline *He is* and *She is*. Tell students that these words can form contractions. Invite volunteers to predict what contractions can be formed from *he is* and *she is*. Write on the board the following sentences: *He's a nice boy. She's a nice girl.*

Go over the activity directions on pages 160 and 161. When students have finished each activity, review their answers.

Extension

Play a guessing game with students in which you give them clues about a noun you are thinking of. Include nouns that name things and nouns that name people. After each clue, allow students to write a sentence that tells what the noun might be. Have students begin each sentence with *it's*, *he's*, or *she's*. (Examples: *It's a stapler. He's a writer.*) Invite volunteers to read aloud their answers after each clue.

The Contractions
We're and *They're*   **Page 162**

Students Should

- understand how to form the contractions *we're* and *they're*

Teaching the Lesson

Review how to form the contractions *it's, he's,* and *she's.* Point out that these contractions tell about one. Review that the pronouns *we* and *they* tell about more than one. Remind students that *we* and *they* use the verb *are.* Write on the board the following sentences: *We are happy to be here. They are happy to be here.* Underline *We are* and *They are.* Tell students that these words can form contractions. Invite volunteers to predict what contractions can be formed from *we are* and *they are.* Write on the board the following sentences: *We're happy to be here. They're happy to be here.*

Go over the teaching. Say sentences that begin with *We are* or *They are* and have students repeat the sentences, substituting *we're* for *we are* and *they're* for *they are.*

Go over the activity directions. When students have finished each activity, review their answers.

Extension

Draw a tick-tack-toe grid on the board. Write in each square of the grid one of the following: *I am, I will, it is, he is, she is, we are, they are, were not,* and *was not.* Ask the class to form two teams, Xs and Os. Have the teams play a game of tick-tack-toe. Have one team choose a square. To claim a square, the team must say the contraction formed, spell it, and use it in a sentence. Continue until one team has claimed three squares that form a line horizontally, vertically, or diagonally.

Contractions Review   **Page 163**

Students Should

- understand how to form contractions with being verbs
- understand how to form the contraction *I'll*

Teaching the Lesson

Use flash cards to help students review the contractions *I'm, I'll, it's, he's, she's, we're,* and *they're.* Invite volunteers to say sentences that use the contractions.

Go over the activity directions. When students have finished the activity, review their answers.

Extension

Write on note cards contractions students have studied in this chapter. Write on other note cards words that make up the contractions. Have small groups use the note cards to play concentration.

Show What You Know   **Pages 164–165**

Students Should

- identify and use contractions correctly

Teaching the Lesson

Explain the directions for each activity. Assist students if necessary. When students have finished each activity, review their answers. Show What You Know may be used as a review or a test.

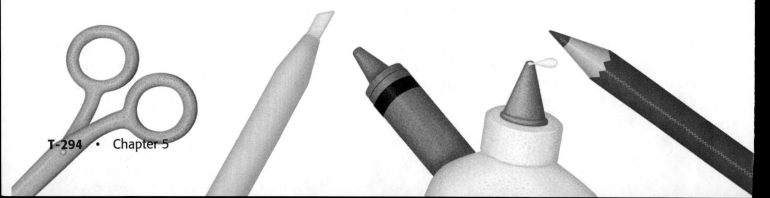

Get Ready to Write

What Is a Book Report? Page 166

Students Should

- identify the elements and characteristics of a book report
- understand the purpose of writing a book report

Teaching the Lesson

Invite volunteers to name some of their favorite books. Ask students to describe the characters in those books and to explain what the characters did. Encourage students to tell why the books are their favorites. Invite students to describe times that they talked about a book with a friend or family member. Explain that when they tell someone about the characters and what happens in a book, they are giving a book report. Then ask a volunteer to read aloud the title. Say: *Writing a book report is a way of telling others about a book. It's a way to help other people decide if they want to read the book.*

Have students turn back to the book report on page 143. Ask students to tell what the title of the book is. *(Get Well, Good Knight)* Remind students that the title of a book in a book report is underlined. Review whom the book is about. *(a Good Knight and the three little dragons he meets)* Ask students whether the writer liked the book and why. *(The writer liked the book because the Good Knight is very funny and helpful.)* Talk about whether this book report makes students want to read the book.

Go over the first paragraph on page 166. Emphasize that the writer of the model book report on page 143 told what the book is about. He also told why he liked the book. Tell students that when they write their own book reports, they will tell about books and share how they feel about the books.

Go over the next paragraph. Explain that when writing a book report, the title of a book is always underlined. To emphasize this concept, write on the board the title of a book and underline it.

Read aloud the next paragraph. Point out that *author* is another word for *writer*. Hold up a few books and point out the authors. Tell students that all books have authors.

Go over the next paragraph. Tell students that characters are the people or things that a book is about. Ask students to name characters in books they have read. Emphasize that characters aren't always people. Encourage students to talk about characters that are animals or objects, as well as characters that are people.

Go over the model book report on page 166. Guide students to complete the activity as a class. Invite students to explain their answers.

Extension

Obtain a copy of *Anatole* by Eve Titus. Read aloud the book and allow students to look over the cover and illustrations. Then have students draw pictures about what the character does in the book. Talk with students about whether they agree with the opinion of the writer of the book report on page 166. Invite volunteers to share their work.

Parts of a Book Report

Students Should

identify the parts of a book report

Teaching the Lesson

Invite students to tell what a book report is. *(a way of telling others about a book; a way to help other people decide if they want to read the book)* Explain that a book report should name the book's title, author, and characters, and should tell how the writer feels about the book.

Have a volunteer read aloud the title. Then go over the first two paragraphs. Direct students' attention to the model book report on page 166. Invite volunteers to tell where the book's title and author are named. *(in the first sentence)* Have students tell where they first read about the character. *(in the second sentence)* Say: *The book's title, author, and main character are named right away. When we write the beginning of a book report, these are the first things we write about.*

Go over the next paragraph. Tell students that what happens in a story can include what the characters do and what the characters say. Review the middle of the book report on page 166. *(Anatole has to find food to feed his family. He gets an unusual job.)* Emphasize that students should tell what happens in a book in the middle of their book reports.

Go over the last paragraph. Ask students to tell whether the writer of the book report on page 166 liked the book. *(yes)* Say: *At the end of a book report, you tell whether you liked the book. You also tell why you liked it.* Ask students to identify why the writer liked the book. *(It shows how smart a mouse can be.)*

Go over the first activity. Guide students to complete the activity as a class. Then have students complete the second activity independently. When students have finished, invite volunteers to share their answers with the class.

Extension

Ask students to choose their favorite book and to draw on separate sheets of paper three important things that happen in it. Have students put the events in the order in which they happened. Then have them write one sentence about each picture, telling who the characters are and what is happening in the pictures. Have students present their pictures to the class and tell why they liked the book.

Complete a Book Report
Page 168

Students Should
* understand how to write a complete book report

Teaching the Lesson

Review the parts of a book report. Ask students to explain what each part of a book report should tell. *(The beginning tells the title, author, and characters. The middle tells what happens in the book. The ending tells how the writer feels about the book.)* Talk about some books that you have read in class. Ask students to say the titles, who the characters are, and whether students liked the books. Tell students the names of the authors.

Ask a volunteer to read aloud the title. Emphasize that a book report should have all its parts so that readers can understand what a book is about and whether the writer liked it. Explain that if parts of the book report are missing, readers might become confused or they might not believe what the writer says. Point out that knowing the title and author allows a reader to find the book if he or she decides to read it.

Go over the activity directions. Guide students to complete the first activity as a class. Help students understand why the missing information is important to the book report. Then read aloud the second activity paragraph. Allow time for students to complete the activity independently. Invite volunteers to share their answers with the class.

Extension

Help students make lists of books they have read. Then allow time for students to draw a smiling face by each title if they liked the book and a frowning face by each title if they did not like the book. When students have finished, invite volunteers to share their lists with the class. Ask students to choose from their lists one book and say one reason why they liked or disliked it.

Plan a Book Report
Page 169

Students Should
* understand how to plan a book report

Teaching the Lesson

Review the parts of a book report. Remind students that a book report should have all its parts so that readers do not become confused. Emphasize the importance of telling how they feel about a book and saying why they feel that way.

Ask a volunteer to read aloud the title. Tell students that when they write a book report, they should think about and plan their ideas. Direct students' attention to the chart. Point out that using a chart can help them organize their ideas and can help them remember all the important parts of the book they are writing about.

Go over the directions and have students complete this activity independently. Encourage students to write or to draw in the spaces for Characters and What happens. When students have finished, invite them to share their charts with the class.

Extension

Invite volunteers to name books that you have read with the class. Write their responses on the board. Help students to name the author of each book. Then have students choose a book and draw pictures for the beginning, the middle, and the ending of a book report. Encourage students to include in their ending a picture of themselves with a speech balloon that tells their opinion of the book. When students have finished, invite them to share their work with the class.

Writer's Workshop

Prewriting— Pick a Topic   Page 170

Students Should

- brainstorm topics for a book report
- identi_y_ appropriate topics for their book reports

Invite v_o_lunteers to name books they have read indepe_n_dently, as well as those you have read togeth_e_r in class. Ask students to tell what happens in ea_c_h book and to say who the main characters are. _A_sk students to explain whether they liked the boo_k_s. Then say: *When we write book reports, we ha_ve_ to choose a book to write about. All the books th_at_ we have talked about would make good topics for a_ b_ook report.*

_A_sk a volunteer to read aloud the title. Then go _o_ver the first paragraph and Dermot's list. Point _o_ut that Dermot brainstormed a lot of books that he had read. Explain that each book might be a good topic for a book report. Ask a volunteer which book Dermot chose and why he chose it. (*Get Well, Good Knight; Dermot thinks his classmates would enjoy hearing about it.*) Say: *When we write a book report, we tell the title and author of a book, what happens in it, and whether we liked it. When we do prewriting for book reports, we think about books we have read and how we felt about them. Then we decide which books to write about.*

Model on the board brainstorming a list of books. Remember to underline each book title. Explain why you think each title might be a good topic for your book report. Then choose one topic by circling it. Choose a book with which students are familiar. It may be helpful later in the Writer's Workshop when you decide which parts of the story you choose to include in your book report. Talk to students about why you have chosen the book and emphasize why it will make a good topic for your book report.

Go over the last paragraph. Then allow time for students to brainstorm their lists of book titles. As students work, circulate among them to be sure that they are listing appropriate book titles. Then encourage students to pick the book that interests them the most.

Prewriting—Plan Your Book Report   Page 171

Students Should

- plan their book reports

Review the importance of planning a book report. (*to make sure the book report has all its parts; to organize ideas*) Talk about ways students have planned their previous writing assignments. (*drawing pictures, making charts*) Explain that planning their book report means writing and organizing ideas in a way that makes sense.

Have a volunteer read aloud the title. Remind students that planning a book report means thinking about what they should include in their first draft. Emphasize that the beginning should name the title of the book, the author, and the characters; the middle should tell what happens; and the ending should tell how the writer feels about the book.

Go over the first paragraph and direct students' attention to the model chart. Invite students to tell the title of the book, the author, and the characters. (*Get Well, Good Knight; Shelley Moore Thomas; the Good Knight, three little dragons*) Then go over the rest of the chart. Tell students that Dermot uses the chart to help him think about and organize what he wants to write in each part of his book report.

Model on the board how to organize information for a book report. Begin by writing a chart for your own book report. Emphasize that the title of the book is underlined. As you complete the What happens section, point out which parts of the story you want to include in your book report. Tell students that you do not want to tell everything that happened, just a few important things. Explain that they should not give away the ending of the book. In the How I feel about this book section, point out why you liked the book.

Go over the rest of the page. Allow time for students to draw their charts and organize their information in their notebooks. As students work, help them make sure that they have written their titles correctly and have included everything their charts require. Emphasize the importance of including a reason why they feel the way they do about their book.

Drafting   Page 172

Students Should
- use prewriting notes to write their first drafts

Invite a volunteer to read aloud the title. Talk with students about their experiences writing drafts for previous writing assignments. Remind students that writing a first draft is their first opportunity to put their ideas into sentences. Emphasize that they will have time to make changes later. Say: *Now we will write our drafts. We will put our ideas from prewriting on paper. Once we see all the ideas together, we can look for places to make the draft better.*

Go over the first paragraph and direct students' attention to Dermot's draft. Talk about how each part of the draft relates to the book report chart that Dermot made during prewriting. *(Examples: The sentences that tell what happens come from the section What happens, and how Dermot feels comes from the section How I feel about this book.)*

Model for students how to use your prewriting notes to write the first draft of your book report. Be sure to include in your draft at least one mistake from the Editing Checklist on page 173 and one mistake from the Proofreading Checklist on page 174. Save your draft for use during editing.

Go over the rest of the page. Allow time for students to complete their drafts. As students work, circulate among them to provide support. Remind students to

include in their drafts all the parts of a book report. Encourage students to include titles for their book reports.

Editing   Page 173

Students Should
- edit their book reports

Have a volunteer read aloud the title. Talk with students about what happened when they edited previous writing assignments. Ask students to tell how their writing improved after editing. Say: *When we edit book reports, we make sure that all the parts are included. We make sure that we tell why we feel the way we do about the book. We also look for places where readers might get confused, and we fix those problems.*

Go over the first two paragraphs and the Editing Checklist. Pause after each checklist item to help students understand what each question means and how they might check for that item in their drafts.

Go over the next paragraph and the thought bubble. Ask students which item on the checklist helped Dermot find the mistake in his draft. *(Do I have a beginning that tells the title, author, and characters?)* Ask students how Dermot fixed his draft. *(He added the sentence* It's about a Good Knight and three little dragons.*)* Talk about why the sentence Dermot added makes his book report better. *(It tells who the characters are so that the reader isn't confused.)*

Direct students' attention to your book report. Guide students to use the Editing Checklist to edit your draft. Help them find the mistake in your draft. Remind students that all writers make mistakes, and that all writers edit their work to make it better.

Go over the last paragraph of this section. Then allow time for students to edit their drafts. Circulate among students to be sure that they are giving appropriate consideration to each item on the checklist. Check students' justifications for making or not making changes to their work. For those students who have grasped the concept and value of editing, check to be sure that they are not making arbitrary changes. Guide these students to understand which editing changes they mark are appropriate.

If students read each other's drafts, remind them of the proper language and behavior for peer-editing sessions. Emphasize that they should double-check the mistakes their friend finds. Guide students to ask questions when they are unsure of a marked change. Remind them they can also ask a teacher, a parent, or another friend for help.

Revising   Page 173

Students Should

- use editing changes to revise their drafts

Ask a volunteer to read aloud the title. Say: *When we revise our writing, we make changes so that the writing is better and less confusing.* Remind students that some changes are our ideas, while some might come from a friend or a teacher.

Go over the first paragraph. Demonstrate with your draft how you will correct the mistake that the class found during editing. Rewrite your draft on the board, including the change you made. Do not forget to include your mistake from the Proofreading Checklist on page 174. Remind students that a new copy of the draft can help them see any other mistakes that might be in the book report. Remind students that although the book report is better, there are still ways to improve it.

Go over the last paragraph. Allow time for students to revise their drafts. As they work, circulate among students to be sure that they are correctly writing their editing changes on their drafts. Emphasize the importance of not adding any new mistakes into the revised draft.

Proofreading   Page 174

Students Should

- proofread their revised drafts

Read aloud the title. Say: *We do proofreading to make sure that words are spelled correctly and that we have written sentences correctly. Proofreading is important because book reports that have spelling mistakes or sentences that are wrong can be confusing for the reader.*

Go over the first paragraph and the Proofreading Checklist. Help students understand what each checklist item means and how they can check for it in their drafts.

Go over the partial student model and the next paragraph. Ask students what proofreading mistake Dermot found and which question helped him find the mistake. *(He misspelled the contraction* don't; *Are contractions used correctly?)* Talk about how the proofreading marks function within the draft and how Dermot used it to correct his mistake.

Model on the board proofreading your revised draft, using the Proofreading Checklist. Guide students to use the checklist and to help you find the proofreading mistake in your book report. Ask students how the mistake might be corrected and have a volunteer mark the correction in your draft.

Go over the rest of the page. Remind students to put an *X* next to each checklist question to which they can answer yes. Then allow time for students to proofread their drafts. Remind students to check for only one kind of mistake at a time. As students work, circulate among them to offer guidance and support. Remind students to use reference materials such as a picture dictionary, a word wall, and the student book to check and correct mistakes.

If time allows, have partners trade drafts and proofread each other's work. Remind students that a friend might catch mistakes that they have missed. If you choose this option, circulate among students to be sure that they are using appropriate peer-conferencing language. When students have finished, remind them to double-check their friend's suggestions. Encourage students to ask a parent, teacher, or other friend for help if they are unsure whether a marked change is correct.

Publishing   Page 175

Page 142e provides a full-sized, reproducible copy of the student's Book Report scoring rubric. Students can use the rubric when assessing their own book reports.

Page 142f provides a full-sized, reproducible copy of the Teacher's Scoring Rubric for book reports. The rubric can be used when assessing students' understanding of the genre.

Students Should
- produce final copies of their book reports

Invite a volunteer to read aloud the title. Review with students how they published previous writing assignments. Say: *Publishing is the time that writers share their work with an audience. An audience is anyone who wants to read the book report.* Remind students that the audience can be anyone interested in learning about the book.

Go over the first paragraph. Tell students that because Dermot wants people to read the book he wrote about, he takes special care when publishing his book report. Emphasize that Dermot recopied his book report carefully to make sure that no new mistakes were added.

Model for students how to produce a final copy. You might write your final copy on the board, or you might use one of the publishing ideas listed in the student book. As you work, talk with students about who the audience for your book report will be. Encourage students to think of ways to publish that the audience will find interesting. Tell students to practice using their best handwriting when they publish their book reports.

Go over the rest of the page. Talk with students about how their book reports should be published. Then allow time for students to make a final copy of their book reports. Remind students to write slowly and carefully, and to check each sentence to make sure they do not make any new mistakes. Then allow time for students to create artwork to accompany their book reports.

When students have finished, distribute copies of the student's Book Report scoring rubric. Guide students to understand what each item means and how to apply it to their own writing. Then allow time for students to self-evaluate their book reports.

Remind students to keep a copy of their final book reports in their portfolios. Point out that having a portfolio will help them keep track of the improvements they are making in their writing throughout the year.

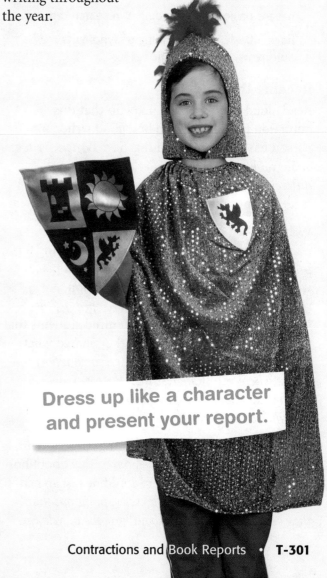

Dress up like a character and present your report.

CHAPTER 6

Word Study and Research Reports

Chapter 7 of the student book provides lessons and activities that teach students how to use reference tools. You may find it helpful to teach Chapter 7 prior to or concurrently with Chapter 6 in order to prepare students to write their research reports.

Introducing the Chapter   Pages 176–177

Students Should

- have a basic understanding of research reports
- have a basic understanding of synonyms, antonyms, and homophones

Reading the Model

Read aloud the quotation. Explain that this quotation is saying that to be a good writer, a person has to practice writing. Say: *Writers write about all kinds of things. They write for many different reasons.* Review the genres of writing students have practiced throughout the school year.

Write on the board *research report*. Underline *research* and explain that research is searching for information about something. Talk about places where people might look for information. *(Examples: the library, books, encyclopedias, the Internet)* Underline *report* and remind students that when they wrote book reports, they shared what they knew about a book. Say: *A research report is a report where you share research. First you look for information about a topic. Then you share the information with readers.*

Invite students to name things that interest them. Write their responses on the board. Talk about how the things that interest them could be researched. *(Example: If students said bicycles, point out that they could find out more about how the bicycle was*

invented or about popular bicycle races throughout the world.) Emphasize that research reports are about something real. Explain that writers often research because they find something interesting and they want to learn more about it. Point out to students that learning about things they like will make research fun.

Read aloud the model research report on page 177. Then invite a volunteer to tell what this writer researched and wrote about. *(ladybugs)* Tell students that ladybugs are the topic of this research report. Ask students which sentence tells the topic of the research report. *(the first sentence)* Explain that the beginning of a research report includes a topic sentence that tells what the report is about.

Read aloud the second sentence. Point out that this sentence tells a fact. Explain that a fact is information that is true. Invite volunteers to tell other facts they learned from the research report. Say: *When you do research, you look for facts. You collect all your facts in your notes. Then you share your facts in your report.*

Write on the board the sentence *Aphids are bugs that can harm crops.* Underline the word *harm.* Invite volunteers to name another word they could use that has almost the same meaning as *harm.* *(hurt)* Write below the first sentence *Aphids are bugs that can hurt crops.* Point out that the sentences have almost the same meaning because the words *harm* and *hurt* have almost the same meaning. Say: *These words mean almost the same thing. Words that mean almost the same thing are called synonyms.*

Ask students to name a word that means the opposite of *harm.* *(help)* Write on the board *Aphids are bugs that can help crops.* Point out that this sentence means the opposite of the first sentence because *harm* and *help* have opposite meanings. Draw a line from *help* to *harm*. Say: *This word means the opposite of* harm. *Words with opposite meanings are called antonyms.*

Read aloud the last sentence of the model. Then write on the board *The next time you sea a ladybug, remember that it is a useful bug.* Read the sentence aloud and guide students to find the mistake. *(sea should be* see*)* Erase *sea* and write *see*. Talk about what the words *sea* and *see* mean. Point out that the sentence sounds the same with the incorrect word. Say: *These words sound the same. Words that sound the same but have different meanings and spellings are called homophones.*

Synonyms   Page 178

Students Should
- understand what a synonym is

Teaching the Lesson
Pantomime for students the word pairs *big-large, sad-unhappy, happy-glad, small-little,* and *jog-run.* For each pantomime invite volunteers to guess words that name what you are pantomiming. List on the board in separate columns students' responses to each pantomime. If students name only one word for the pantomime, talk about other words they might have used.

Demonstrate for students that the words in each column have almost the same meaning by showing that you can pantomime each set of words the same way. Write on the board above each column *synonyms.* Explain that the words in each column are synonyms. Tell students that synonyms are words that have almost the same meaning.

Go over the teaching. Then have two volunteers read aloud the examples. Point out that *cold* and *chilly* are synonyms because they mean almost the same thing. Invite volunteers to say their own sentences with *cold* and *chilly.*

Go over the activity directions. When students have finished the activity, review their answers.

Extension
Write on the board sentences that use the synonym pairs *big-large, sad-unhappy, happy-glad, small-little,* and *jog-run. (Examples: Nancy was sad about leaving. I felt unhappy when she left. My dad runs every day. He jogs in the park.)* Invite volunteers to circle the synonyms in each pair.

More Synonyms *and* Working with Synonyms   Pages 179–180

Students Should
- recognize synonyms

Teaching the Lesson
Use the teaching on page 179 to review that synonyms are words that have almost the same meaning. Review synonym pairs students have learned. Then write on the board *The big airplane had big wings.* Point out that *big* is used twice in the sentence and that the sentence might be improved with a synonym. Write on the board *The big airplane had large wings.* Guide students to understand how the sentence was improved with a synonym. Write on the board *My friend Paul has a friend named Xena.* Explain that *pal* is a synonym for *friend.* Invite a volunteer to replace one instance of *friend* in the sentence on the board with *pal.* Explain that many words have synonyms.

Go over the activity directions on pages 179 and 180. When students have finished each activity, review their answers.

Extension
Have students recite the poem on page 179. Help them decide on a pantomime for each pair of synonyms in the poem. *(Example: pumping arms as if running for* quick *and* fast*)* Then have students recite the poem again, pantomiming each word in each synonym pair as they say it. Invite volunteers to say sentences using the synonyms in the poem.

Synonyms Review
and
More
Synonyms Review Pages 181–182

Students Should
- identify synonyms

Teaching the Lesson
Use flash cards to review the synonyms that students have studied. Show students one word of a synonym pair and invite the class to name its synonym. Write students' responses on the board. Accept other correct synonyms students may suggest. Then invite volunteers to use the words on the board in sentences.

Go over the activity directions on pages 181 and 182. When students have finished each activity, review their answers.

Read aloud the Writer's Corner on page 181. Talk with students about things they like to do during the summer to cool off. Have students draw pictures of those activities. Then have students write their sentences under the pictures.

Extension
Students may benefit from learning other synonyms. Introduce new synonym pairs by writing words in two columns. Have volunteers draw a line from one word in the left column to its synonym in the right column.

Antonyms Page 183

Students Should
- understand what an antonym is

Teaching the Lesson
Use classroom objects to illustrate some antonyms. *(hard-soft, big-little)* Then pantomime *over-under* and *happy-sad*. Explain that these words are opposites. Write on the board *fast, slow, hot,* and *cold*. Circle *fast* and *slow*. Invite pairs of volunteers to pantomime these words. Repeat with *hot* and *cold*. Explain that words that have opposite meanings are called antonyms. Write *antonyms* over each pair of circled words.

Go over the teaching and examples. Reinforce the idea of opposite meanings by having volunteers name things that are hard and things that are soft.

Go over the activity directions. When students have finished the activity, review their answers.

Extension
Assign partners pairs of antonyms. Have students draw a picture for each word. Then invite partners to present their pictures to the class. Have students describe their pictures without using the antonyms. Then have the class guess the antonyms.

Synonyms, synonyms, we know quite a few.
Quick and *fast, shout* and *yell, glad* and *happy* too.
Synonyms, synonyms, how our list will grow.
Words that we call synonyms are jolly friends to know.

More Antonyms *and* Working with Antonyms
Pages 184–185

Students Should
- recognize antonyms

Teaching the Lesson
Use the teaching on page 184 to review that antonyms are words that have opposite meanings. Write on the board *big, happy, cold, over,* and *fast.* Invite volunteers to name antonyms for each word. Then write on the board *go, down, out, short,* and *off.* Explain that each of these words has an antonym. Say each word and invite volunteers to name a word that means the opposite.

Go over the activity directions on pages 184 and 185. When students have finished each activity, review their answers.

Extension
Read aloud a story with which students are familiar. As you read, replace some words with their antonyms. Have students say *antonym* when they hear a word that does not belong. Write that word on the board and have a volunteer name an antonym of that word. Then have students recite the poem on page 184.

Antonyms Review *and* More Antonyms Review
Pages 186–187

Students Should
- identify antonyms

Teaching the Lesson
Review that antonyms are words that have opposite meanings. Write on the board in one column *hot, little, down, in, sad, on, under, fast, go,* and *tall.* In a second column write *out, off, slow, short, big, cold, happy, over, stop,* and *up.* Invite volunteers to draw a line from a word in the first column to its antonym in the second column. After each volunteer identifies an antonym pair, invite other volunteers to use each word in a sentence.

Go over the activity directions on pages 186 and 187. When students have finished each activity, review their answers.

Read aloud the Writer's Corner on page 186. Brainstorm on the board a list of things that can be open or shut. Then allow time for students to write their sentences.

Extension
Students may benefit from learning other antonyms. Introduce new antonym pairs by writing words in two columns. Have volunteers draw a line from one word in the left column to its antonym in the right column.

> Antonyms, antonyms, we know quite a few.
> *In* and *out, up* and *down, sad* and *happy* too.
> Antonyms, antonyms, how our list will grow.
> Words that we call antonyms are jolly friends to know.

Homophones *and* More Homophones   Pages 188–189

Students Should
- understand what a homophone is
- recognize common homophones

Teaching the Lesson
Write on the board the words *meet* and *meat*. Talk about what each word means. Then write the following sentences: *Will you meet me tomorrow? Dad put meat on the grill.* Invite volunteers to read aloud the sentences. Point out that the words *meet* and *meat* sound the same. Write on the board *homophones*. Explain that words that sound the same but have different meanings and spellings are called homophones.

Go over the teaching on page 188. Invite a volunteer to read aloud the example and identify the homophones in the sentence. Invite other volunteers to tell what each word means. Erase *meet* and *meat* from the sentences and rewrite them in the wrong sentences. Read the sentences aloud and point out that the sentences sound the same but that they are not written correctly.

Go over the activity directions on pages 188 and 189. When students have finished each activity, review their answers.

Extension
Have eight students come to the front of the room. Say a sentence that uses one of the homophones listed on pages 188 and 189. Then have the first student spell the homophone. If he or she is correct, allow that student to proceed to the next round. If he or she is incorrect, have that student return to his or her seat. Repeat with each student in line, using a different homophone from the list in each sentence. Continue by using the same homophones in new sentences until one student is left. Repeat with a new group of volunteers.

The Homophones *Meat-Meet* and *Blew-Blue and* The Homophones *No-Know* and *Ate-Eight*   Pages 190–191

Students Should
- distinguish between the homophones *meat-meet, blew-blue, no-know,* and *ate-eight*

Teaching the Lesson
Write on the board the following sentences. *Does your dog eat meet? Let's meat my friend.* Read the sentences aloud and explain that there is something wrong with each sentence. Invite a volunteer to correct each sentence. Review that the words *meat* and *meet* are called homophones because they sound the same but are spelled differently and have different meanings. Write on the board the words *blue* and *blew*. Read aloud the words and point out that they are homophones. Talk about what each word means and invite volunteers to use each word in a sentence. Repeat with the homophones *no-know* and *ate-eight*.

Go over the activity directions on pages 190 and 191. When students have finished each activity, review their answers.

Extension
Have students recite the poem on page 190. Then help students come up with a pantomime for each of the homophones in the second line. Have students recite the poem again, pantomiming the homophones as they say them.

The Homophones *Sale-Sail* and *One-Won*
and
The Homophones *Dear-Deer* and *Hear-Here*   Pages 192–193

Students Should

- distinguish between the homophones *sale-sail, one-won, dear-deer,* and *hear-here*

Teaching the Lesson

Review that homophones are words that sound the same but are spelled differently and have different meanings. Then write the following sentences on the board: *There is a sale on buttons. The boats sail across the sea. One person can go. Who won the contest?* Help students find the homophones in the sentences. Talk about what each word means. Repeat with the following sentences: *My grandma is a dear person. The deer ate corn from my hand. Do you hear something? Is there a fly in here?*

Go over the activity directions on pages 192 and 193. When students have finished each activity, review their answers.

Read aloud the Writer's Corner on page 192. Invite volunteers to tell what the words *night* and *knight* mean. Allow time for students to write their sentences. Invite volunteers to share their work with the class.

Extension

Write on the board the following words: *knight, night, sale, sail, one, won, dear, deer, hear,* and *here.* Have small groups work together to write a story about a knight. Challenge students to use as many of the words on the board as they can. When students have finished, invite volunteers to read aloud their stories.

The Homophones *See-Sea* and *To-Two-Too*
and
Homophones Review   Pages 194–195

Students Should

- distinguish between the homophones *see-sea* and *to-two-too*

- identify homophones

Teaching the Lesson

Review that homophones are words that sound the same but are spelled differently and have different meanings. Use flash cards to review the homophones that students have studied. Then write on the board *The sailor went to sea to see a whale.* Invite a volunteer to underline the homophones in the sentence. Have other volunteers explain what each word means. Write on the board the words *to, two,* and *too.* Explain these three words are all homophones that writers sometimes write incorrectly. Talk about what each word means. Have volunteers use each word in a sentence.

Homophones, homophones, we know quite a few.
Dear and *deer, here* and *hear, to* and *two* and *too.*
Homophones, homophones, how our list will grow.
Words that we call homophones are jolly friends to know.

Go over the activity directions on pages 194 and 195. When students have finished each activity, review their answers.

Extension

Have students fold a sheet of paper into quarters and then unfold it. Ask students to select two sets of homophones. Have them draw a picture in each quarter to illustrate each homophone's meaning and write the appropriate homophone underneath the picture. Invite volunteers to share their work with the class.

Show What You Know
Pages 196–197

Students Should
- identify synonyms and antonyms
- distinguish between homophones

Teaching the Lesson

Explain the directions for each activity. Assist students if necessary. When students have finished each activity, review their answers. Show What You Know may be used as a review or a test.

Get Ready to Write

What Is a Research Report?   Page 198

Chapter 7 of the student book provides lessons and activities that teach students how to use reference tools. You may find it helpful to teach Chapter 7 prior to or concurrently with Chapter 6 in order to prepare students to write their research reports.

Students Should
- identify the elements and characteristics of a research report
- understand the purpose of writing a research report

Teaching the Lesson

Talk with students about wild animals that interest them. Invite students to explain what the animal looks like, where it lives, and what it eats. Say: *These animals would all be good topics for a research report. A research report gives information about something. We write research reports to learn about something that we are interested in. Research reports can be about almost anything.*

Ask a volunteer to read aloud the title. Then go over the first paragraph. Talk about research-report topics. Emphasize that the topic of a research report can be a person, a place, a thing, or an event. Invite students to name possible research-report topics. List their responses on the board. *(Examples: Abraham Lincoln, New York City, squirrels, Halloween)* Point out that any of these might make good research-report topics.

Have students turn back to the research report on page 177. Have students identify the topic of the report. *(ladybugs)* Ask students what the report says that ladybugs eat. *(aphids)* Explain that this sentence tells information about ladybugs. Invite a volunteer to find in the report the sentence that tells what color ladybugs are. *(Ladybugs are red with black spots.)* Explain that telling information is a part of writing a research report.

Go over the activity directions and the model research report. Guide students to answer the questions as a class. Talk with students about what they learned about the tyrannosaurus from reading this research report.

Extension

Distribute to small groups a variety of research materials about the tyrannosaurus. Have students work together to find one additional piece of information about the tyrannosaurus. When students have finished, invite each group to share their information with the class. Talk with students about how the information might be added to the research report on page 198.

Choosing a Topic   Page 199

Students Should

- identify narrow topics for a research report

Teaching the Lesson

Talk with students about what they know about research reports. *(They tell about something real. They give information about a topic.)* Then talk about topics that might make good research reports.

Ask a volunteer to read aloud the title. Then go over the first paragraph. Explain that the topic of a research report is what the report is about. List on the board the following topics: *Cinderella, bicycles, dragons, horses.* Talk about whether the topics would be good ones for research reports. Emphasize that research-report topics are about real people, places, things, or events.

Go over the next paragraph. Explain that there have been many presidents and that it would take a long time to tell about all of them. Write on the board *bugs.* Explain that the topic bugs would be too big for a research report. Invite volunteers to suggest smaller topics about bugs. *(Examples: crickets, butterflies, bumblebees)*

Go over the activity directions. Work with students to complete the first item as a class. Then have

students complete the rest of the activity independently. When they have finished, invite volunteers to share their answers with the class.

Extension

Distribute a variety of age-appropriate magazines, such as *Sports Illustrated for Kids, National Geographic for Kids, Ranger Rick,* or *Highlights.* Allow time for students to look through the magazines. Have students list three topics that they might like to write a research report about. When they have finished, talk about whether the topics students listed are appropriate for a research report.

Topic Sentences   Page 200

Students Should

- identify a topic sentence in a research report
- understand how to write a topic sentence

Teaching the Lesson

Remind students that research-report topics are about real people, places, things, or events. Emphasize the importance of choosing a topic that isn't too big.

Ask a volunteer to read aloud the title. Then go over the first paragraph. Point out that a topic sentence is an important part of the beginning of a research report. Explain that a topic sentence should tell readers what the topic is. Tell students that an interesting topic sentence will make their audience want to read more about their topic.

Go over the directions for the first activity. Guide students to complete the first item as a class. Then have students complete the rest of the activity independently. When students have finished, invite volunteers to share their work with the class.

Go over the directions for the second activity. Invite volunteers to suggest topic sentences for the first item. Write their answers on the board. Then have students complete the second item independently. When they have finished, invite volunteers to share their sentences with the class.

Extension

Ask students to choose a research-report topic that they have talked about in class. Then have students draw a picture of their topic. Ask them to write at the bottom of the picture a topic sentence that might be the beginning of a research report. When students have finished, invite volunteers to share their work with the class.

Finding Facts   Page 201

You may wish to teach page 201 in the library.

Students Should
- identify facts for a research report

Teaching the Lesson

Review that topic sentences tell the topic of a research report. Invite students to name some topics for a research report. Write their responses on the board. Then ask volunteers to say topic sentences for each topic.

Ask a volunteer to read aloud the title. Then go over the first paragraph. Display an object that has a distinct shape. Ask students to tell the shape of the object. Tell students that the shape of the object is a fact about that object. Emphasize that facts are true information about a topic. Tell students that if they do not know about a topic, they must find facts about it in encyclopedias, in other books, or on the Internet. Explain that when students find facts about a topic, they are doing research.

Go over the next paragraph and the questions. Explain that these questions can help students find facts about their topic and can be helpful when doing research.

Go over the last paragraph. Demonstrate writing a fact in your own words. Read aloud a fact from a reference book. Write on the board the fact in your own words. Then read aloud other facts and help students say those facts in their own words. Explain that by writing facts in their own words, students will show that they understand the facts. Tell students that reading and writing facts will

help them learn more about topics that are interesting to them.

Go over the activity directions. Then allow time for students to complete the activity. When students have finished, invite volunteers to share their answers with the class.

Extension

Have students select a topic that they researched on this page. Allow time for students to write a topic sentence about that topic. When students have finished, invite volunteers to share their work with the class.

Organizing Facts   Page 202

Students Should
- understand how to organize facts

Teaching the Lesson

Review where facts can be found. *(in encyclopedias, in other books, and on the Internet)* Remind students that facts are information that is true. Then review the importance of students writing facts in their own words. Point out that writing facts in their own words shows that they understand the facts.

Invite a volunteer to read aloud the title. Then go over the first paragraph. Say: *We write facts on note cards so that we don't forget them. This way, we don't have to find the facts again. We write each fact on a separate note card so that we can easily organize the facts.*

Go over the second paragraph. Explain that putting note cards into piles will help students organize their facts. Help students understand that sorting their note cards will make writing their research reports easier.

Go over the activity directions. Guide students to complete the first item as a class. Then have students complete the rest of the activity independently. When students have finished, have them share their answers with the class.

Extension

Assign the class a topic for a research report. *(Example: tarantulas)* Then assign each student a research question about the topic. *(Examples: What does a tarantula eat? Where does a tarantula live?)* Have students research their questions independently and write one fact on a note card. When students have finished, collect the note cards. Read the note cards aloud and ask students to help you organize the facts into piles of similar information based on the research questions you assigned.

Writing an Ending   Page 203

Students Should

- understand how to write an ending for a research report

Teaching the Lesson

Review writing and organizing notes on note cards. Go over the information that belongs on a note card. *(a fact written in the writer's own words)* Then review how to sort note cards into piles. Remind students that taking notes and organizing those notes can help writers plan and organize their research reports.

Ask a volunteer to read aloud the title. Then go over the first paragraph and the model research report. Say: *Endings are an important part of any kind of writing. They sum up information or tell what the writer has learned. An ending in a research report sums up the topic of the report. It might also sum up important facts that readers have read.* Ask a volunteer to identify the ending of the model report. *(Bats are strange, but they are not scary.)* Talk about how the ending sums up the report. Tell students that an ending often retells the topic sentence.

Go over the activity directions. Help students complete the first item as a class. Then have students complete the rest of the activity independently. When students have finished, invite them to share their answers with the class.

Extension

Have students choose one of the topics in the activity on page 201. Ask students to draw a picture of their topic. Then have students use the facts that they found to write at the bottom of their picture a research-report ending. Invite volunteers to share their work with the class.

Writer's Workshop

Prewriting—
Pick a Topic   Page 204

Students Should

- brainstorm research-report topics

- identify appropriate topics for their research reports

Talk with students about animals, people, places, or events that interest them. *(Examples: goldfish, Johnny Appleseed, Alaska, the moon landing)* Talk about what students might like to learn about those topics. Say: *When we write research reports, we choose a topic. The topics that we have talked about would make good topics for research reports. Research reports are a good way to learn more about a topic and to share with others what you learn.*

Invite a volunteer to read aloud the title. Then go over the first paragraph and Tara's notebook page. Say: *When we write a research report, we tell a reader information about a topic. When we do prewriting for research reports, we think about things we want to know more about. We write down our topic ideas. Then we decide which topic to write about.* Talk with students about the topics that Tara has listed. Point out that each topic would be a good topic for a research report.

Model on the board how to brainstorm a list of topics for your own research report. Write your topic ideas on the board. Explain why you think each topic might be a good topic for a research report. Include a topic that might be too broad for a research report. Talk with students about why the topic might be difficult to write about in a short research report. Then choose one topic by circling it. Talk about why you have chosen the topic and emphasize why it will make a good topic for a research report. Point out that the topic you have chosen is not too big to write a research report about.

Go over the rest of the page. Then allow time for students to write their topic ideas. Encourage students to use the topic prompts to get started. As students work, circulate among them to provide support. Be sure that students are listing appropriate topics. Help students who list broad topics to narrow their topics. Emphasize that students do not have to choose a topic they know much about, because they will learn about the topic by doing research.

Prewriting—Plan Your Research Report   Page 205

Students Should

- plan their research reports

Review the importance of planning a research report. Talk about ways that students have planned their previous writing assignments. *(drawing pictures, making charts)* Remind students that when they plan a research report, they will do research, write note cards, and sort the cards into piles.

Ask a volunteer to read aloud the title. Then go over the first two paragraphs. Talk with students about their experiences finding facts in books, encyclopedias, and on the Internet. If necessary, review pages 218–221 to emphasize encyclopedia and library skills.

Go over the next two paragraphs and Tara's note cards. Invite volunteers to identify the fact on each note card. *(Ladybugs eat aphids that can harm crops. The spots on a ladybug fade as it gets old.)* Point out that after Tara found facts, she sorted her note cards into piles. Ask students what the information in each pile might be. *(The first pile might be about*

what ladybugs eat. The second pile might be about what ladybugs look like.) Remind students that when they write their own note cards, they should write only one fact on each card and then they should put similar information into separate piles. Remind students that by planning and organizing her draft now, Tara will be able to write her research report more easily later.

Model for students how to research the topic you selected for your own research report. Be sure to have available research materials, such as books, encyclopedias, and the Internet, from which to find your facts. You may also consider conducting this part of the lesson in the library to optimize the resources available to you. As you work, explain your decisions for choosing and writing each fact that you gather. It may be helpful to draw note cards on the board or on a large sheet of paper so students can see how you write each fact. Emphasize how to write facts in your own words.

Go over the rest of the page. Allow time for students to research their topics, to write their facts on note cards, and to sort the note cards. As students work, circulate among them to provide assistance and support. Help students retell their facts in their own words. Assist students who are having trouble sorting their note cards into piles of related information.

Drafting   Page 206

Students Should

- use prewriting notes to write their first drafts

Talk with students about their experiences drafting previous writing assignments. Remind students that when they write a first draft, they use the notes they wrote during prewriting to help them. Explain that when they write research reports, their notes are very important, because they contain the facts that students will include in their reports.

Invite a volunteer to read aloud the title. Then go over the first paragraph and direct students' attention to Tara's draft. Invite a volunteer to identify Tara's topic sentence. (*A ladybug is a helpful and pretty bug.*) Point out that the topic sentence tells the reader right away what the report will be about. Guide students to identify in Tara's draft the facts that she wrote on her note cards on page 205. Remind students that Tara organized all her note cards into two piles, one pile of note cards about what ladybugs eat and one pile of note cards about what ladybugs look like. Invite volunteers to identify in Tara's draft another fact that came from the pile of note cards about what ladybugs eat. (*Aphids are bugs that can harm crops.*) Then invite volunteers to identify in Tara's draft another fact that came from the pile of note cards about what ladybugs look like. (*Ladybugs are red with black spots.*) Emphasize that grouping similar facts into piles helped Tara write her draft. Tara also grouped together these similar facts in her draft.

On the board model for students how to use your note cards and facts to write your research report. Begin by writing a topic sentence and explaining your decision to include it at the beginning. Point out that your topic sentence names the topic. As you write, explain how the facts in the middle of your research report relate to the note cards you wrote in prewriting. Explain that students should not mix up the order of their facts, but should put all related information together in the middle of the report. As you write the ending of your research report, explain how your ending sums up

the report. Be sure to include in your draft at least one mistake from the Editing Checklist on page 207 and one mistake from the Proofreading Checklist on page 208. Save your draft for use during the Editing stage.

Go over the last paragraph. Then allow time for students to complete their drafts. As students work, circulate among them to provide support. Help students who are having trouble grouping their facts appropriately in their drafts. Emphasize the importance of keeping related information together in a research report. Remind students that they will have time to fix mistakes in spelling and grammar later and that now is a time for them to capture their ideas.

Editing   Page 207

Students Should

- edit their research reports

Talk with students about their previous experiences editing drafts. Invite volunteers to explain why editing is important. (*Editing is the time that writers fix mistakes in the ideas of a draft.*) Explain that when students edit research reports, they should look at how well the facts tell about the topic.

Invite a volunteer to read aloud the title. Then guide students through the first paragraph and the Editing Checklist. Help students to understand each question and how they should check their drafts for each question when editing.

Go over the next paragraph and the thought bubble. Ask students which item on the checklist helped Tara find the mistake in her draft. (*Does the middle have important facts?*) Ask students how Tara fixed her draft. (*She took out the sentence There are many ladybugs in my backyard.*) Help students understand how Tara's deletion improves the report.

Direct students' attention to your research report. Guide them to edit your report, using the Editing Checklist. Help students use the checklist to find the mistake in your draft. Invite students to act as your editors and to suggest ways that you might fix your mistake.

Go over the next two paragraphs. Remind students that reading their drafts aloud is a good way to catch mistakes that were made while drafting. Then allow time for students to edit their drafts. Check that students are giving appropriate consideration to each item on the checklist. Check students' justifications for making or not making changes to their work. Have students pay particular attention to making sure their research reports include a topic sentence.

If partners read each other's drafts, remind them of the proper language and behavior for peer-editing sessions. Remind students to check their friends' changes, using the checklist. Emphasize that they can also ask a teacher, a parent, or another friend for help.

Revising   Page 207

Students Should
• use editing changes to revise their drafts

Review with students the purpose of revising. Remind students that some of the changes we include in revised drafts are our ideas, while others might come from a friend or a teacher. Emphasize that writers make a new copy of their draft to more clearly see other possible mistakes when they proofread.

Go over the title and the first paragraph. Then demonstrate revising your draft. Talk about how your editing change improves the draft. Then rewrite your draft on the board, incorporating into the new copy your marked change. Remember to include your mistake from the Proofreading Checklist on page 208.

Go over the last paragraph. Then allow time for students to revise their drafts. As they work, circulate among students to be sure that they are correctly writing their editing changes on their drafts.

Proofreading   Page 208

Students Should
• proofread their revised drafts

Remind students that when we do proofreading, we make sure that the sentences are written correctly and that there are no misspelled words. Talk about students' previous experiences proofreading. Invite volunteers to describe how proofreading improved their drafts.

Invite a student to read aloud the title. Then go over the first paragraph and the Proofreading Checklist. Talk with students about what each checklist item means and how they might check for it in their drafts.

Go over the next paragraph and direct students' attention to the partial student model. Talk about how the proofreading marks function within the draft. Then ask students to identify which question on the checklist helped Tara to find her mistake. (*Are homophones used correctly?*) Invite a student to tell how Tara fixed her mistake. (*She deleted* two *and replaced it with* too.)

Using your revised draft, model for students how to proofread. Guide students to use the Proofreading Checklist to find your mistake. Demonstrate how to mark the change. Remind students that proofreading helps them make their drafts better.

Go over the last two paragraphs. Then allow time for students to proofread their drafts. Remind students to check for only one kind of mistake at a time. As students work, check that they are giving appropriate consideration to each item on the checklist. Remind students to use references such as a picture dictionary, a word wall, or the student book to check and correct mistakes.

If time allows, have partners trade drafts and proofread each other's work. Remind students that a friend might catch mistakes that they have missed. If you choose this option, circulate among students to be sure that they are using appropriate peer-conferencing language. When students have finished, remind them to double-check their friend's suggestions.

Publishing   Page 209

Page 176e provides a full-sized, reproducible copy of the student's Research Report scoring rubric. Students can use the rubric when assessing their own research reports.

Page 176f provides a full-sized, reproducible copy of the Teacher's Scoring Rubric for research reports. The rubric can be used when assessing students' understanding of the genre.

Students Should

- produce final copies of their research reports

Review ways that students have published previous writing assignments. Talk about why publishing is important. *(because it is when a writer shares his or her work with an audience)* Explain that textbooks, magazine articles, news stories, movies, and TV shows require research. Say: *The audience for a research report is someone who is interested in reading about your topic. This person is interested in learning the facts that you wrote about.*

Invite a volunteer to read aloud the title. Then go over the first paragraph. Remind students that sharing a report with a teacher and classmates is publishing. Emphasize that Tara was careful writing her final copy because she was going to share it with her audience.

Model for students how to produce a final copy. You might write your final copy on the board, or you might use one of the publishing ideas listed in the student book. As you work, talk about who the audience for your report might be.

Go over the rest of the page. Allow time for students to make final copies of their research reports. Remind students to write slowly and carefully, and to check each sentence to make sure they do not make any new mistakes.

When students have finished, talk about how the class will publish their research reports. Allow time for students to create any artwork or other items that might help readers understand the facts in their reports.

When students have finished, distribute copies of the student's Research Report scoring rubric. Guide students to understand what each item means and how to apply it to their own writing. Then allow time for students to self-evaluate their research reports.

Have students add to their portfolios their finished research reports. Remind students that their portfolios have helped them to see how their writing has improved throughout the year. Encourage students to examine their portfolios at this time to view their progress from the beginning of the year.

Ladybugs
A ladybug is a helpful and pretty bug. Ladybugs eat aphids. Aphids are bugs that can harm crops. That is why farmers like ladybugs too. Ladybugs are red with black spots. As a ladybug gets old, the spots fade. The next time you see a ladybug, remember that it is a useful b

Research Tools

Introducing the Chapter

Pages 210–211

Students Should

- have a basic understanding of the library
- have a basic understanding of research tools

Using the Model

Read aloud the quotation. Explain that when people do research, they learn about a topic. Say: *I am a teacher. If I didn't learn about things, I would have nothing to teach you. Research means finding out about a topic and then sharing what you learned with other people. This quotation means that you need to learn about a topic if you want to share important information with someone else.* Explain that this quotation is especially true when writing research reports. Tell students that learning to use research tools in the library will help them write better research reports.

Direct students' attention to the picture on pages 210 and 211. Tell students that libraries may look a little different from one another, but that every library has the things in the picture. Ask students what a library is. *(a place to borrow books and to find facts and other true information)* Invite volunteers to talk about times they have gone to a library and to explain why they went. Tell students that the library contains many research tools, such as dictionaries, encyclopedias, nonfiction books, and computers.

Point out the Librarian callout. Ask students what they think the librarian does. *(He or she helps people find what they need in the library.)* Say: *Librarians go to school to learn how libraries are organized, what the rules of the library are, and how to help people who use the library. Librarians are one of the best research tools that we have.* Tell students that they should ask a librarian whenever they need help finding materials in the library.

Go over the Circulation Desk callout. Tell students that the circulation desk is where people check books and other materials out of the library. Explain that checking out a book means borrowing the book for a period of time. Emphasize that students should take good care of materials they check out of the library so that others can use those materials later. Then point out the Book Return slot. Explain that if students have books to return to the library, they can drop the books into the slot and the librarians will check them in later.

Direct students' attention to the Fiction Section, the Nonfiction Section, and the Reference Area callouts. Explain that books are usually put in certain parts of a library to make them easier to find. Tell students that in the fiction section they will find made-up stories. Ask students to name some fiction books they have read. Tell students that in the nonfiction section they will find books with true information about real topics. Then tell students that in the reference section they will find special books such as dictionaries, encyclopedias, and books of maps. Explain that because these materials are used often by many people, they usually can't be taken out of the library. Emphasize that if students need to use books found in the reference section, they should take notes or make photocopies of the pages they need because they cannot take the books home.

Point out the Computer Area callout. Say: *Most libraries have computers so people can use the*

Internet. These computers can be used to do research. Computers at the library can also help you find books about a topic. These computers are called electronic card catalogs. You can type a topic into a computer, and it will list books that the library has about that topic.

Go over the Reading Area callout. Explain that the reading area is for everyone, but that people must be quiet when in the reading area. Tell students that noise in the library makes it hard to read and to study. Emphasize that when students go to any library, they should remember to be quiet at all times.

ABC Order *and* Practice with ABC Order
Pages 212–213

Students Should

- understand how to put words in ABC order

Teaching the Lesson

Talk with students about times they have stood in a line according to the ABC order of their names. Talk about other things that can be put into ABC order. *(Examples: words, book titles, animal names, DVD titles)* Tell students that ABC order is one of the most common ways that people organize things.

Go over the teaching and the alphabet on page 212. Explain that when words are put in ABC order, they should be arranged by the first letter of the

word. Guide students to understand that using ABC order is an easy way of organizing because most people know the order of the letters in the alphabet. Then show students a dictionary. Say: *This dictionary has thousands of words in it. The dictionary is organized in ABC order to make finding words easier.*

Go over the activity directions on pages 212 and 213. When students have finished each activity, review their answers.

Extension

Have students draw on separate sheets of paper three different animals whose names begin with different letters. Tell students to write at the bottom of each picture the name of the animal. Circulate among students to be sure that they are spelling the names of their animals correctly. Then have students exchange their drawings. Tell students to put the drawings they receive in ABC order. When students have finished, invite them to share their work with the class.

Names in ABC Order
Page 214

Students Should

- understand how to put names in ABC order

Teaching the Lesson

Invite five volunteers to come to the front of the room. Guide students to line up alphabetically by the first letters of their first names. Then invite students to say aloud their names in ABC order. Remind students that using ABC order is an easy

Aa Bb Cc Dd Ee Ff Gg Hh Ii Jj Kk Ll Mm

Nn Oo Pp Qq Rr Ss Tt Uu Vv Ww Xx Yy Zz

way of organizing because most people know the order of letters in the alphabet. Then have the same volunteers line up alphabetically by the first letter of their last names. Explain that because many people have the same first names, names of people are often put in ABC order according to their last names. Talk with students about any times at which they were put in ABC order according to their last names.

Go over the teaching and the activity directions. When students have finished the activity, review their answers.

Extension

Have students draw pictures of imaginary visitors from outer space. Tell students to write at the bottom of their pictures a first and last name for the space visitor. Then invite volunteers to come to the front of the class and stand in ABC order according to the last name of their space visitors. Have students hold their pictures in front of them so the rest of the class can see them. Invite volunteers to say in ABC order the last names and then the full names of their visitors.

Dictionary Skills
and
Practice with Dictionary Skills
and
More Practice with
Dictionary Skills   Pages 215–217

Students Should
- understand how to use a dictionary

Teaching the Lesson

Write on the board the following words: *ache, disturb, imitate, koala, quarrel.* Ask students whether they know what each word means. Tell students that if they don't know the meaning of a word, they can find it in a dictionary. Explain that

dictionaries tell the meanings of many words. Read aloud from a dictionary the meaning of each word on the board. Tell students that they can also use a dictionary to check the spelling of a word. Point out that knowing the meanings and spellings of words can help them better understand what they read.

Go over the teaching on page 215. Then direct students' attention to the example dictionary page. Point out the guide words *garden* and *gym*. Explain that all the words on a dictionary page come between the guide words in ABC order. Write on the board the entry words in alphabetical order, circling the two guide words. Point out that the guide words and all the words on the page begin with the letter *g*. Explain that when words begin with the same letter, they are alphabetized by the second letter. Cover up the letter *g* in each of the words on the board. Point out that the second letters are in alphabetical order. Tell students that the words are in ABC order, so all the words on this page come between the guide words. Explain that when we look in a dictionary to find a word, we use the guide words to see how close we are to the page that has the word we are looking for.

Point out the callouts. Explain that although dictionaries can look different, all dictionaries will tell the meanings of the words. Tell students that some dictionaries use pictures and example sentences to help readers understand the meanings of words.

Go over the activity directions on pages 215, 216, and 217. When students have finished each activity, review their answers.

Extension

Have students choose two words from a dictionary. Tell students to write on separate sheets of paper each word and what the word means. Have students include with each word their own picture that helps illustrate the word's meaning. Invite students to share their dictionary entries with the class.

Encyclopedia Skills   Page 218

Students Should

- understand the parts and function of an encyclopedia

Teaching the Lesson

Review that dictionaries list words in ABC order and that they give meanings of words. Tell students that encyclopedias are groups of books that have true information about topics and that they are organized in a way similar to dictionaries. Talk with students about times they have seen or used an encyclopedia. Tell students that when they write research reports, they may use an encyclopedia to find facts about their topic. Then look up the entry for *cat* in an encyclopedia. Read aloud the first paragraph of the article. Talk about some facts about cats that students have learned from the article. Say: *We use dictionaries to find out what words mean. We use encyclopedias to find information about topics. Encyclopedias are organized like dictionaries, but they have a lot more information.*

Go over the teaching and direct students' attention to the picture of the spine of a volume. Point out the title of the encyclopedia, the volume letter, and the volume number. Then display an encyclopedia volume. Point out that the volume has topics that all begin with the same letter or letters. Tell students that other volumes of the encyclopedia cover topics that start with other letters. Say: *Most encyclopedias have one volume for each letter of the alphabet. Letters that may not have as many topics, such as X, Y, and Z, might be put together in the same volume.*

Open the encyclopedia to the beginning of an entry and display the entry for students. Point out the article on the page. Talk with students about how an encyclopedia is similar to a dictionary. Remind students that entries are listed in ABC order.

Go over the example encyclopedia entry on page 218. Ask students to tell facts they learned about snakes from reading the article. Emphasize that the information in an encyclopedia can be used to learn more about a topic and that it can also be used in a research report to teach others about a topic.

Go over the activity directions. When students have finished the activity, review their answers.

Extension

Have students form small groups. Assign each group an interesting animal. *(Examples: armadillo, meerkat, kangaroo rat, spiny dogfish)* Have students use encyclopedias to do an Animal Investigation to find three interesting facts about their animal. Have groups share with the rest of the class the information they found.

Fiction and Nonfiction   Page 219

Students Should

- distinguish between fiction and nonfiction books

Teaching the Lesson

Display a selection of age-appropriate fiction and nonfiction books. Talk about books that students have read. Invite students to tell whether the books were made-up stories or if they had true information. Talk about how students know that a story is made up. Tell students that books with made-up stories are called fiction books.

Go over the first paragraph of the teaching. Point out the fiction books that you have displayed. Emphasize that fiction books are stories that are made up by the writer. Invite students to name fiction books with which they are familiar. Explain that because the information in fiction books is made up, we do not use fiction books when we write research reports. Ask students to turn back to the picture on pages 210 and 211. Point out the area labeled Fiction Section. Say: *Librarians don't want people to get confused when they try to find books. So they put fiction books in a special part of the library. All the fiction books are put together. That way when you need to find a fiction book, you can go to that part of the library.*

Go over the second paragraph of the teaching. Explain that nonfiction books do not have made-up information. Say: *When you put* non- *at the front of a word, it's like saying* not. *So if* fiction *means "made up,"* nonfiction *means "not made up." Nonfiction books are books with true information.*

Remind students that encyclopedias are research tools that have true information about topics. Explain that encyclopedias have entries with information about a topic, while in most nonfiction books, the whole book is about one topic. Emphasize this point by displaying an encyclopedia article and a nonfiction book that are about the same topic. Then have students turn back to the picture on pages 210 and 211. Point out the Nonfiction Section. Explain that librarians put all the nonfiction books in a different part of the library than the fiction books so that people can easily find what they're looking for.

Go over the activity directions. When students have finished the activity, review their answers.

Extension

Make a list of book titles in the library from the fiction and nonfiction sections. Read titles from the list and have students guess whether the book is fiction or nonfiction. Talk about clues in book titles that can help students distinguish between fiction and nonfiction books.

The Cover of a Book   Page 220

Students Should

- identify information located on the cover of a book

Teaching the Lesson

Talk about things that students need to include in the beginning of a book report. *(the title of the book, the author of the book)* Tell students that they can find a lot of important information on the cover of a book.

Go over the teaching. Direct students' attention to the example book cover. Talk about each callout and help them pronounce any terms they have difficulty with. If students do not understand what these words mean, invite a volunteer to look them up in a dictionary. Explain to students that when they write reports, they often need to know the title and author of the book in which they found information.

Go over the activity directions. When students have finished the activity, review their answers.

Extension

Ask students to choose a book from your classroom library and to draw a picture of the book cover, including the book's title, author, and illustrator if listed. Then have students write callouts similar to those on page 220, noting each part of the cover in their drawings. Invite students to share their work with the class.

Using the Internet Page 221

Students Should

- understand that the Internet can be used as a research tool

Teaching the Lesson

Talk with students about their experiences using the Internet. Invite volunteers to name things that the Internet allows them to do. *(find information, play games, buy products)* Explain that the Internet is a powerful research tool because a great deal of information is available on the Internet.

Go over the first paragraph. Explain that the Internet has billions of Web pages stored on computers for people to see. Tell students that these Web pages can be written and published by people, businesses, universities, and other organizations. Explain that there are Web pages on almost every topic and that people can find these Web pages from any computer. Tell students that using the Internet can save a lot of time and work when doing research for a research report. Then say: *As helpful as the Internet is, we have to be careful when we use it. Anyone can make a Web site, and sometimes people make Web sites that have false information or information that we can't trust.* Tell students that when they use the Internet to do research, they should always check the facts that they find on at least two other Web sites or in a nonfiction book or an encyclopedia. Explain that by checking Internet facts, they can be sure the information isn't made up.

Direct students' attention to the example Web page. Talk about features of the Web page, such as the search field and links to information on other pages. Then go over the paragraph following the Web page. Point out that this example Web page is from a kid-friendly search engine. Emphasize that a kid-friendly search engine can find Web sites that have real facts and that have information that is OK for children to look at.

Go over the last paragraph. Then share with students the following rules for Internet safety:

1. Never share personal information online.

2. Tell a parent or an adult if anything you see on the computer makes you feel scared, uncomfortable, or confused.

3. Never meet in person anyone you talk with on the Internet.

Go over with students an Internet safety resource, such as NetSmartz.org, SafeKids.com, or iKeepSafe.org, that offers students, teachers, and parents guidelines for safe Internet use.

Extension

Supervise students as they use a kid-friendly search engine to find two facts about an animal of their choice. Have students write down each fact and the address of the Web site on which they found the fact. Then have students check the fact in a nonfiction book or an encyclopedia. Remind students that facts found on the Internet should be checked on at least two other Web sites or in a nonfiction book or an encyclopedia.

Index

Acknowledgments

Illustration

Anni Betts: iii bottom, 14, 18, 28, 42 top, 47, 51, 59, 65, 79, 87, 93, 98, 100, 119 top, 126, 149, 152, 162, 166, 167, 176–177, 208, 219, 221, T-229, T-243, T-245, T-250, T-295

Holli Conger: iv bottom, 8, 9, 22, 32, 44, 46, 57, 83, 92, 99, 111, 117, 122, 131, 142–143, 158, 186, 198, 202, 203, 216

Deborah Melman: iv top, 16, 33, 40–41, 49, 78, 88, 94, 115, 118, 133, 147, 160, 165, 178, 179 top and middle, 188, 189, 210–211, T-240, T-282, T-306, T-320, T-321

Cindy Revell: v bottom, 11, 13, 15, 19, 21, 23, 26, 30, 31, 42 bottom, 43, 48, 52, 53, 58, 67, 76, 82, 85, 86, 90, 91, 97, 108–109, 113, 114, 119 bottom, 124, 128, 130, 144, 145, 146, 148, 157, 161, 164, 179 bottom, 182, 184 bottom, 190, 194, 199, 206, 214, T-225, T-228, T-232, T-234, T-242, T-244, T-246, T-247, T-252, T-259, T-262, T-268, T-271, T-275, T-277, T-278, T-280, T-286, T-289, T-292, T-296, T-297, T-304, T-305, T-307, T-308, T-312

Christine Schneider: iii middle, iv middle, 6–7, 25, 50, 54, 60, 61, 81, 89, 96, 101, 116, 120, 135, 150, 159, 168, 180, 184, 196, 212, 213, T-248, T-294

Melanie Siegel: 10, 20, 45, 56, 74–75, 84, 110, 121, 132, 151, 156, 163, 183, 195, 215, 217, T-273

Photography

Phil Martin Photography: 7, 37, 39, 41, 71, 73, 74d, 105, 107, 139, 141, 142d, 173, 175, 207, 209, 210c, T-239, T-241, T-253, T-255, T-267, T-269, T-284, T-287, T-301, T-315

Literature

Quote from Betsy Byars found in *Scholastic Treasury of Quotations for Children.* Copyright © by Adrienne Betz. Published by Scholastic Inc.
All rights reserved.

Quote from *I Can Read with My Eyes Shut!* by Dr. Seuss, copyright ™ and copyright © by Dr. Seuss Enterprises, L.P. 1978. Used by permission of Random House Children's Books, a division of Random House, Inc.

Acknowledgments for Literature Links

Chapter 1–Personal Narratives

Cover from *Diary of a Spider* by Doreen Cronin. Illustrations by Harry Bliss. Copyright © 2005. Published by Joanna Cotler Books, an imprint of HarperCollins Publishers.

Cover from *There's an Alligator Under My Bed.* Copyright © 1987 by Mercer Mayer. Used by permission of Penguin Books for Young Readers. All rights reserved.

Cover from *My Name is Yoon.* Text copyright © 2003 by Helen Recorvits. Illustrations copyright © by Gabi Swiatkowska. Published by Frances Foster Books, an imprint of Farrar, Straus and Giroux.

Chapter 2–Friendly Letters

Cover reprinted with the permission of Atheneum Books for Young Readers, an imprint of Simon & Schuster Children's

Publishing Division from *Yours Truly, Goldilocks* by Alma Flor Ada, illustrated by Leslie Tryon. Illustrations copyright © 1998 Leslie Tryon.

Cover from *The Jolly Postman* by Janet and Allan Ahlberg. Copyright 1986 by Janet and Allan Ahlberg. First published in Great Britain 1986 by William Heinemann. Published by Little, Brown and Company, part of the Time Warner Book Group.

Cover from *Corduroy Writes a Letter* based on the character created by Don Freeman. Copyright © 2002 by Penguin Putnam Inc. Used by permission. All rights reserved.

Chapter 3–How-to Articles

Easy Art Fun: Do-It-Yourself Crafts for Beginning Readers by Jill Frankel Hauser. Illustrations by Savlan Hauser. Copyright © by the author. Published by Williamson Books, an imprint of Ideals Publications.

Cover from *My First Book of How Things Are Made* by George Jones. Copyright © 1995 by Pond Press. Reprinted by permission of Scholastic Inc.

Cover reproduced from *The Usborne Book of Masks* by permission of Usborne Publishing, 83-85 Saffron Hill, London EC1N 8RT, UK. Published in the USA by EDC Publishing, 10302 E. 55th Place, Tulsa, OK 74146, www.edcpub.com/corp. Copyright © 1993 Usborne Publishing Ltd.

Chapter 4–Descriptions

Cover from *Frog and Toad All Year.* Copyright © 1976 by Arnold Lobel. Published by HarperCollins Children's Books.

Cover reprinted with permission of Atheneum Books for Young Readers, an imprint of Simon & Schuster Children's Publishing Division from *Henry and Mudge: The First Book* by Cynthia Rylant, pictures by Sucie Stevenson. Illustrations copyright © 1987 Sucie Stevenson.

Book cover from *I Went Walking* by Sue Williams, illustrations copyright © 1989 by Julie Vivas, reproduced by permission of Harcourt, Inc.

Chapter 5–Book Reports

Cover from *Chang's Paper Pony* by Eleanor Coerr. Copyright © 1988 by Deborah Kogan Ray. Used by permission of HarperCollins Publishers.

Cover from *Babe the Gallant Pig* by Dick King-Smith, illustrated by Mary Rayner, copyright © 1983 by Dick King-Smith. Illustrations copyright © 1983 by Mary Rayner. Used by permission of Crown Publishers, an imprint of Random House Children's Books, a division of Random House, Inc.

Cover from *If You Give a Pig a Party.* Text copyright © 2005 by Laura Numeroff. Illustrations copyright © 2005 by Felicia Bond. Published by HarperCollins Children's Books.

Chapter 6–Research Reports

Cover from *The Magic School Bus: Inside the Human Body.* Illustrated by Bruce Degen. Illustrations copyright © 1989 By Bruce Degen. Reprinted by permission of Scholastic Inc.

Cover of *From Seed to Plant* by Gail Gibbons. Copyright ©1991 by Gail Gibbons. Used by permission of Holiday House. All rights reserved.

Cover from *What's It Like to Be a Fish?* Text copyright © 1996 by Wendy Pfeffer. Illustrations copyright © 1996 by Holly Keller. Published by HarperCollins Children's Books.